D1327280

CRITERIA OF CERTAINTY

CRITERIA OF CERTAINTY

Truth and Judgment
in the English Enlightenment

KEVIN L. COPE

THE UNIVERSITY PRESS OF KENTUCKY

Publication of this work is made possible in part
by a grant from the Hyder E. Rollins
Publication Fund of Harvard University.

Library of Congress Cataloging-in-Publication Data

Cope, Kevin Lee.
  Criteria of certainty : truth and judgment in the English
Enlightenment / Kevin L. Cope.

    p. cm.
  Includes bibliographical references.
  ISBN 0-8131-1750-X
  1. English literature—18th century—History and criticism.
  2. Great Britain—Intellectual life—18th century. 3. Philosophy,
English—18th century. 4. Philosophy in literature.
  5. Enlightenment. I. Title.
  PR448.P5C6 1990
  820.9'005—dc20   90-12264

Contents

FOR WALTER JACKSON BATE

Friend of the Human Spirit

Acknowledgments

One of the great pleasures of writing a book on a wide-ranging topic like the literature of certainty is the opportunity to hear the advice and acquire the friendship of many scholars involved in the "mighty maze" of Restoration and eighteenth-century scholarship. Of all the debts that I have incurred during the preparation of *Criteria of Certainty*, the heaviest and most general is the one that I owe to the American, the International, the Canadian, and the various regional Societies for Eighteenth-Century Studies—organizations whose members, from Percy Adams to Rose Zimbardo, have always been eager in their encouragement, wise in their criticism, and welcoming in their reception of my work. Particularly helpful in the way of encouragement have been James T. Engell, Howard Weinbrot, O M "Skip" Brack, James Thorson, John Shawcross, Colby H. Kullman, and Connie Capers Thorson; in the way of patient, learned, and indispensable criticism, John J. Richetti; and, in the way of courteous reception, J.M. Armistead, Robert Maccubbin, Gerald Kirk, John Burke, and David Vieth. Many unknown colleagues have read and reviewed the manuscript of my book; I want to recognize them all, wherever and whoever they may be, for their persuasive, constructive, and graciously candid suggestions. I would also like to recognize Nancy Atkinson for her superior copyediting. For their unwavering confidence in, support for, and assistance with this book as well as with many other enterprises, I want to say a special word of thanks to two faithful friends, Paul J. Korshin and Paula R. Backscheider.

Criteria of Certainty has emerged over a long and happy period of study, with the result that I now have the privilege to acknowledge the contributions of several persons from several walks of life who, sometimes unknowingly but always generously, have made contributions to my scholarship. For their influence on the earliest stages of my work, I thank Phyllis Noyes and Arthur Schor, of San Diego,

California; Albert Wachtel, James Bogen, Stephen Glass, and the late Beverle Houston, of Pitzer College; President Patsy H. Sampson, of Stephens College; and the late John L. Mackie, of University College, Oxford. Gwynne Blakemore Evans, Herschel Baker, the late Dame Helen Gardner, Larry Benson, and Jerome Hamilton Buckley joined with James Engell and W.J. Bate to surround me, during my years at Harvard, with an atmosphere inspiring a respect for both scholarship and the dignity of mankind. More than once in my scholarly life, both my studies and my morale have benefited from the kinds words of Hazard Adams. For continuing support of my research at Louisiana State University, I offer my appreciation to John R. "Jack" May, Carolyn Hargrave, Billy Seay, Gale Carrithers, and especially my fellow bayou *dix-huitièmistes*, John Irwin Fischer and Jim Springer Borck. For her daily, ever-delightful revelations, I thank my graduate student disciple, "Protoprofessor" Deborah Jacobs. I argue in my book that philosophizing is the public form of vigorous belief and rigorous coherence; I can think of no better example of a soul giving a championship performance in the arena of common sense than my good friend Dale Brown, of LSU. Any smudges picked up during my daily jousts on the philosophic fields have been washed away by that geyser of wit and wisdom, my wife, Susan J. Kotler-Cope. To Susan I am deeply indebted for countless bits of information concerning contemporary cognitive science, a few of which have percolated through to my introduction and epilogue.

Bishop Sprat warns that Abraham Cowley relishes theory but neglects budgetary concerns. Lest I commit the same error, I would like to thank the Hyder E. Rollins Fund of the Department of English and American Literature and Language of Harvard University for a generous grant, which aided in the publication of this volume. My grateful applause goes to Robert Kiely, of this same department, for his more-than-cameo role in securing this award.

I would like to summarize my acknowledgments by reaffirming my often-expressed (but still inadequate) esteem for the dedicatee of this book, Walter Jackson Bate, whose example of liberty, honesty, genius, courage, and humanity will remain with me for a lifetime and with the commonwealth of scholars forever.

PROLOGUE

Literary critics often tell the truth, but they seldom take truth as their subject. Who would want to do a job that Lord Bacon (and his unlikely witness Pilate) turned down? Who would dare to define the world's most perplexing noun? The idea of a "literary" criticism, after all, seems to distinguish literature from ordinary experience and to protect it from crude attempts at verification. Bacon's successor in the art of taxonomy, Northrop Frye, has set the tempo for our age by insisting, however paradoxically, that the science of criticism must restrict itself to the purportedly literary attributes of texts. The flood of ideologies, counterideologies, and nonideologies that has precipitated from the work of Frye and others has all but sunken the fundamental question of truth *in* literature.

I italicize *"in"* in order to underline what I believe to be one provisional solution to the problem of capturing the truth *of* literature. The battle over truth in literature is usually transposed into a battle over the truth of literary criticism. This latter battle most often takes the form of a fight between those who test an essay against historical fact and those who demand that an essay deploy a critical technique or an ideology. The writer's purposes, like the application of literature to his, her, or our lives, gets lost in the shuffle. Historical researchers like Douglas Patey and Howard Weinbrot, for example, have inflicted deep wounds on both poststructuralist critical theory and its Marxist counterparts. These critics, however, have not so much eliminated as reshaped their enemies. By attacking the imperialism of many contemporary critical speculators, they champion a more complex, more theoretical engagement with both the past and the present. They open up the possibility of reconstructing what Lincoln Faller calls, in his brilliant synopsis of criminal biography, the "sociopoetics" and the "psychic realities" of the past.[1] Patey, Weinbrot, Faller, and others make it possible to think of an elusive yet objective thing like truth as part of a universe of discourse, but they also remind us that this universe was, is, and always will be filled not only with signs, but also with those courtiers, scribblers, philosophers, ideologues, actors, itinerants, shopkeepers, and laborers who read, accept, reject, and act in response to them.

To raise the perplexing problem of truth is to revise expectations about literature. To read texts philosophically is to upset comfortable conceptions about the character of writers. British authors of the late seventeenth and eighteenth centuries would not recognize our highly professionalized system of disciplines and genres. George Berkeley thought of himself as a philosopher, poet, traveler, cleric, and social reformer; Addison was no mere journalist. One unfortunate consequence of new criticism and its nineteenth-century antecedents has been the prizing of the aesthetic and the downplaying of the philosophical and the historical. Neither post-Romantic aestheticism nor new critical analysis, however, can blunt the hard philosophical edge of *Gulliver's Travels*, an edge sharpened by Paul Korshin and many others.[2] Neither Dryden nor Rochester can be properly appreciated without the recognition of their commitment to philosophical debate. There are certainly easier ways to entertain a literary audience than to pen a work like *The Hind and the Panther*; it boggles the imagination to think that Pope would steep himself in Leibniz, Bolingbroke, and Shaftesbury if he had only been interested in demonstrating rhetorical proficiency. It can be argued that the philosophizing writers of the eighteenth century either underread, overread, or otherwise misread their philosophical sources, yet careful research has shown, for example, that Pope paid more attention to the details of philosophical arguments, and thus evidenced greater concern for philosophical issues, than is commonly recognized.[3] By way of countering the resistance to the philosophical reading of literature, Barbara Shapiro has wisely declared that the discussion of truth suffused virtually every writing of the seventeenth century.[4] Although the issue of a philosophical reading of literature is far from settled, it is nevertheless clear that criticism is at last preparing to open the wax museum of literary history and engage the human originals of its effigies in the fully literary discourse of truth. It is time, as it has always been time, to take authors seriously.

A philosophical interpretation of literature, especially one centering on so complex an issue as truth, requires a thesis that is at once simple and polyvalent: simple, so that it may be clearly defined; polyvalent, so that it may account for the enormous variations within any historical period. I want to argue that late seventeenth- and eigh-

teenth-century writers treated explanatory systems as a kind of master
genre, that they regarded explaining and systematizing as a literary
mode with a vitality and a methodology of its own. My job will not
be to reduce authors to proponents of this or that system, but to deal
with systematizing as a technique for confronting, organizing, manipulating, and subduing experience. Writers, of course, have always
discussed experience, but, for reasons that I shall describe below, the
discussion became, during the Restoration and eighteenth century,
an attention-getting confrontation. In my project I am seconded by
that most popular of Restoration writers, Abraham Cowley, and by
that most projective of Restoration historians, Bishop Thomas Sprat.
Rejecting Cartesianism and Scholasticism, Sprat and Cowley suggest
that the traditional division of the world into mind and matter (or any
of a dozen other dualisms) will not suffice for a cultivated society.
Modern writers should promote the development of a third realm,
that of "Mediate Creatures" or "Mans Creatures": laws, procedures,
strategies, conventions, sciences, and artifacts.[5] The purpose of this
self-consciously artificial realm is to mediate between (and eventually
displace) divergent dualistic domains, whether those of spirit and
flesh or those of kings and commoners.

Following up on Sprat's and Cowley's concern for the priority of
the artificial, I shall demonstrate that explanatory systems gradually
took on most of the evidentiary functions that the "scientific" movement had initially reserved for experience. One of these functions
was, of course, to serve as a subject for literary representation. I shall
further argue that explanatory systems grew more extensive and complex as the period progressed; that, accordingly, they became more
and more eligible as objects for imitation and representation (in Pope,
for example); and that writers of the period were solving an ethical
and a psychological as much as a philosophical problem: namely, that
of eliciting consent to, and gaining artistic control over, artificial (and
artifactual) explanatory systems. My book therefore begins with Rochester, who spins out short poems on his often desperate attempts to
fit any of several explanations to any of several highly distressing,
highly unstable phenomena. It proceeds through Locke, who aims to
produce a complete, coherent, and autonomous domain for explanatory rhetoric. And it ends with Pope and Smith, who enlarge and
manipulate explanatory systems for aesthetic and moral effect, and
who must, as a result, find some way to assert their moral authority
over their ever-expanding explanatory discourse.

Criteria of Certainty recounts the story of the development, in the
English Enlightenment, of an epistemology of engagement. By evalu-

ating the enlargement of the process of explanation, it evaluates the role of system and system making, first in the act of believing, and, second, in the commitment of an author to the production of a didactic artifact. By attending to the *act* of explanation, I recover the process by which a collective, cultural concern with systematizing the world—with, for example, the epistemological defeat of ontological gaps like those endemic to Cartesianism—inscribes itself in the experience of particular authors. Cowley's tripartite world, after all, seeks stability by promoting a constructive instability. The asymmetry of its extreme terms, spirit and substance, entails the perpetual mobilization of the intermediate term, "Mans Creatures." Artificial things must not only *be*; they must explain, mediate, reconcile, and, most of all, act. The greater the division, distance, or tension between limiting terms like mind and matter, the more expansive the mediating system, and the more aggressive the mediator.

The importance of this "Mans World" (for which I shall substitute the ungendered term "human world") is therefore far greater than its insubstantial character might suggest. Although a seemingly abstract index of procedures and conventions, it bears directly on daily moral experience. It overshadows and eventually absorbs its more substantial counterparts. The artificial "human world" houses the components of, and justifications for, moral action. For the authors of my period, the making of art and things artificial counts as a particularly prestigious sort of action. This book offers a history of the expansion and enlivening of artificiality. It explores the enabling of the "relation"—first, as a foundation of knowledge; second, as the key ingredient in identity; and, finally, as a tool for linking the private act of consent with a publicly accessible, communal system of mediation. My argument therefore proposes revisions in modern criticism. It allows for the sense of engagement that characterizes new historicism, but it locates this engagement on the psychic and literary battleground, a battleground whose boundaries have been but inadequately surveyed by semiotics and neostructuralist criticism.

Statements about theses and approaches must be amplified by facts. A full account of seventeenth-century intellectual history is beyond the scope of this book, but the most influential factors in the development of a literature about truth can be set forth briefly.

The seventeenth-century preoccupation with certainty signals both a renewed confidence in human intellectual powers and a collective doubt concerning the availability of truth. On one hand, startling social and intellectual developments—the civil war, the vogue for skepticism, exposure to New World peoples, and the challenge of a more pluralistic world—had tarnished the reputation and reliability of truth. On the other hand, the pursuit of a non-Scholastic basis for science, the search for a useful knowledge, and the need to legitimize an increasingly secular government gave the question of truth an unusual urgency.

At the center of debate in the later seventeenth century was the "Rule of Faith" controversy, in which Tillotson, Chillingworth, and Wilkins were the chief disputants.[6] Squabbling over the discovery of a means for choosing between religions, these controversialists drew less attention to the rightness of a given doctrine than to the criteria for consenting to it. Overall, the seventeenth-century discussion of "certainty" played down veracity but played up verification. Chillingworth, for example, ventured that "moral certainty," a tenuous "assurance" that allows for organized action in the face of philosophical doubt, might have more practical value and offer more psychological comfort than might intellectual certainty about abstract truth. This Chillingworthian process of systematically replacing and responding to a missing truth, I would suggest, corresponds to the production of a mediating "human world."

The issue of "moral certainty" reverberates through most seventeenth- and eighteenth-century writing. The appeal of "moral certainty" to those whom Shaftesbury would call "the moralists"— under which heading he includes poets—results from its artificial, hybrid character. "Moral certainty" combines both the social and the skeptical in a single psychological process. It uses philosophical doubt to spur constructive social action. Divines like Chillingworth have no special claim on this way of thinking. Seventeenth-century probability theory, for example, constructed useful systems out of random events.[7] It allowed for belief in "laws"—laws that experience, in its randomness, could never evidence. Metaphysics fell on similar expedients. Cartesian dualism had blunted hopes for a unified, final truth. Oddly enough, the practical English had a more difficult time than did their Continental counterparts in accepting Descartes's valiant efforts to affirm, theoretically, the coherence of the divided universe. Rather than reason away the fragmentation of Descartes's world, they opted to look for a third party, a mediator. Cambridge wizards like Ralph Cudworth and Henry More, for example, concocted a mystical "plastic director" to mediate between God and nature. The same drama unfolded in the theater of religious speculation. Of the many factions that made up religious life in the seventeenth century, that complex array of congregationalist divines who fell into the "Puritan" movement were probably the most enamored of a dualistic distinction between the church and the world. Political expediency demanded that these fractious parties devise ad hoc justifications for interacting with the world and among themselves, the ultimate example, of course, being the near-legitimizing of the Interregnum government.

Last but not least, Restoration science stressed cooperative, practical research. The social by-products of scientific activity—academies, colleges, social reforms—attained an equal footing with the products of research. Reformers like Glanvill, Sprat, Wilkins, and Boyle would have made fine conventioneers. They talked a great deal about the priority of experience, but their first step toward its study was the proposing of visionary societies, especially "courts of eloquence." "Experience" could only be made available through an artificial, mediating construct. The usual mediators, reason and revelation, could not do the trick. Reason and revelation, which work within the mind, lack artificiality and sociability. An artificial mediating device, like Cowley's odes on the relation of nature to science, must draw on shared, publicly accessible conventions. The fact that an *artificial* mediator must itself be incongruent with the natural world and the real minds that it would reconcile may well doom it to failure, yet this incongruence also keeps open the process of artful explanation and explanatory confrontation. Were they alive today, the virtuosi (and the poets who glorified them) would revise Marxist criticism, for they would value the intellectual alienation that encourages the production of explanatory discourse. They would, however, also distrust the formalist ideal, for they would link the production of systematic explanations with the production of moral value and potentially destabilizing belief. It is no accident that an eccentric young enthusiast like Adam Smith should end up as a taxonomist of public policy, nor is it odd that an architect of public policy like the Marquis of Halifax should carry out his political projects by writing literary characters.

The mention of Halifax, an author who talked around, but seldom about, his topics, leads naturally to the question of "approach." Approaches can be defined either negatively, by what they exclude, or positively, by what they admit. It's always wise to end on a happy note, so I'll begin by differentiating myself from my admired predecessors.

Any large-scale study risks dismissal as "synoptic." Dr. Johnson may grumble that people need reminding more often than they need instructing, but contemporary scholarship has marginalized attempts to index whole eras. And with good reason. Too often these intellectual odysseys do little more than string together paragraphs better suited for service as anthology headnotes. Even the best of the early handbooks, those of A.D. McKillop and George Sherburn, freely reduce complex movements into neat headings like "neoclassicism" or "minor poets."[8]

From critics like McKillop and Sherburn I shall differ in obvious ways, most importantly by rejecting their implicitly biographical model of explanation. By emphasizing writers' lives and careers, these encyclopedists insinuate that biographical events control—or, worse, cause—writers' literary activity. I plan to avoid altogether what these authors would deem a synoptic study. Rather than passing briefly through dozens of occasionally great men of literary history, I shall offer extended readings of seven, emphasizing the ways in which individual writers *generate* (and also deviate from) rather than react to their intellectual milieu. My authors postulate rather than report on their literary mode; they energize this mode by also postulating their deviation from it.

A second, more sophisticated type of synopsis has afforded me a great deal of guidance, but it has not exhausted the resources of its genre. Basil Willey, Leroy Loemker, Donald Greene, Paul Fussell, and Henrik Van Leeuwen constitute the ancients in this company; Barbara Shapiro and Douglas Patey appear as their modern counterparts. These searching authors evidence an excruciating, almost penitent awareness of the problems of historical explanation. Hounded by editors and bitten by new critics, these ambitious authors offer what they timidly describe as "background" books. Each of these scholars accepts a pat, authoritarian distinction between a "foreground," what Willey chillingly calls "pure" literature, and a "background," its social-cultural-philosophical-religious milieu. This awkward distinction leads to perplexities in the study of writers like Mandeville, who must surely be the strangest pure philosopher in town, of dramatists like Wycherley, who revels in the mixing of modes, or of latter-day lawgivers like Blackmore, who versifies metaphysics. For this reason, Basil Willey's "background" book contains no chapters on what is usually thought of as "pure" literature; Leroy Loemker suggests that every writer in the directory of seventeenth-century studies was "struggling" out of a background, toward some elusive "synthesis"; Paul Fussell, in listing twelve ideas that constitute "humanism," forgets that ideas (as well as "ethics and imagery") derive from far more flexible attitudes; and Donald Greene, while masterfully detailing the background events of the eighteenth century, seems to lose sight of the variety of its literature.[9] Greene's book is especially puzzling, for it rejects the sloppy use of a term like "Augustan" only to introduce another equally vague one, "Augustinianism," with the surprising result that Dryden and Cowper appear in the same register of orthodoxy.[10]

My approach denies this dichotomy of "background" and "foreground" and argues instead for what strikes me as a commonsense viewpoint: that "background" is best understood through the interpretation of those who played their works against it, those for whom it was, in fact, the foreground. Backgrounds, in any case, have a way of changing places with foregrounds; Dryden is in the background of a history of skepticism, but skepticism is in the background of a study of Dryden. The problem of backgrounding is in many ways most acute in the recent entrants into the "background" sweepstakes. Barbara Shapiro and Douglas Patey have hoarded vast treasuries of background data. Yet both critics, superb as they are, fail to find the "distinct intellectual style" of their era, let alone the "mental process of joining such parts into a whole in the process of reading."[11] What is missing in Patey's and Shapiro's magisterial studies is a sense of the immediate experience of that background; Patey, for example, reduces the novels of the later century to a system of "probable signs," making little effort to reconstitute the spontaneous, energetic experience of thinking about and consenting to this system. In one study of systematicity in later eighteenth-century fiction, Eric Rothstein talks about the procedural character of systems—about their role in mental actions like evaluating, deciding, predicting, and acting.[12] I wish that Rothstein had not limited systematicity to one genre, but I admire and emulate his feeling for the vitality of the act of explanation.

A third type of synopsis would be best designated as the "progress." In its most innocuous form, the progress traces the historical transformations of what Arthur O. Lovejoy called "unit ideas."[13] In its most dangerous form, the progress charts the successive reactions of writers to some figure, usually a great man, like Newton or Bacon, who has interests outside literature.[14] In its most studied form, the progress documents the transformation of one age into its successor, the best example being Walter Jackson Bate's *From Classic to Romantic*.[15]

The difficulty with the progress arises from its tendency to discover progress. A progress must nominate some beginning point, like a great man, then must force this historical marker into the rear guard of a larger social movement, then must finally arrive at the Jerusalem of a later age. Even Bate casts the unlucky Descartes into that miserable *bolga*, the beginning, then leads his panting student toward the paradise of Romanticism. In my study, I hope to avoid this "progressive fallacy" by dealing with individuals before movements, by exemplifying a full range of possible variations on the systematizing mode, and by suggesting that the road between the Cavalier and the Romantic is a two-way street, nay, a ring road. I shall challenge the still-common view of the period as a long march toward sentimentality or naturalism. By analyzing Locke's discussion of the relation of the individual to that most public of artifacts, language, for example, I aim to play down the role of privacy and self-expression in Romanticism (and, conversely, to play up their role in earlier writers). By treating processes like systematizing and complication, I shall question attempts to understand a change in "mode" as a change in one or more dominant themes, whether the privileged theme be imagination, nature, genius, classicism, allusive poetry, probability theory, Palladianism, or prophecy. I shall vest systematicity not in an issue or a genre but in the consenting impulse that animates the "human" world.

To speak by way of affirmation rather than differentiation, I would say that my own project adds a psychological and epistemological dimension to the social and historical criticism practiced by my predecessors. My enterprise attempts to recover the moral and psychological experience of a specific, and for the most part privileged, reading community. I aim, however, not for a neo-Romantic apotheosis of the self, but for a sense of the individual as both an integral and an integrating member of this community. Hence I've selected Locke as one of my keynote authors—not simply because Locke appears in every synopsis, but because Locke's contractual account of society provides a road map for the trip between the self and the community.

It might be argued that the study of a logical entity like truth is inconsistent with a socially and psychologically alert criticism. This objection would stem from a contemporary prejudice: the habit of thinking of the self as alienated from the system, a habit that is seldom found among seventeenth- and eighteenth-century authors. For these writers (and, I think, for us), the discussion of the "philosophical" applications and meanings of texts entails a discussion of the motivations leading to their production. Those who tackle a philosophical problem generally have a solution in mind or an agenda to fulfill. Explanation expresses moral desire. Philosophical interpretation inevitably raises the issue of authorial intention, an issue that, however long out of vogue, simply refuses to go away. Like critics from Dr.

Johnson to Douglas Patey, I affirm that literary signs serve a moral as well as an intellectual purpose, that they would not exist were they not *intended* to reveal referents, whether or not they achieve that goal.

Following the lead of that greatest of reconcilers, the Marquis of Halifax, I designate my critical approach in two converging ways. First I invoke the example of that once great but lately impugned reformer, Deng Xiaoping. During his halcyon days, Deng sweetened his capitalist policies by describing them as "Chinese style socialism." Were I to follow his example, I would call my criticism "all-American Marxism." One aberration of our era is the assumption that all criticism dealing with historical milieux must derive from leftist intellectual traditions. That peculiar new term "new historicism" has come to signify the analysis of large-scale, allegedly historical dialectics, processes that operate across whole classes of people but seldom register the influence of individuals. The czar of imperial neo-Marxism, Louis Althusser, is fond of reducing even such suitably rebellious thinkers as Spinoza into "detours" in the historical juggernaut's path.[16] Even moderate literati like Max Horkheimer and Theodor Adorno write off examples of individual deviancy as devious illusions. Orson Welles's "departures from the norm" emerge as "calculated mutations which serve all the more strongly to confirm the validity of the system."[17] But who made this "system"? Who, to use that new historicist buzzword, will take *responsibility* for it?

My criticism co-opts the Marxist program. Following the lead of John Locke, that latter-day Puritan and intellectual ancestor of entrepreneurial American criticism, I discuss the production of social structures from the actions of single (and singly talented) citizens. I attend to the production of the work and to the function of writers in a community, but I evaluate production with regard to the experience— and the fact—of the individual who produces. Likewise, I try to cure that obsession with commodities that leads Marxists to treat works as impersonal products rather than personalized productions. This fixation with products sustains Antonio Gramsci's enthusiastic attempt to align "intellectual elaboration" with "muscular nervous effort."[18] It leads an otherwise sensitive reader of eighteenth-century texts like Arnold Kettle to declare baldly that "the whole history of realism" is "bound up" with "material success" and (again) "bound up" with "control and power" without bothering to elucidate the cause-and-effect relationships or to name the responsible agents implied by the verb "bound."[19]

Throughout my book, I shall speak of a "collected" rather than a collective idea of society, thereby pointing up the priority of sepa-

rate, generative individuals over generated products or overempow-
ered states. Sir Lewis Namier warned that any project in period history
will end up attending to an "extraordinary club" of persons who, like
the members of Parliament, have emerged as representatives of their
times, or who, like writers and revolutionaries, have otherwise nominated themselves as social reformers.[20] More recently, J.C.D. Clark
has demanded that critics and historians recognize "categories which
those [past] societies present to us," categories, like "authority," "belief," and "rebellion," that fit poorly with the orthodox Marxist processes of "class conflict" or "revolution."[21] Rather than follow the
lead of an austere writer like Pierre Macherey, who talks about silence,
about what writers leave unsaid, and about what the finished product
doesn't disclose, I talk about what is said by writers who are talking,
announcing, and loudly producing, who are fully conscious of what
they are doing, who present themselves as leaders of their societies,[22]
and who expect, like Marx himself, to construct the self within a world
system that is both social and objective, both ideological and verifi-
able.[23] A neocapitalist critique, my book values those intentions that
produce value-conscious writing, those mediating processes through
which explanatory systems are produced, and those ethical and social
systems that surround literature. In a recent study of Bernard Mandeville, M.M. Goldsmith explains that Marxism follows a "C-M-C" format: commodities are exchanged for money, which in turn is
converted back into more commodities. Capitalism, he further explains, follows an "M-C-M" format, in which money obtains commodities in order to convert them into more money.[24] I think of my
approach as essentially "capitalist" in that it proceeds from value-
producing intentions, to works, and finally to that fuller system of
intentions that constitutes society. It encourages interpretation, the
capitalizing of the work into that system of meaning and value produced by both the data of history and the attitudes of its denizens.

   For my second description of my method, I call up another new
term, "engaged semiotics." Structuralism and its deconstructing successors derive from the critical philosophical traditions of the Enlightenment. Still, the concern of the English Enlightenment with action
and instability, especially in their psychological or political manifestations, disquiets the practitioners of this intensely theoretical critical
mode. Derek Attridge has recently constructed his deconstructive
reading of Western literature around the "three obvious turning
points" of "Renaissance, Romanticism and Modernism," dropping
our period into the great gulf of *différance*.[25] As Hazard Adams re-
spectfully cautions, writers like Derrida and de Man "assume a nar-

row and monolithic view of language, not as a creative power," but as "reactionary play within an infinite enclosure," as a system of signs "radically cut off from meaning."[26] Taking the mandate from Adams, himself a student of that system-smashing Enlightenment genius William Blake, I examine the *source* of our own deconstructed, language-saturated universe: those system-generating writers of the late seventeenth and eighteenth centuries who recognized both the comprehensiveness and the arbitrariness of their works but who also believed in those systems, who, in struggling to gain authorial hegemony over them, charted an escape route from the potential prison of semiotics, who lived both within and without the hermeneutic circle, and who, like Halifax's deconstructed post-Stuart monarch, would both make and abide by the law.

Jonathan Culler says that deconstructionists doubt the possibility *of* systematic knowledge;[27] I intend to show that authors in the Restoration and the eighteenth century were less concerned with a distant knowledge *of* than a coherent knowledge *in* systems, a knowledge that *is* system and that begins *in* systematizing acts. While Derrida dares "to think only in signs" and "to think play radically," writers from Rochester to Smith, I respond, dare to play with signs, to build signifying but also significant systems, and to retain the authority to preempt those systems. For them, the occasional breaking of the hermeneutic circle confirms the relevance of explanatory constructs to an engaged, authoring mind.[28] Paul de Man points to the "anxiety traces," "hesitations," and unexpected "theological allusions" that pop up in the most language-conscious texts of the eighteenth century.[29] In coining the term "language-conscious," I initiate my own project to explain such unexpected deviations from the monolithic semiotics of both our own age and the Enlightenment by writing about—by textualizing—the consciousnesses that produced them. When Michel Foucault declares that the "rules" composing his "archive" are "caught up in the very things that they connect," he implies that any discussion of the source of these rules, the collection of persons who constitute society, would also be "caught up" in this system of "statements"; yet, while it may well be "impossible for us to describe our own archive," it might be possible for the archive to describe us, to serve as an instrument of disclosure and as a treasure-trove of explanatory rhetoric rather than as a veil over the empty temple of inaccessible knowledge.[30]

My argument, I affirm, has been enriched by the contribution of poststructuralist and semiotic criticism. Perhaps the central issue in my work is the matter of "relations" and relational ideas in eighteenth-

century writing. For me, moreover, this issue is central, not decen-
tered. Unlike deconstructive critics, I am prepared to privilege this
relation, to examine the empowering fullness of the "trace" or "sup-
plementarity" and to allow this fullness to turn a mere system of
signs into a meaning*ful* system of value. I am prepared to establish
a relation between our own critical discourse and that of the past, to
disclose rather than to veil the "antecedents" of contemporary deconstructive critics. Like George Berkeley, I assume that the system
of language always engages us in a constructive action as well as a
reflective interpretation. Interpretation itself is something of an action. Action need not serve any one ideology; as I will show in my
chapter on Swift, it can very well be directed at the reification of
systematicity in general.

A word should be said about the relation of my approach to my
selection of authors. A practical concern for the size of my volume
and a reserve about traditional synopses have prevented me from
including every author who might fit with my argument. My selection
of writers is necessarily based on arbitrary but useful criteria: their
relevance to my theme, their stature, and, to some extent, their in-
teracquaintance. I have not hesitated to include biographical and historical data when appropriate, but I have tried to avoid the confusion
of my interpretative project with a study of influences and associations. Writers have been selected because they seem to represent more
clearly than other candidates successive permutations and enlarge-
ments of the "human world." Rochester's poems pit the world and
the poet against one another, bringing about a fragile reconciliation
through (and giving substance to) the sheer act of hypothesizing;
Halifax devises a more stable but still foundationless system for the
prolonged balancing of warring political forces; Dryden charts a
course for the expansion of a reconciling world of debate; Locke devises a system that prizes coherence but that stands in a fragile ana-
logical relationship with ordinary experience; Swift tries to lend a kind
of moral stability to Locke's system; Pope devises more and more
systems to manage and stabilize the proliferation of systems; and,
finally, Smith returns to Rochester's confrontational mode, this time
wrestling with a system that, like experience, threatens to undercut
his moral authority. My approach is therefore Addisonian or Butleri-
an; like a "character," it heightens the features and outlines the limits
of an elusive quantity, the collected "personality" of an age.

This project is an unrepentant exercise in centrality, but it does
legislate an expansion in the canon. Dryden, Locke, Pope, and Swift
have been central to their respective canons since their own time. For

vastly different reasons, Rochester, Halifax, and Smith have been sent packing from the contemporary awareness. Yet Rochester was central to both the court and popular cultures of his era; Halifax's natural habitat was the pinnacle of power; the influence of Smith and the Scottish school has been vastly underestimated.[31] I have tried, however incompetently, to suggest that historians may maintain the idea of a mainstream mode yet recognize that that mode allows for extraordinary deviation. What I call the "epistemology of engagement" has naturally led me to what one reader of this text has called the "social reconstruction of the self," the charting of a map to the deviant individual mind as it is projected on the greater mind that constitutes culture.

All authors flatter themselves with the expectation that great consequences will accrue from their labors. From this vanity I am not exempt. Although my principal concern is with the late seventeenth and eighteenth centuries, I hope that this book makes four points of a more general interest.

First, I want to suggest the possibility of a renewed discussion of the literary period. No one would want to return to a mystical *Geistesgeschicte* approach. Reductive approaches, however, can go too far. No one will ever satisfactorily define terms like "Augustan" or "neoclassical," yet any fool can distinguish the milieu of 1726 from that of 1826. Organizations like the American Society for Eighteenth-Centuries Studies would not exist were there no commonsense notion of their titular periods. Nonetheless, serious questions have been raised, most recently by John Steadman, concerning whether a concept like "period style" can have any meaning.[32] Like Dr. Johnson, Steadman finds numerous instances in which similar literary conventions serve contrary ends. Steadman's reticence results from his analysis of "period style" from the outside. Looking at literary conventions from a remote vantage point, he undermines attempts to tie them to specific ideas. Steadman downplays the possibility that authors may consciously choose to deploy those conventions that, in their milieux, seem to manifest an idea. I shall explore the thought of the late seventeenth and eighteenth centuries from the inside, recapturing the attempt of authors to deploy their evolving mode against an all-too-new, all-too-vital notion of experience. I hope to set the notion of "period style" on what we would now call "psychosocial" grounds, although I shall repeatedly stress that the authors of my period would only credit the "psychological" when it announced itself through the manufacture, identification, and organization of some publicly accessible object or system. Writers throughout the eighteenth century, for example, were fond of the term "common sense," yet this common sense invariably presented itself in judgments by individuals—individuals whose commonsense judgments could only be credited if, circularly, their society recognized them as persons of common sense.

My second point concerns the premier philosophical movement of the era, empiricism. Open any anthology of literature and you will find empiricism, the gospel of objectivity, associated with psychology, the apocrypha of subjectivity. This paradoxical association is often felt but seldom proved to be viable. My presentation of empiricism will reveal a philosophical tradition that is less a myth of observation than a mode of consent, less a way of widening or closing than of proceeding across the mind-body chasm. Semioticians have been eager to lay claim to Locke, the self-professed practitioner of 6ημειωγικὴ, but they have missed the fact that Locke is more interested in the production of "identities," in the manufacture of a public language of "objects," than in the reading of signs. Empiricism was, from its beginning, more literary than empirical; Lockean cognition looks a great deal like literary authorship. Writers as diverse as Locke, Berkeley, Shaftesbury, Hutcheson, Hume, and Smith were uniformly concerned with the establishment of explanatory and admonitory formats for experience, but only marginally concerned with experience itself. Ever expressive, empiricism values the voluntary reconciliation of inconsistent facts, forces, and experiences. Despite its nominal privileging of experience, empiricism could only lead to a sententious, reconciling poetry like Pope's—to the favoring of satire, a mode that attacks uncooperative experience.

My third point concerns genre. Critics of a tender constitution may object to my mixing of genres, especially to my eliciting of philosophical significance from literary texts. Some may suggest that lovely poems and crabbed treatises should never mingle. I have already mentioned the reluctance of earlier authors to enclose themselves in a sterile, bellettristic literature. All of the authors in this study grant to art the power to disrupt, displace, and finally systematize experience; conversely, all see philosophy as a literary mode, a way of solving ontological problems through the reorganization of language. Smith's impartial spectator looks to us more like Mighty Mouse than Superman, but Smith allowed his monster to pass moral judgments because he allegedly understood the rule of good taste. In discussing mediating systems, I hope to restore some credibility to Pope's injunction that none can compass more than they intend—that intention, function, and motivation are contributing factors to the formation of a genre. A pastoral may function equally well as a mediating act, as may a polemic. Critics will have more luck identifying Mandeville's *Fable of the Bees* if they attend to what Mandeville intends than if they puzzle over its formlessness. In his ground-breaking *Philosophical Writing*, John Richetti has argued for the analysis of texts in terms of their rhetorical power.[33] I shall continue his argument by stressing the literary significance of philosophical texts; I shall hope to enlarge it by amplifying his implicit call for the philosophical interpretation of literary works. The authors of the late seventeenth and eighteenth centuries understood that the biggest of all generic distinctions, that of literature from philosophy, was at best a provisional hypothesis. And hypotheses, for these same authors, were meant to chart paths between apparently disparate phenomena.

My fourth and sharpest point concerns the validity of criticism generally. This book is not a treatise on critical theory, but it does hope to redirect, by a few degrees, the course of critical inquiry. Literary criticism of the last twenty years has been split between what Halifax would call the gentleman-admirals (structuralists, deconstructionists, semioticians, and others locked up in the officer's quarters of hermeneutics while sailing off the horizon of reference) and the tarpaulins (Marxists, feminists, and other advocates of groups—all mutineers from the great tradition but all unable to assume the rank and privilege needed to captain the literary sloop). I want to set aside the question of the propriety of applying post-eighteenth-century ideology to eighteenth-century texts, and ask instead whether these movements have adequately registered developments in contemporary thought. Responsible criticism ought to be true, and not just to evidence drawn from critics; if it is to retain its credibility, it must avoid Scholasticism.

The central topos of this book is the confrontation of the individual writer with experience, or, as it were, with nature. The contemporary reevaluation of nature has, alas, largely escaped the notice of contemporary critics. In his mammoth *Sociobiology*, Edward O. Wilson (who is fond of citing Butler, Kant, and Leibniz) establishes the groundwork for a description of human behavior, including "aesthetic" behavior, in terms of the complete genetic history of the organism. Wilson's discovery of almost unlimited "plasticity" in social behavior short-circuits any attempt to think in collectivist terms. Talk about "classes" or about stages of history applies to so small a segment of humanity that it carries little explanatory force.[34] One contribution of deconstruction, with its unremitting emphasis on difference, is the debunking of superstitious notions of class. Even the most fervid

Marxists confess that "the deconstructive rewriting of the classical dialectic removes the justification for the conservative Marxist model of a linearly evolutionary and finalistically resolutive progress to socialism."[35]

Explorations of the systematicity of the individual and of the limitations of individual systems would have accomplished this end even without the complicity of Derridians. Cybernetic theory offers good news for critics interested in justifying the reconstruction of the individual experience: artificial intelligence has elicited from an artifact, a machine, the simulacrum of volition; computer science has made it possible to describe systematically what takes place inside at least one "black box," one simulated mind; ideas concerning freedom and "chaos" have spread through most of the sciences; and cognitive psychology has made it possible to reconstruct internal processing algorithms, systems that evidence the operation not only of consciousness, but of the "unconscious" as well.[36] The sciences of "expert systems" and of neurobiology have converted material into information, information into processes, and nostalgic materialism into dynamic functionalism. The key to this preliminary retrieval of inner experience has been an insistence on the association of private consciousness with systematicity and publicity, whether through the use of programming conventions or through the assumption that elusive, quasi-Freudian entities like "the unconscious" may be induced to announce (and demystify) themselves in an artificial language. My point here is that it is quite in accord with contemporary research to talk, as I do, about the association of conscious or moral processes with their announcement in modes, systems, and functions. I am in agreement with most contemporary students of the subject when I assert that intention is a type of information, and, moreover, that information can only be understood when it is processed, applied, conventionalized, and finally personalized.

PART I

Restoration of Certainty

CHAPTER ONE

ROCHESTER

Confrontational Systems

The Earl of Rochester, alias John Wilmot, alias Dr. Bendo, alias everyman: like truth, ever elusive, but like certainty, ever pursued. The poems of Rochester open as wide an entry as possible into the subject of a verifying literature, a literature that transforms irregular experience into the foundations of coherent belief. Like experience itself, Rochester's poems never fail to draw a full range of responses; like the topic of certainty, his writings have been easy to trivialize or dismiss. As late as 1953, censors of Vivian de Sola Pinto's edition could only see the pornographic jester, not the philosophizing poet. Yet, like truth itself, Rochester won't quite go away. Year after year, annals of popular taste like the *Norton Anthology* cannot quite edit out this "dangerous seducer" and "natural man."[1]

The confused reaction to Rochester results largely from the well-intentioned efforts of his critics to read him in too redemptive a way. In order to lend legitimacy to their courtly satyr, Rochester's advocates try to explain him with regard to what he *is* rather than to what he *does*. Rochester becomes either the world's greatest index of literary conventions or the world's greatest libertine thinker, but he never becomes a libertine thinker who uses literary conventions in philosophical ways. Attempts to say what Rochester *is* may not have spread from China to Peru, but they do extend from Hawaii to New York. Dustin Griffin opens his masterful study with a list of Rochester's reading in skeptical philosophers, never asking what type of influence such a strange collection of disaffected aristocrats and devilish rogues might exert; Kristoffer Paulson invests oversize meaning in a sermon by Stillingfleet; C.F. Main champions the legacy of Montaigne; J.W. Johnson seconds the French Epicureans; David Farley-Hills resorts to inverting St. Augustine; Raymond Whitley and Thomas Fujimara brand Rochester a generic "pessimist" and a "translator" of Hobbes.[2] It is, of course, important to remember that anyone who has studied the subject has become convinced that Rochester has deep philosophical concerns and has realized that he devotes an unusually large portion of his work to the offering of a variety of theories and explanations for a variety of things and problems. The trouble with all of the aforementioned critical projects is that they enroll Rochester in this or that particular school, whereupon he becomes a naughty student indeed, with the result that the critical project succumbs to ridicule. Is the author of "To the Postboy" really a "translator" or an "Augustinian"?

To take Rochester's poetry seriously, critically, is to take his explosive "frivolity" seriously—to read him not as the burlesquing scribe for some philosophical tradition, but as a sort of philosopher himself, or, better, as a philosophizer, a user and manipulator of philosophical rhetoric. A theorizing poet, Rochester sets his poems in highly hypothetical situations. He creates those situations by raising questions about them, and he confronts experience by speculating about its relation to his philosophizing discourse. Dislocating moral value, sporting with audience expectations, and systematically manipulating every literary convention in the book, Rochester's poems irreverently demolish, reconstruct, and relocate the foundations of human knowledge. As Howard Erskine-Hill brilliantly argues, Rochester's poetry not only questions the *results* of the exploration of the world, but it questions the *value* of the exploration itself.[3] It draws painful, awkward laughter by using familiar literary techniques, especially those of comedy and satire, to confront, abuse, and wring intelligibility from a world that not only is not, but vigorously refuses to be, intelligible. Unlike lesser poets, Rochester takes more pleasure in the wringing than in the knowledge, in the confrontation with, rather than in the discovery of, truth.

I want to deal with the three most important items on Rochester's agenda. First, Rochester wants to substitute the attainment of certainty, a psychological process, for truth. As a poet, Rochester is ideally suited to a distinctly modern mode of philosophizing: to the multiplying and experiencing of theories with less concern for their truth than for their moral and aesthetic effect. Rochester wants to dialogue with experience, to avoid putting an end to the fun by terminating this continuing process of philosophical confrontation in a closed philosophical system. Second, Rochester wants to define a "human world" in which explanatory systems can generate certainty and, thence, moral and aesthetic action. He wants to set philosophical systems in the context of motivation, to regard his own highly conventionalized poetry as a means of forcefully and voluntarily approaching and moralizing a reluctant world. Third, Rochester wants to fill his world with as many artificial, systematically defined things— laws, rules, conventions—as he can make. Not infrequently he styles himself as a shrill, poetic voice discoursing about and between two more real things, usually God and nature. Serving as a third, artificial "thing," as the unnatural source of "Mans Creatures," Rochester confronts, dualistically, the duality of spirit and matter. As G. Douglas Atkins, citing Hillis Miller, observes, the relation between author and text implies a third party to whom these two parties are related, a party that might be a mere "trace," but might be a full-fledged "God";[4] and so, for Rochester, the confrontation between worlds and ontologies implies the presence of a human world, a world that may be groundless, that may be a ground of something significant, or that may, in grounding a world of artificial human creatures, be both at the same time.

Rochester's poetry, I shall argue, experiments with the paradox of necessary moral commitment to a contingent world of artificial systems, of theories, conventions, and explanatory systems. He reduces philosophical argumentation to poetic technique, but he also presents technique as a means of defining that "strange prodigious creature man." Rochester "loved to talk and write of speculative matters" in which he held not the slightest belief, for he was less interested in the answers to the problems of philosophy than in the process of responding to them. By framing responses to his favorite "Cartesian" problem, the relation of the mind to the world, he makes "certainty" into something more than idiosyncratic belief.[5]

My revisionist presentation of Rochester as perpetual reviser will be divided into four parts. In the first, I shall talk about Rochester's treatment of philosophical approaches to the world as the substance of poetic experience. I shall show how Rochester uses artificial poetic conventions to counteract the violent instability of a far more substantial experience. In my second part, I shall discuss Rochester's attempt to assert the continuity of explanation with the world explained. I shall examine Rochester's experimentation with literary forms, arguing that he treats this kind of literary play as a counterpart to philosophical hypothesizing, and, hence, as an important factor in the process of eliciting belief. In my third part, I shall show how the assertion of the continuity of explanations with objects turns into a battle, and how the combat between theory and experience leads to the intensification of Rochester's unremitting campaign of explanation. And, in the fourth, I shall talk about how Rochester binds himself up in a complex dilemma—how he perpetuates the art of explanation by exempting it from crude verification, and how, in thus depriving explanation of its presumed use, he opens the problem of finding another use for it.

SUBSTANTIATING THE APPROACH

Rochester always writes from an exaggerated pose. "Exaggerated" is a key word: posing permits Rochester to exaggerate his incongruity with himself, with his poems, with his persona, with his world, and, finally, with the literary tradition on which those poses depend. In Rochester's enlarged world, incongruence becomes opposition, opposition opens up epistemological distance, epistemological distance encourages hypothesizing, and hypothesizing initiates the psychological motion toward certainty. One need only look to Bishop Burnet's biography in order to see how one terrifying pose, that of the deathbed penitent, could convert a life dedicated to skeptics, libertines, and assorted disbelievers into a melodramatic motion toward belief.

Rochester's obsessive experimentation with and subversion of poetic forms underwrites his program to ground literature in the speculative act. It enables him to produce a kind of experience that cannot be contained in preestablished poetic traditions, traditions that assume a ready-made, mimetic relation between literary conventions and experience. By exaggerating the conventionality of his poems while trivializing their "social" subjects, Rochester orchestrates a mock-heroic confrontation between convention and experience.[6] In social satires like *A Ramble in St. James's Park* or in *A Letter from Artemisia in the Town to Chloe in the Country*, for example, overwrought heroic couplets do battle with a bland review of the social vices. Chloe bores on for "two hours, some grains of sense" being "mixed with volleys of impertinence" (*Artemisia to Chloe*, ll. 255-56) while stately heroic verse points up the triviality of her society. Comic fact and heroic form together fail to draw coherence from a world that, generically, they divide in two. From the decadently social yet paramilitary "command" that opens the poem to the fatigued comments that command its ending, *Artemisia to Chloe* tears itself apart. Various social, gender, and poetic expectations are "dashed" by (and against) assorted heroical and rhetorical sallies (see *Artemisia to Chloe*, ll. 1-15). Such so-called "social satires" form the largest part of Rochester's oeuvre, and in all of them Rochester follows this same strategy: dichotomizing the poem between its shape and substance, exaggerating this dichotomy so as to suggest that glamorous conventions always conflict with wretched experiences, and, finally and implicitly, suggesting that the approach to, and explanation of, experience, whether poetic, social, or natural, might make a more substantial subject for poetry than might experience itself.

Rochester could be said to be interested in "substantiating" the approach. He presents his poems as both the locus and the product of an epistemological rift. The epistolary form of *Artemisia to Chloe*, for example, suggests that the recipient, or at least the addressing of a recipient, is of some importance to the poem. But by forcing readers to know that addressee as only a postulate, as little more than the recipient of Artemesia's unreliable reports or as the inappropriately passive audience for Artemesia's inappropriately heroic journalism, this poem prevents its reader from knowing either Chloe or the world behind Artemesia's rhetoric. Yet *Artemisia to Chloe* and similar "social" poems keep Rochester and his readers on the move. Never resolving on a form, a tone, or an attitude, they remain lists of events, observations, and disconnected notions, forcing their readers to keep trying to devise some approach to the problem of knowing the world and the people in it. Because this task can never be finished, the approach *to* becomes the experience *of* the poem.

Rochester, appropriately, almost always presents his poems as capsulized (and complex) dualisms. His genre always counterpoints his subject, and his own pose counterpoints both. In *A Ramble in St. James's Park*, for example, Rochester carefully observes all the rules of satire. He counterpoints his conventionality by calling attention to his strict observance of one obsolete rule, that satire should be rough.[7] Posing as an author who is only trying on poses, he exaggerates his difference from the miniature worlds of his poems—a strategy that, in turn, exaggerates the isolation of the explaining writer from the experience he would explain.[8] Rochester chooses the lyric, pastoral mode for almost half his poems, for no other mode could so contrast with his sometimes angry and sometimes rakish persona. In a poem like "Fair Chloris," pastoral elegy supports a fantasy about coy innocence and visionary rape. The topic that interests Rochester, the accidental masturbation that occasions Chloris's dream, undercuts both the lurid tenor of the story, a rape, and its vehicle, the pastoral poem. In "Love a Woman? You're an Ass," romantic lyric and satire both conflict with the practical lesson of the poem, that boys work as well as girls in inspiring raptures—a power extended in "M.G. to

O.B." to excrement. In *The Disabled Debauchee*, Rochester uses the high-tone Gondibert stanza to enforce so great a separation between his lofty form and his plodding subject that it becomes impossible to determine (but easy to speculate) whether heroic form satirizes pathetic subject, vice versa (as Dustin Griffin suggests), or both.[9] Rochester's poems open up a great deal of distance between reader, writer, poem, tradition, form, and subject, with the result that the closing of this distance, the approach of one part of the poetic experience to another, becomes the central concern of the poem.

This discourse of approaches and exaggerated dichotomies is always at play in the background of Rochester's verse. His lightest fancies take on a negative form, escapism, the self-titillating reaction against a serious threat through the casual singing, chatting, or storytelling it away. Even Rochester's short poems come off, sometimes to his chagrin, as still more, if still negative, approaches to experience—as further strategies for engaging epistemology.[10] When, for example, Rochester describes Lucretius's gods ("Translations from Lucretius"), when, for another example, he teases the Disabled Debauchee as one who "Transported, thinks himself amidst the foes / And absent, yet enjoys the bloody day" (*The Disabled Debauchee*, ll. 11-12), he may well strum the lyre of Stoicism, but he also sounds the possibility of an intermediate type of engagement, of a convinced participation in the building of an artificial but public world.[11] Lucretius, after all, describes several gods, collectedly "Rich in *themselves*" (Second "Translation from Lucretius," l. 5; my italics), publicly sharing their amusements. Rochester's various characters and personae, likewise, always intend to perform those actions that they forecast. The fact that they forecast rather than perform actions is only a way of lending substantiality to the forecast itself.[12] When these poetic persons forecast but don't do anything else, the reader interprets the forecast as the predicted action.

Rochester's poems, then, take a speculative, narrative form. They move from hypothetical situations to hypothetical solutions. The anticipated action never materializes, but the psychological preparation for it creates a kind of extrapersonal experience in which this action seems to occur. Experience is replaced first by theories about the nature of the expected experience, then by the belief in those theories. The preeminent example of this hypothesizing mode is the song "The Platonic Lady." Rochester opens the poem with an invocation to a conventional Petrarchan ladylove. His Laura, however, lacks any specific identity. Lacking even a particular name, she *is* the collating of theories, many of them conflicting, about women and their relation to men. Not content with replacing sex with Neoplatonic theories about it, Rochester substitutes a qualified account of what "may be termed" his own desires for the discussion of the desires themselves:

> I hate the thing is called enjoyment:
> Besides it is a dull employment,
> It cuts off all that's life and fire
> From that which may be termed desire;
>   Just like the bee whose sting is gone
>   Converts the owner to a drone. [ll. 7-12]

The qualification "may be termed" also suggests that all this may happen to the artificial Rochester, his persona, rather than to Rochester himself. Language, Rochester shows, may serve speculation rather than referentiality. To name a desire is to connect it either with its inadequate possessor or with the desired object. Either linkage will convert the desire into its various negations: the irresolution of the desirer or the inadequate gratification afforded by the desired object. Better to puzzle about what "desire" *might* mean. The conclusion of the poem therefore announces that desires are "the only sweets of love"; were orgasm obtained, Rochester "would neglect it with flat disdain," preferring instead his commitment *to* sexual experience.

"The Platonic Lady" lays out a master story line for Rochester's satires. A kind of extended tautology, "The Platonic Lady" could be called a "static" poem in that it doesn't go anywhere. It opens with a hypothesis—"I could love thee till I die, / Wouldst thou love me modestly" (ll. 1-2)—then ends, still in the first person, in the same conditional mood: "I'd give him liberty to toy . . . " In the same way, the opening sexual paralysis of *The Imperfect Enjoyment* leads nowhere but to more sexual paralysis. In this poem, Rochester barely manages to keep his erotic fantasy going. His penis, "the base deserter of my flame" (l. 46), an "unmoving lump" (l. 36), threatens to lay down and go to sleep.[13] *Upon Nothing* also follows the "static" plan, for it ends up flowing back into the nothingness that it initially invoked. And so the Disabled Debauchee, "Deprived of force, but pressed with courage still" (l. 2), commands the armada of experience from the armchair of "impotence," in which the entire poem remains confined.

Although the plots of his poems refuse to advance from the hypothetical to the actual, Rochester commits himself to the approach *to* reality. In "The Platonic Lady," the implied retrograde motion—from nature, to sex, to literary models of sex, and finally, in the concluding ironic allusion to Marlowe, to literary models for abstinence—

is not a one-way proposition. The ability to do theoretical modeling of sexual experience postulates the theorist's past acquaintance with the subject. This insinuation constructs an artificial, rhetorical simulacrum of sex in a poem that, in fact, contains no sexual activity. Theory produces a sense of experience; models move into life. Even when Rochester analyzes "Nothing," he treats nothing as though it were something, for the act of analysis imputes a paradoxical semblance of reality to the thing being analyzed. Anxiety and expectation, the moods suffusing "The Platonic Lady," end up generating our sense of the objectivity of those experiences to which these feelings are, in fact, only a response—and only an emotional, not a sensual, response at that. By remaining in the conditional mode, this most motionless of poems puts readers into a great deal of motion. It forces them to join in the act of theorizing, to treat the artificial poem as a constitutive substitute for its real topic.

This same motivational technique is used more angrily in that antitype of "The Platonic Lady," *The Imperfect Enjoyment*, a poem about an abbreviated—or inadequately emphasized—approach to orgasm. Rochester spends the first eighteen lines of this poem reflecting on the generic thrills of intercourse with yet another nameless—but not fleshless—generic ladylove. He so exaggerates the division of thought from thing that the idea of acting out his fantasy becomes self-contradictory. While Rochester's mind conveys "Swift orders that I should prepare to throw / The all-dissolving thunderbolt below" (ll. 9-10), the talk about copulation both turns on and dwindles down to sheer speculation. Mind can't find any systematic means to relate to, let alone command, alienated matter, yet mind can't, in its angry impatience, think about anything else. As a result, a consumptive chaos ensues; fantasy may relate to, be implemented by, or poetically fabricate any material thing at all:

> In liquid raptures I dissolve all o'er,
> Melt into sperm, and spend at every pore.
> A touch from any part of her had done 't:
> Her hand, her foot, her very look's a cunt. [ll. 15-18]

Rochester "enjoys" his erotic imagination, but the enjoyment remains "imperfect" because it represents the failure of the mind to break out of itself.[14] Desperate to move out of his static poem, to turn disembodied fantasy into an organizing, embodying approach, Rochester spends the rest of the poem perorating on sexual failure, seemingly happy for something as concrete as a deflated penis to embody his mental processes. Scolded by his literary lady for his failure to "pay a debt *to* pleasure" (l. 24, my emphasis), the spokesman of the poem belatedly realizes that fantasies, theories, and anxieties postulate their application *to* something, if only the paradoxical "something" of failure.

It is not only in his pseudo-Ovidian love poems that Rochester fastens attention on those anxieties, convictions, and moral forces that generate approaches but distance goals.[15] In *A Satyr against Reason and Mankind*, he scowls that "thoughts are given for action's government; / Where action ceases, thought's impertinent" (ll. 94-95). Reason is charged with managing the approach to gratification:

> I own right reason, which I would obey:
> That reason which distinguishes by sense
> And gives us rules of good and ill from thence,
> That bounds desires with a reforming will
> To keep 'em more in vigor, not to kill.
> Your reason hinders, mine helps to enjoy,
> Renewing appetites yours would destroy. [ll. 99-105]

Right reason sustains those inner tensions that drive the cycle of desire and gratification. Experience does little more than provide an object for speculation. Too close an encounter with experience destroys that anxiety-producing distance from experience that allows right reason to exercise its powers. Rather than distinguish among sense data, reason distinguishes moral rules by and through them. Later in this poem, too empirical an analysis of this cycle reduces these motivating, rhetorical anxieties to real, repugnant fears: "The good he acts, the ill he does endure, / 'Tis all from fear, to make himself secure" (ll. 155-56). "Sacred jealousy," complaint, and grief yield "The only proof 'twixt her and me / We love, and do not dream" ("The Mistress," ll. 27-28). Pain, the response *to* something external, indicates the completeness of knowledge, but the "fantastic fantasies" of ratiocinative philosophy yield only the "frail joys" found in experience.[16] Fear, jealousy, and pain, dispositions toward, and responses to, experience, prove more substantial than the world to which they apply. "Sweetness" or "light" may be facts or may be illusions, but anxiety is human, clear, and distinct.

Rochester cultivates a poetry of failure because it provides a medium for the exciting, hence informative, experience of dissatisfaction. Dissatisfaction, unlike general depression, requires conscious reflection on the inferiority of experience. A person who relishes dissatisfaction prefers the process of incomplete knowing to the dead-end fact of direct experience. Rochester therefore takes more interest in the pleasing construction of moral theories than in that luscious failure, experience. "His wisdom did his happiness destroy, / Aiming to know that world he should enjoy" (*Satyr*, ll. 33-34). A quest for raw truth not only fails to reach reality, but leads to the production of aesthetically dissatisfying conceits—"flaming limits," pierced limits of the universe, flying sots, mysteries fabricated only to be unwoven, and Diogenes's preference of his "tub" to more decent accommodations (ll. 69-93). A kind of dramatic philosopher, Rochester gives us a choice between actively knowing the world—approaching it through actable theories—and allowing the world to spatter us with the evidences of our incompetence.

ASSERTING CONTINUITY

Hierarchies are measures of power. By making the means superior to the substance of knowledge, Rochester empowers epistemology and trivializes facts and things. As *The Imperfect Enjoyment* and *Upon Nothing* show, the privileged act of explanation may postulate the existence of an inferior thing or state of affairs for the sole purpose of explaining it. Rochester never doubts that miserable experience should be forced to serve as a target for heroic explanation, nor does he hesitate to assert the continuity between explanation and what he calls "Something." Critics are fond, for instance, of finding background sources for Rochester's theriophily, but this theriophily is better understood less as an interest in animals than as a respect for the power of instinct to implement its demands, to manifest itself through experience. Analogous to certainty, instinct generates, often violently, bestial plans of action comparable to those conventions and procedures that make up the human world.[17]

Rochester calibrates certainty to psychological forces rather than to objective standards. Human knowledge terminates not in real things, like God or nature, but in moral forces, like hope and fear. These passions mark the boundaries beyond which certain human knowledge confronts uncertain theology or physics. Hope and fear are passive, nonconstructive responses to epistemologically remote, objectively real goods or evils, not active mental motions like the construction of systematic knowledge. Yet passions can be useful. By positioning the art of explanation between reactions like hope and fear, Rochester can insinuate that an idiosyncratic, moral impulse, a desire to explain or believe, can prove more productive than philosophy, which says a lot but does very little. This art of explanation may in fact do far more than explain. While ordinary philosophy reports or approximates the laws of God and nature, explanatory activity responds to or even substitutes for them.

The assertion of the continuity of explanation with experience comes to the foreground of Rochester's poetry. As *The Imperfect Enjoyment* and many other poems illustrate, nothing is more subject to destruction by experience than an abstraction, a fantasy, or a theory that neither approaches nor commandeers experience. Poems like *The Imperfect Enjoyment* point up Rochester's commitment to aggressively explanatory theories. They show him responding to the failure of theory by devising still more theories, by asserting that fantasy, behavior, and body may be voluntarily coordinated through some master approach. The frustrating second segment of *The Imperfect Enjoyment* features such an assertion of continuity:

> This dart of love, whose piercing point, oft tried
> With virgin blood then thousand maids have dyed;
> Which nature still directed with such art
> That it through every cunt reached every heart—
> Stiffly resolved, 'twould carelessly invade
> Woman or man, nor ought its fury stayed:
> Where'er it pierced, a cunt it found or made. [ll. 37-43]

Rochester's failure may well result from his making more of a commitment to Platonizing conceits than to sex itself. Yet he responds to the catastrophe with a more violent affirmation of these fictions— with a claim that his penis can force anything and everything to become, first, a female sexual organ, and, second, as the allusion to the "dart" shows, the foundation for a unifying (and sexually empowering) courtly myth.

Anthropomorphic conceits allow Rochester to invigorate objects like reluctant penises with an artificial personality and, thence, with the simulacrum of moral commitment, with the practical conviction that his theories will work. So in *Tunbridge Wells*:

> Faith, I was so ashamed that with remorse
> I used the insolence to mount my horse;
> For he, doing only things fit for his nature,
> Did seem to me by much the wiser creature. [ll. 172-75]

Plunging himself into the value system of the Wells, Rochester once again asserts that anything can be a sex object. This assertion provides the groundwork for more than an orgasm (alas, we don't know what happens in the sequel, after the mounting). It begets a theory about the conformity of creatures to their natures and, thence, a reciprocal theory about human nature. This most extreme of actions, mirrored in this most extreme of conceits, ends up, however unexpectedly, promoting the adaptation of private impulses to a mode of behavior appropriate for the "nature" of a "wiser creature"—for, as it were, the public, collected character of horsedom.

The form of many of Rochester's poems may be partly explained by his decision to assert rather than to discover the continuity of formal explanations with substantial experience. A static poem like "The Platonic Lady" substantiates the approach to experience, but it risks reducing the approach to a motionless, disabled abstraction. To avoid this reduction, Rochester tries to describe approaches to experience not only in "substantial" terms, but also as aggressive attacks on experience, as powerful instruments that might actually reach, displace, or overwhelm the world to which they only apply. He tinctures his sophisticated, explanatory discourse with the brutal language of experience. In the *Satyr*, for example, he twists a theorized account of nature into a physical heap of theories, twists theoretical talk into natural imagery, and torques his way to the top of a Scholastical mountain piled up in his all-too-physical "brain":

> Reason, an *ignis fatuus* in the mind,
> Which, leaving light of nature, sense, behind,
> Pathless and dangerous wandering ways it takes
> Through error's fenny bogs and thorny brakes;
> Whilst the misguided follower climbs with pain
> Mountains of whimseys, heaped in his own brain. [ll. 12-17]

This reactive process—distorting nature into theory then reactively forcing theory back into nature—allows a character like the Disabled Debauchee to clamber up his rigid heap of fantasy as though it were a genuine rubbish pile. It makes the approaching party, the character or reader or author, take the approach seriously, as something continuous with real experience. Hence the "dual" structure that critics have noticed in many of Rochester's poems. *The Imperfect Enjoyment*, the *Satyr*, "Fair Chloris," *Tunbridge Wells*, *St. James's Park*, "The Fall," *Disabled Debauchee*, and *Upon Nothing*, among others, begin with theories about experience. In the first part of these poems, various theoretical approaches to experience are piled on top of one another. In the second part, this increasingly autonomous body of approaches

encounters that brutal experience from which they purportedly derive. The reciprocal shock demolishes both theory and experience,
and the poems end with epic catalogues of chaos.[18] The third realm
of human artifice disintegrates as mind comes to oppose nature, as
the fragile theory, the unifying approach, collapses along with the
poem. More positively, the resulting heap of rubble acquires a degree
of palpability not found in the earlier, more airy speculations in these
poems.

Rochester's many formal projections of the collapse of explanation
are intended to free, not to indict, the approach. Indeed, they sustain
his program for treating explanation as a truly medial mode. The
dichotomy of approach and experience is, after all, unstable. Experience is much bigger and heavier than theory. Rochester regularly
professes to know nothing of God, nature, or even his own mind;
moderating explanation is always close at hand, but explanation's
objects are always running away. Explanatory talk should be aggressive, but it is not self-sustaining; it needs to work at the nexus of
conflicting influences, to postulate and to approach, but not to touch,
"Whats" like God, nature, and the mind.

Many of Rochester's longer satires can be seen as discussions of
elusive forces that interact with explanatory rhetoric but that remain
outside of, define, and balance its medial world. In the *Satyr on Charles
II* or in *Signior Dildo*, for example, a disruptive sexuality is nominated
as one of these dark balancing forces. Signior Dildo's potency generates the story, hence the narrative character, of the poem, but its
threatening, antinomian power remains outside of, and in counterpoint to, this witty, dainty work. In *St. James's Park* and *Tunbridge
Wells*, similarly, chaos is allowed to speak in counterpoint to the
poems. In both these satires, the disconnected parts of experience
have a life of their own—a right to refuse to form a coherent poem
or lead up to any moral or critical rule. Another force, like a speculating mind, must convert what is not only a list, but a list of militantly
disorderly things and events, into an organized narrative satire. Hence
the loudness of the narrator, who must counteract a chaos that could
destroy the poem. In *Artemisia to Chloe*, on the other hand, a negative
force, entropy, reduces to absurdity a purely empirical approach.[19]
After two hundred lines of undifferentiated "impertinence" and
"folly," the speaker allows fatigue to assert a kind of anti-rule for
poetic productions:

> By the next post such stories I will tell
> As, joined with these, shall to a volume swell,

> As true as heaven, more infamous than hell.
> But you are tired, and so am I. [ll. 261-64]

Only an arbitrary act, by someone like the speaker, can pull this world into the paradigm of boredom.[20] The poem means nothing without the concluding remark, "But you are tired, and so am I."

The *Satyr*, conversely, postulates implausible explanations—a bogus Hobbesian account of "freedom" in which no agent is really free, as Rochester claims, to change himself into an animal, in a concluding vision that demands a paradoxical belief in the inconceivable[21]—in order to suggest that many topics are better left as counterpoints *to* rather than as part *of* "Mans" discourse:

> Were I (who to my cost already am
> One of those strange, prodigious creatures, man)
> A spirit free to choose, for my own share,
> What case of flesh and blood I pleased to wear,
> I'd be a dog, a monkey, or a bear,
> Or anything but that vain animal
> Who is so proud of being rational. [ll. 1-7]

The manifest invalidity of this casuistical diatribe, the fact that Rochester plays with his own inability to believe in what he says (it is, after all, the unlikelihood that anyone would want to be an animal that gives this passage its startling, contrast-rich character), implies the presence of vague influences, like Rochester's own outrage, which operate around but not in his rhetoric. Rochester's detextualizing of those forces that produce, manage, or counterpoint the poem plays up, paradoxically, the continuity of the poem (and the human world) with these dark domains. It implies that Rochester is establishing a definite place for explanatory discourse—that this discourse has a context of its own, a story that can be balanced against other dark, untold tales. Like "instinct," nature discourses from a low, natural foundation, empirical evidence; God talks from on high, from his divinized production, revelation; people discourse from an intermediate ethical podium, from apparently groundless theories in which, as Dryden says, they "must believe" (*The Medall*, l. 135) Rochester, says Burnet, scoffed at prayer because it dealt only with abstract rationality and natural necessity, but not with the morality in between.[22] The long satires bequeath an encumbered legacy: an assertive narrative voice and a demand that all artificial discourse, whether poetic or philosophical, assert both its continuity *with* and its relation *to* a vast array of unknown balancing forces.

ASSERTING ENGAGEMENT

Whether or not he reacts directly to dualism, Rochester co-opts its conceptual system. He establishes the need for a unifying discourse of explanations by exaggerating the conflicts between theism and libertinism, mind and body, speaker and poem, and God and nature. He habitually argues by negation and contrast. If the world is really as bad as he says it is, Rochester shouldn't bother with writing poems; yet Rochester insinuates that the badness of the world somehow entails the emergence of his moralizing voice. Similarly, he suggests that the human world can interact with, and mediate between, its natural and supernatural counterparts precisely because it differs from them, because difference justifies a process of reunification.

Rochester's long, mature, and bitter satires, especially the "social" ones, are therefore far more than crusades of destruction. They perform the same service for human nature that apophatic theology performs for the nature of God. By depicting the inadequacy of natural persons to the artificial idea of human nature, *A Ramble in St. James's Park* catalogues those ordinary, repulsive folks who might block the development of a truly "human" society:

> Rows of mandrakes tall did rise
> Whose lewd tops fucked the very skies.
> Each imitative branch does twine
> In some loved fold of Aretine,
> And nightly now beneath their shade
> Are buggeries, rapes, and incests made.
> Unto this all-sin-sheltering grove
> Whores of the bulk and the alcove,
> Great ladies, chambermaids, and drudges,
> The ragpicker, and heiress trudges.
> Carmen, divines, great lords, and tailors,
> Prentices, poets, pimps, and jailers,
> Footmen, fine fops do here arrive,
> And here promiscuously they swive. [ll. 19-32]

By exaggerating the animality—or vegetality—of his quasi-human mandrakes, Rochester can quickly proceed to his undifferentiated, negative vision of human society. Repulsion goes further than analysis in generating a compelling, "certain" definition of what "man" should *not* be. By refusing to contrast this scene to some Pollyannish review of nice but still particular persons, Rochester makes way for the counterassertion of a more clearly differentiated, more general pattern for human behavior. The danger of this negative approach, of course, is that everything will be excluded from the idea of "humanity":

> Bless me! thought I, what thing is man, that thus
> In all his shapes, he is ridiculous?
> Ourselves with noise of reason we do please
> In vain: humanity's our worst disease. [*Tunbridge Wells*, ll. 166-69]

Yanking the clothes off the disintegrating "mandrake," man, Rochester, like Jonathan Swift, exploits his implied difference from this all-too-common "humanity." From the rags of the natural man he negates the costume of a committed spokesman.

Rochester's rhetoric of negation is in the business of producing artificial replacements for rejected things or ideas. Negation absorbs dualism; it assimilates and transforms what it negates. Rochester frequently toys with the thought that the most serious responses to experience must occur within artificial, poetic worlds, worlds that aggressively differentiate themselves from, and eventually displace, experience, at least in the reader's attention. In "The Fall," Rochester takes as his working but paradoxical hypothesis the utility of a state with no relevance to day-to-day experience, the Garden of Eden: "How blest was the created state / Of man and woman, ere they fell" (ll. 1-2). Although the prelapsarian state afforded a perfect harmony between mind, impulse, and body—"Enjoyment waited on desire; / Each member did their wills obey" (ll. 6-7)—this poem does little more than dispassionately discuss the contrasting state of affairs in this world, from which the poem is to be differentiated. The conclusion is especially poignant:

> Then, Chloris, while I duly pay
>   The nobler tribute of my heart,
> Be not you so severe to say
>   You love me for the frailer part. [ll. 13-16]

Differentiating himself from the roles of both a real man and an ideal literary suitor, Rochester pleads with his Petrarchan lady to pretend that the natural body does not pertain to this less frail, theoretical love. Joys "lessen still as they draw near" (l. 11); the less hypothetical, the less real.

The problem for Rochester with a strict commitment to hypotheticality is that such a commitment contradicts itself. By isolating the human world, it makes the definition of this world impossible. It altogether cuts off those worlds of reason and sense from which the human world must only be differentiated and to which it must be engagingly related. When Rochester ridicules the Disabled Debauchee, he shrinks the old soldier down to the "flashes of fire" thrown from the points of his eyes, then locks him in the "impotence" of monomania, the pinhead of his personality.[23] "The Fall" extrapolates this paradoxical relation between autonomy and engagement. If the mediating human world is to mediate, it must be engaged; if it is to have a measured existence apart from the infinitesimal of individual consciousness or the infinities of religion, it must be independent of them. Rochester, after all, loathes the reasoning "that makes a mite / Think he's the image of the infinite" (*Satyr*, ll. 76-7), that fixes on the private mind or the infinite God but leaves the intermediate moral world vacant. The utter isolation of "The Fall" is an impossibility; failure to extend an artifact with an aggressive discourse will shrink it into nonentity. Even in "The Fall" itself, Rochester shoves his clean prelapsarian world into the jumbled world of action. The poem opens in the hypothetical state of paradise, but it ends with the presentation of the problem, the imminence of a frightening sexual encounter. There is, alas, no going back to the beginning, even rhetorically. This potentially "static" poem not only leaves the literary Garden of Eden, but relentlessly progresses toward and asserts its engagement with those threatening, sexual forces that led to its conception. In the same way, even the disengaged Disabled Debauchee thinks only of directing his imaginings at an audience, at the "cold-complexioned sot," at "Chloris," and at the "well-looked linkboy." Thought becomes an artificial "thing" when it is being directed at something, when it is purposive and moral.

SUBSTANTIATING VERIFICATION

"The Fall" is not the only poem of Rochester's to end in a sudden devaluation from the poetic to the natural, the repulsive, or the horrific.[24] Rochester's imperative—the designing of a coherent world of artifice and explanation that engages but does not belong to experience—entails many a contrary motion. The sometimes jarring forces that animate his poems eventuate in anticlimaxes, even in his most erotic narratives. An inveterate lover of disguises who, Burnet tells us, "would go about in odd shapes" (*Passages*, pp. 27-28), Rochester always fears that unseen mental and physical forces might suddenly burst his artificial bubbles. We have already seen how Rochester can end a poem in a horse's tail. Devaluation, for that matter, may occur in the middle as well as at the end of a poem. The earthquakes that rock the conclusions of the *Satyr* and of *Artemisia to Chloe*, for example, are anticipated by lesser tremors. A malicious, "voluntary" "wantonness" could instantly shatter the "smiles, embraces, friendship, praise" of social convention (*Satyr*, ll. 135-37); at "the bottom of his [man's] vast design" (l. 153) swirls a whirlpool of knavery and fear. In Artemisia's letter to Chloe, "That cordial drop [love] heaven in our cup has thrown / To make the nauseous draught of life go down; / . . . / Is grown, like play, to be an arrant trade" (ll. 44-51). Cultivated "love" could instantly collapse into economic warfare—a devaluation emphasized by the reference to gambling, a science that devalues rules into randomness.

The many sudden devaluations in Rochester's poems always coincide with an upset in the delicate, tripartite balance of mind, artifice, and nature. For Rochester, this balance *is* the poem. Artifacts, like the human world, *are* the process of balancing and mediating. Still, Rochester's poems lead to the upset of this balance.[25] His inquiring eye looks into the artificial mirror on nature, but in looking into this imitating medium, it sees only itself and nature. The result is predictable: medium and percipient collapse into the most aggressive image, that of nature. Counterbalanced by no mind, the balance of nature, artifice, and mind tips first into nature and finally into chaos. The tragic effect of Rochester's greater satires results from this loss of a powerful, hypothesizing art in an abortive attempt at the mimesis of an unknowable, and hence inimitable, nature.

This tragic effect, however, registers more than a loss. It also announces the painful emergence of an expressive, explanatory experience, a type of "human" experience born of the response to those real forces that produce but that also disorder experience. Orgasm is therefore one featured topic of Rochester's art and a model for his explanatory rhetoric. A process like orgasm may rise from the body or the mind, but it cannot, as *The Imperfect Enjoyment* proves, be resolved into either one. Orgasm and the artifacts that Rochester draws from it articulate a response to inarticulate realities; Rochester regards both as a fortiori more knowable than their natural or mental origins. One doesn't know what "nature" or "body" or "God" might mean, but one can theorize ad infinitum about orgasm. Rochestrian orgasm, as *The Imperfect Enjoyment* shows, is a displacement of the body, an assertion that something knowable—a poem, a speech, a feeling—can be forced from the interplay of unintelligible objects. The case is the same with Rochestrian explanatory discourse. Spiritual vanity and raw animality push "truth" out of the overcrowded *Satyr*, but the convinced, unquestioned, and, as it were, instinctive voice of the narrator manages to guide the reader through the mob of philosophers whose thoughts don't please. Certain of what he thinks, the narrator of the *Satyr* demands that we demolish the dialectic of proof and disproof, that we literally verify the poem by applying it *to* experience. Rochester's poems cannot be falsified because they themselves enact certainty and enable judgment.

Rochester's culminating crises and devaluations are never complete. The sheer persistence of his poems shows that, despite what Rochester says, literary artifice and the psychological force behind it simply won't disappear. No passage, for example, so evidences logical reasoning and rhetorical convention than does the outraged, almost deranged dive into "Hobbesian" nature that crowns the *Satyr*.[26] What remains after Rochester's devaluations is thus the sheer motion toward, the sheer presentation of and commitment to, intelligible order. A paradox pervades Rochester's poetry: Rochester wants to define human nature from an objective viewpoint, but he must do so from within the human world, for definitions belong among "Mans Creatures." He cannot fully project himself into the "viewpoint" of nature, God, or anything else, nor can balanced human nature be defined from any single, unbalanced perspective. He can only define human nature as an unfinished finishing process, as, to quote the *Satyr*, "what human nature craves" (l. 168).

As Rochester finds the substance of the poem in the approach to experience, so he finds the substance of the approach in the affirmation of its explanatory, verifying power, its ability to turn most everything into a "human creature." As startling as the pigsty setting of "Fair Chloris" may be, Rochester's witty disgust is deflected toward Chloris herself and toward her unwitting capacity for converting the natural into the aesthetic: "And her own thumb between her legs, / She's innocent and pleased" (ll. 39-40). Through one "amorous groan," she realizes, in her genitals, the intersection of fantasy with flesh. She makes herself, a filthy object, into an eroticizing process, a process in which nature can be conjectured to be exciting, even when it most certainly is not. In *The Imperfect Enjoyment*, likewise, Rochester's vision of the fallen world centers not around experience, not even around "hogs" retrieved from "Fair Chloris," but around the penis, a part of the human anatomy that, however natural it may be, cannot be disengaged from moral and aesthetic impulses:

> Worst part of me, and henceforth hated most,
> Through all the town a common fucking post,
> On whom each whore relieves her tingling cunt

As hogs on gates do rub themselves and grunt,
Mayst thou to ravenous chancres be a prey,
Or in consuming weepings waste away;
May strangury and stone thy days attend;
May'st thou ne'er piss, who didst refuse to spend
When all my joys did on false thee depend. [ll. 62-70]

The more Rochester addresses his penis as an object, the more it sets him to the giving of judgments, the making of analogies, and, in short, the doing of deeds appropriate to a human world.

Rochester finds himself at cross-purposes. He tries desperately to conceive of artifice under some "objective" category.[27] The theriophily of the *Satyr*, for example, connects the human world with the animal kingdom. Every time that Rochester makes an effort at grounding the human world in something else, though, he finds that the effort itself reinforces the novelty of humanity. "Humanity's our worst disease" (*Tunbridge Wells*, l. 169). In the end, Rochester cannot occupy the human world that he explores. He dives into nature or flies up after God. Yet Rochester's readers find their ascents or descents blocked by a reasoning voice—not so much by its reason as by the conviction behind it. Hence Rochester appends to the *Satyr* his strangely incongruous portrait of the Christian, "a meek, humble man of honest sense, / Who, preaching peace, does practice continence" (ll. 212-13). Rochester offers the social personality, the man who forms, believes in, and acts on otherwise unfounded hypotheses, as a shining example of human knowledge—a human knowledge that stands on the very brink of the black hole of truth. For Rochester, there is a human world, but it *is* in the act of affirming that it is *over there*, that the human world is not a thing at a place, but a moral motion toward the discursive vanishing point where explanation turns into engagement.

Rochester commits himself to the telling of a cyclical tale. The more he tries to associate "Mans Creatures" with something natural or supernatural, the more arbitrary, rhetorical, and intractably human he discovers them to be. Yet the closer he zooms in on things artificially human, the more tempted he is to engage them with individual consciousness or external reality. Like the rising and descending Disabled Debauchee, the categories of ontology either approach or recede from, but never quite touch, the human world:

Is or Is Not, the two great ends of Fate,
And True or False, the subject of debate,
That perfect or destroy the vast designs of state—

When they have racked the politician's breast,
Within thy bosom most securely rest,
And when reduced to thee, are least unsafe and best.
                                    [*Upon Nothing*, ll. 31-36]

The wilder Rochester's ontological forays and the more stark his categories, the more likely he is to defer or "reduce" queries, but also the more likely he is to substitute the moral and critical "best" for the rational "is or is not."

No one could accuse Rochester of relativism. Even masturbation entails, in "Fair Chloris," the framing of a publicly intelligible narrative and the organized use of a system of familiar conventions. Rochester makes use of artificial organizing systems, whether those of love poetry or of Scholastic philosophy, to chart a course *toward* the objective. David Vieth headnotes *Upon Nothing* as an excursus on the problem of creation ex nihilo, yet the topic of this poem is neither God nor nature, but the technique for bringing something out of vacuity. God's program for creating nature parallels Rochester's program for bringing organized poetry out of nothingness. In a cheeky parallel, Rochester portrays a God (or the "Nothing" who stands in for him) who, like himself, is organizing a universe from a bundle of philosophical commonplaces and a void field of uninformative experience. Together, God and the godless rake organize a "Something," a hypothetical system of explanations that Rochester courageously propels toward, and engages with, the void:

Ere Time and Place were, Time and Place were not,
When primitive Nothing Something straight begot;
Then all proceeded from the great united What.

Something, the general attribute of all,
Severed from thee, its sole original,
Into thy boundless self must undistinguished fall. [ll. 4-9]

Like Rochester himself, "Nothing"—which encompasses both nature *and* God—is the first (and unknowable) half of the dialectic of reality and artificiality. This "Nothing" is defined through the act of giving knowable order.[28] Rochester's "boundless" God divides himself between the abstract categories of Scholastic philosophy and the undefined abyss of empty space. Only the conviction to create "Something," a world with times, places, and a history, brings him into resolution.

Rochester's witty parallels convert the process of artificing and theorizing, of making a productive language, into the principal task of philosophy. The opening invocation of *Upon Nothing*—"Nothing! thou elder brother to a Shade"—charges a mere abstraction, "Nothing," with a certain vitality. This invocation does, in fact, make nothing into something, in that it invokes a poem and engages the reader in its experience. Rochester conceives of his own explanatory artifacts as such evocative, organizing acts. Poetry must reenact that "vast Necessity," that irresistible act, which, as Rochester told Burnet, would solve all the paradoxes of philosophy. Even Scholastic philosophers cooperate in this mock ontologizing of art, for their highly schematized categories provide theoretical procedures by which Rochester can impose useful order on the unknown void:

> Yet Something did they mighty power command,
> And from thy fruitful Emptiness's hand
> Snatched men, beasts, birds, fire, water, air, and land.

> Matter, the wicked'st offering of thy race,
> By form assisted, flew from thy embrace,
> And rebel Light obscured thy reverend dusky face. [ll. 10-15]

"Assisted" by philosophical jargon, Rochester violates the void, snatching up creatures—of which "men" are the first—by casting out general taxonomic categories (birds, beasts) that the void could not produce. *Upon Nothing* extracts dichotomies, like "nothing" and "something" or "is and is not" or "truth and falsity," from a bland, undifferentiated epistemic void. The corpus of Rochester's work amounts to such an effort to associate the term "man" with a process of organization and conviction—a process that can hypothesize this creature into existence, that can systematize him from his disorganized physical and mental components.

Rochester's human world is the stable form of an erratic system of seesaws and balances. His composite man teeters on the infinitesimal fulcrum between the intangible soul and the elusive natural world. God himself wavers between his apparent unreality and his theoretical obligation to extend himself through all extent. Perhaps, Rochester suggests, those fulcra that constitute human and divine identity coincide in a single point; perhaps the center of our world is also the ethical center of God. Or, perhaps, the hypothetical center of the human world is only the beginning of a moral ray that points toward an infinitely receding, even nonexistent truth. Rochester's poetry aims to coordinate both possibilities in the most tenuous of artificial worlds, in that sheer ethical process through which contradictions produce provocative theories.

from anything and everything, but they never disengage themselves from practical and philosophical concerns.

A philosophical approach to Halifax might seem less improbable than a philosophical approach to Rochester. Still, the novelty and complexity of such an approach should not be underestimated. Rochester's countless allusions to philosophers bring his philosophical interests to the foreground. Halifax, however, disdains quotation, allusion, and name-dropping. He prefers practical business to precedent hunting. A puzzle to even the most puzzling deconstructor, his discourse abounds in practicality and referentiality, yet conceals— or perhaps spurns—its literary and semiotic antecedents. Avoiding the big philosophical questions that Rochester loves to ask, Halifax might be regarded as less a philosopher but more a philosophizer than Rochester. He discourses on political topics, treating the squabbles of ontologists as just another collection of influences in need of organization. He redirects and engages epistemology by giving advice not systematically, but in bits and pieces; he evidences no Romantic fondness for incompleteness, but he exploits incompleteness to turn the unfinished process of organizing into a permanent state of affairs.

Halifax disciplines a project like Rochester's. A narrow zone between balancing contraries, Rochester's artificial world requires constant defense against those natural and supernatural influences that threaten to overwhelm it. Rochester's human world *is*, quite literally, the process of verification, of making things take on a truth-value. An act of assertion, it perishes with the assertor. It lacks a stately permanence. Halifax, however, is an inveterate statesman and compromiser. One of the few writers who could turn moderation into polemical position, perhaps the only diplomat who would hope for a compromise between James and William, he aims to enlarge, stabilize, and perhaps hypostatize the intermediate world of artifacts, conventions, and explanations. By grounding an enlarged human world in its own inertia, by further dividing it from its natural and supernatural counterparts, he expects to make explanation into a durable medium. Halifax wants to connect his explanatory mode with a more stable, public, and artificial entity than the individual poet, to vest explanatory action, for example, in a personification of a political attitude, the Trimmer, the dependable moderate who "trims" the ship of state until it attains stability and follows a compromising course by steering between extremes. By systematizing the endless battle between ideality and reality, he makes this conflict into a dependable, predictable, and systematic foundation for certainty. Unlike Rochester, Halifax explains that artificial entities, like governments, can become permanent features of experience; but like Rochester, he suggests that these stable "human creatures" must manifest themselves in the most unstable, most confrontational situations. In Halifax, the Rochestrian nexus of forces expands into a large, durable arena for the sustained combat of competing powers. What, he asks, is the status of a large artificial entity like "the state," which transcends, nay, confronts those who made it? What can one make of Halifax himself, who poses as a self-possessed wit but who cultivates the public art of political rhetoric?

Like Halifax's attempt to institutionalize political upheaval, my reflections on Halifax could be described as pseudorevisionist. It is hard to be revisionist when there have been no critical studies to revise, but I hope to revise the expectation that Halifax, if he is treated at all, should be treated as little more than the real man behind the quaint mask of the Trimmer. The well-known editor of Shakespeare, Gwynne Evans, would react to the mention of Halifax with an explosive "The Trimmer!" and no more; I hope to present a Halifax who is more than an astonishing entry in a critical apparatus.

I shall divide my discussion into three sections. In the first, I shall detail Halifax's ambidextrous approach to instability and incoherence. I shall suggest that Halifax enlarges examples of incoherence in order to enlarge the art of resolution, thereby privileging the act of explanation while depreciating its factual basis. In my second section, I shall talk about Halifax's creative use of uncertainty. I shall describe, for example, his perplexing presentation of doubt as a means for empowering his stabilizing rhetoric, and I shall evaluate his attempt to ground government on its flexibility, its artificiality, and, in short, on its groundlessness. In the final section, I shall describe Halifax's efforts to enlarge the human world—to use philosophical discourse inversely, as a means of invoking, co-opting, and systematizing those dangerous, inexplicable, and, alas, doggedly real forces that traditional philosophy relegates to the dark domains of mystery.

INSTABILITY AS SYSTEM

"Stability" is an alluring, even preoccupying idea for Halifax, if only because stability evidences Halifax's favorite quality, artifactuality. Halifax's "trimming" pose implies an explicit commitment to the production of an artifactual stability in the wake of more natural destabilizing forces. Like a happy ending, Halifaxian stability must be approached through the unstable interaction of heterogenous forces. That Oz of the "trimming" latitudinarians, moral certainty, is itself a stabilizing psychological response to instabilities in evidence. What else is a government, if not the institutional form of preplanned, stabilizing responses to erratic threats?

Setting a course for the stable eye of the moral hurricane, Halifax presents almost all of his tracts as compromising, hypothetical, practical, and stabilizing solutions to otherwise insoluble problems— whether finding the virtuous parliamentarian or keeping a husband happy. His favored genre, the maxim, lays down the simulacrum of general procedures for what are, in fact, unusual, highly particularized problems. By eliciting convincing theories from resistant facts, maxims both exaggerate and close the distance between knowable generalities and destabilizing particulars. Like its extension, the character, the maxim, a witty turn on a point, permits Halifax to highlight the act of relating a "truth" to an aggressively problematic experience. Many of Halifax's maxims, after all, originate with him, not in antiquity. Contrasting with old-timey truisms, they declare their recency and artificiality. The Halifaxian maxim thus draws attention to the act of relating a believing reader to a fragmented world, with the result that Halifax's committed reader must believe—or passively assume— that Halifax's master genre, the giving of advice, will somehow mediate between the raw facts of a problem and those dazzling, convincing, and highly structured flashes of wit that fill his pages. Maxims, as polished by Halifax, invite their readers and writers not into Heloise's world of hit-or-miss helping hints, but into a world of moral and aesthetic process—a world institutionalized in Halifax's book of state.

Walter Raleigh and Helen Foxcroft think that Halifax is a man of experience; but the utter incoherence of experience, along with the implied need for a compensatory, explanatory system, is one of the most striking features of his writing. Halifax fights against facts; no "trimming party" ever existed, but the Trimmer did devise a trimming political and philosophical program.[2] It was, indeed, crucial to Halifax's political and literary program that his Trimmer should be purged of anything savoring of simple objectivity or fixed notions about a stable natural or civil order. Halifax's own pose as the Trimmer represents a reaction to Roger L'Estrange's attempt to unsettle normal usage by confounding "moderation" with "self-interest." The Trimmer counterbalances L'Estrange's countertrimming; reactively redefining "moderation," "centrality," and "stability," he counters linguistic destabilization.[3] He *is* a fiction about both contrariety and its defeat. Time and again, Halifax recounts the variable, unstable character of evidence: "When a Man looketh upon the Rules that are made, he will think there can be no Faults in the World; and when he looketh upon the Faults, there are so many he will be tempted to think there are no Rules."[4] As in Rochester, strictly empirical or rationalistic approaches generate their contraries, with the result that Halifax's reader is prompted to look for moral stability between these extremities. Halifax's maxims may rise out of the encounter of mind with experience, but they deflect attempts to reverse this productive encounter by looking for a coherent philosophy in either simple empiricism or rationalism.

Halifax, therefore, presents a world like that in Rochester's *A Ramble in St. James's Park*, where general surveys of experience lead to a general sense of incoherence. Explanatory tools like maxims and characters, he suggests, have one countervailing advantage over experience in general: their particularity. A maxim makes one point about one issue, although that point may coordinate a vast multiplicity of factors. Aggressively identifiable, differentiated from everything else, and yet general in its style, the maxim, as a genre, is the most eligible form with which to begin a program of reunification and organization. Making witty, particular points is a way of rebuffing disorder without introducing philosophical abstractions. Maxims assert the autonomy of explanatory art even while they assert its applicability to anything and everything. By contracting a broad range of ideas into a pointed, explanatory artifact like a maxim, Halifax both differentiates and expands the moral center of the human world:

Philosophy, Astronomy, & c. have changed their Fundamentals as the Men of Art no doubt called them at the time. Motion of the Earth, & c.
     Even in Morality one may more properly say, There *should be* Fundamentals allowed, than that there *are* any which in Strictness can be maintained.
     However this is the least uncertain Foundation: Fundamental is less improperly applied here than any where else. [*Political Thoughts and Reflections*, p. 210]

Experience shows that physics and metaphysics have failed to generate fundamental rules, but the history of their interplay has helped to relocate the foundation of theorizing from the "is" of ontology to the "ought to be" of the aphorist. Halifax here amplifies the discrepancy between reason and experience in order to open up space for his pointed, and once again negative, assertion that *some* fundamentals are viable. These privileged fundamentals, of course, are not fundamental at all, but are ethical and intermediary, part of the third, human realm. Their validity is evaluated morally and aesthetically, by their propriety. The nature of propriety and impropriety must remain vague, for one example of impropriety would be the reduction of Halifax's elusive, moral rhetoric to an overstated, inflexible doctrine. Even fundamental truths must be skewed into particular, flexible maxims.

The use of particular points to elicit flexible processes is best evidenced in Halifax's discussion of utility. Halifax distrusts any simple equation of validity with utility, but evidence of the utility of some plan or proposition in some particular case can elicit a belief in it, or at least a feeling of its certainty. Always thinking through differentiating negation, Halifax argues that anything that cannot be practiced cannot elicit belief. Put more positively (and aesthetically), the successful application of a rule "recommends" its veracity: "It would be too great Partiality to say they are perfect or liable to no Objection; such things are not of this world; but if they have more Excellencies and fewer Faults than any other we know, it is enough to recommend them to our Esteem" (*Trimmer*, p. 53). Halifax champions the interplay of such worthy but incomplete ideas, for this interplay defines a moral and rhetorical world in which a word like "Esteem" can carry an epistemological as well as a moral and aesthetic meaning. The interplay of maxims allows for a kind of disengaged engagement, a collected application of "Mans Creatures" to the experience from which they are singly differentiated.

On a larger scale, the interplay of independent concerns—mind and nature, theory and experience, and so forth—can also work out flexible approaches to particular problems, approaches that merit "our" collected "Esteem." Whether the Navy should be commanded by "tarpaulins" or by gentlemen is one exemplary question: "There must be a mixture in the Navy of *Gentlemen* and *Tarpaulins*, as there is in the Constitution of the Government of *Power* and *Liberty*. This Mixture is not to be so rigorously defined, as to set down the exact Proportion there is to be of each; the greater or lesser Number must be directed by Circumstances, of which the Government is to Judge, and which make it improper to set such Bounds, as that upon no occasion it shall on either side be lessened or enlarged" (*New Model at Sea*, p. 176). The experience of the professional seaman and the abstract right of the gentlemen fail, individually, to yield the science of personnel management, but their reverberation against one another sets up clear "Bounds," guidelines, within which an artificial mediator, the government, may be guided into action. These "Bounds" stake out a defined, hypothetical jurisdiction, those military necessities that may arise. The rule itself remains unspecified, visible only in the practice of (and the discoursing about) naval administration.

What *is* specified is Halifax's generative approach to law. The fact that interests always clash, that mateys always squabble with skippers, suggests that a procedure for arbitrating disputes rather than a single formula for staffing a ship might serve as an outline of a more permanent law. In the *New Model at Sea*, for example, the proper balancing of one crew yields one manifestation of the general procedure for staffing. This balancing procedure is both "true" and a "model" for several reasons: because it remains hypothetical, claiming authority over only one reconciling act, one boat, at a time; because it denies the final authority of any one of its interplaying manifestations; and because it always presents itself as particular, abbreviated, and artificial compromise, as more of a finished law than an *ad hoc* maxim. Halifax prefers the practical merit and the relative permanence of such hypothetical laws to any "true" propositions about a disorderly reality:

This innocent Word *Trimmer* signifieth no more than this, That if Men are together in a Boat, and one part of the Company would weigh it down on one side, another would make it lean as much to the contrary; it happeneth there is a third Opinion of those, who conceive it would do as well, if the Boat went even, without endangering the Passengers; now 'tis hard to imagin by what Figure in Language, or by what Rule in Sense this cometh to be a fault, and it is much more a wonder it should be thought a Heresy." [*Trimmer*, p. 48; italics reversed]

Halifax's originality lies less in his desire for stability than in his selection of a metaphor that precludes the discovery of ultimate answers. One can be a destabilizing party or a stabilizing trimmer, but one's views can't be right. The Trimmer's explanatory rhetoric stabilizes the boat not in order to sail toward a single truth, but in order to provide a platform for the free-floating clash of many drifting interests. The substance of the state may be the apathetic yeomanry, the real water, that floats this tippy canoe, but the pleasure of this cruise results from brawling and balancing on the high seas of civil life. Halifax's position—or positioning—as the balancing pilot depends upon the existence of destabilizing forces. His explanatory criticism of life explains that both life and criticism energize explanation by resisting what Dryden might call "metaphrastic" translation into simple verbal representations or clear-cut, prematurely finished theories. Moreover, Halifax works himself into a position (rather like Rochester's in *Upon Nothing*) where he must react against and balance something, where the moderate position, in standing against a duality of interests, becomes reactionary: "Our Government is like our Climate, there are Winds which are sometimes loud and unquiet, and yet with all the Trouble they give us, we owe a great Part of our Health unto them, they clear the Air, which else would be like a standing Pool and in stead of Refreshment would be a Disease unto us" (*Trimmer*, p. 63). Aiming less at producing a *Civitas Dei* than at keeping the system humming, a good government creates a stabilizing instability.

Passages like the preceding point up the importance of metaphor in Halifax's project. Halifax wants to fuse a pointed, differentiating rhetoric with an engaged, stabilizing political program. Relying on naturalistic imagery, Halifax's elaborate metaphors quickly overgrow, yet always draw energy from, their rootstock. It is worth noting that Halifax's outrageously metaphorical style derives from incompatible sources. He borrows his naturalistic vocabulary from the arch-reductivist Hobbes, but his conceited style derives from the speculative, so-called "metaphysical" poets of the earlier seventeenth century— no small feat of reconciliation. His metaphors both assert and deny their engagement with objective experience; they both recede from and fight with their conflicting literary and philosophical precedents. They lead from their vehicles, things in experience, to a more active tenor, the "trimming" process of balancing and reconciling. Halifaxian metaphors reverse our modern expectations; rather than directing a reader through a vehicle to an array of suggested meanings, they treat the vehicle as a sharply defined, differentiated thing, a contrasting device for bringing into the foreground that reconciling, trimming process that created the metaphor-laden style in the first place. Our "Root"—our real, British character—"produceth in us a Stalk of English Juice" (*Trimmer*, p. 97); the fixed, produced vehicle, English nature, deflects attention to its mobile tenor, the initial production of a moral and political identity. By extension, the branches of Halifax's metaphorical tree fill out a civil world above the soil of nature but beneath the heavenly sky, a world suffused with that "Juice" of ethical engagement that first created it.

Halifax's zest for metaphor reveals less of a Donnean desire to do rhetorical battle with an incoherent nature than a Popean desire to focus on the relation—the distance *and* the engagement—of the artificial human world to real things. The stalk, branches, leaves, and sap of Halifax's civil tree interest him more than its subterranean roots or the pollen in the spiritual breeze. Trees must have roots and pollen, but Halifax wants to imply their presence without distracting attention from the more useful "Stalk." He accomplishes this by treating everything, even God, as a finished metaphorical vehicle that points back to the mobile tenor of his trimming process. In the Disneyland of

Halifax's discourse, every "thing" becomes a vehicle, a cheerful ride toward its own assimilation into a demystifying, moral metaphor: "Our Trimmer, as he hath a great Veneration for Laws in general, so he hath a more particular for our own, he looketh upon them as the Chains that tye up our unruly Passions, which else, like wild Beasts let loose, would reduce the world into its first State of Barbarism and Hostility. . . . God himself thought it not enough to be a Creator, without being a Lawgiver, and his Goodness had been defective towards Mankind in making them, if he had not prescribed Rules to make them happy too" (*Trimmer*, p. 50). Halifax allows a commonplace, metaphorical division of bestial animal passions and divine reason. The beasts and their chains, the laws, are, however, not metaphors *for* nature, man, or God; instead, they are little more than modes of behavior that justify the *giving* of laws.

We only "see" God, man, and nature to the extent that they point back to the trimming process, the process of giving laws and making conceits. God himself becomes a metaphorical "Lawgiver," a systematizing process and an orientation toward the human world. Lawgiving processes, whether natural or divine, work from the center rather than from above the human world: "All Laws flow from that of Nature, and where that is not the Foundation, they may be legally impos'd, but they will be lamely obeyed: By this Nature is not meant that which Fools and Madmen misquote to justify their Excesses; it is innocent and uncorrupted Nature, that which disposeth Men to chuse Vertue, without its being prescribed" (*Trimmer*, p. 50). Nature, like divinity, becomes a vehicle for that most important of tenors, the disposition to "quote" it properly. A public person capable of being quoted, nature becomes the enactment rather than the foundation of kingship.[5]

Cowley points out, in his *Proposition*, that some "human" things, like rhetoric, center on human artifice, while others, like science, point toward extrahuman realities. Halifax habitually seizes the most artificial elements in even the most outward-oriented artifacts. A creation like Parliament, for example, takes into account the most heterogeneous forces—hunger, weather, earthquakes, intransigence—yet it treats emergencies as the precursors of metaphor. Emergencies become vehicles; they become means of deflecting attention to that "Life and Vigour which is necessary to produce great things" (*Trimmer*, p. 65). A supernatural concern like religion, similarly, ought to be less concerned with the "Eternal and Unchangeable" than with its adaptation to the several "Climates and Constitutions" of various peoples (p. 67). Halifax surprises his moderate readers with the announcement that "a Constitution cannot make itself; some body

made it, not at once but at several times. It is alterable; and by that
draweth near Perfection; and without suiting itself to differing times
and Circumstances, it could not live" (*Political Thoughts and Reflections*,
p. 211). Halifax is not, of course, joining with Dryden's Achitophel
in a campaign to resume the social contract. To quite the contrary
effect, he argues that the stability of the constitution proves it to be
a stabilizing artifact generated by an enormous number of heterogenous actions and events. Collating the acts of thousands of collected
"somebodies" at thousands of "times," it verifies that a nation of
deviants living in a world of exigencies has again and again approached, approximated, and consented to this document. It confirms
that the discourse of an ever-various people converges on this flexible,
developing tenor.

A process that moves toward a product, Halifax's rhetoric of rec-
onciled extremes abounds with instabilities. Yet these instabilities also
insure its durability. Particular philosophical systems come and go,
but rhetoricians continue stabilizing experience. Halifax's faith in the
persistence of theorizing discourse is in some ways self-fulfilling, for
it regulates his conception of those natural and supernatural worlds
that could destabilize their human counterpart. It is not so much that
Halifax finds himself lost inside a hermeneutic circle as that, for reasons of state and stability, he voluntarily anchors himself in this re-
assuringly limited, discourse-saturated world. Rochester could whirl
all the way to down to "Nothing" before making a rendezvous with
fundamental categories of ontology like "is or is not." Halifax, however, situates these extremes of ontology in the regulating, artificial
discourse of politics. Lacking a taste for "Nothing," he seldom strays
further from the "wise Mean" of constitutional monarchy than the
categories of tyranny or democracy, both artificial human constructs.
Anarchy, for example, amounts to a nonpolitical form of government,
a rule by idiosyncratic impulses; but idiosyncratic impulses stand outside of Halifax's political discourse, with the result that democracy, a
political system, must serve as a substitute extreme. Politics, not ontology, may be Halifax's topic, but his maxims on religion and philosophy evidence this tendency to limit the world with political and
rhetorical rather than logical or ontological categories: "Factions [in
religion] are like Pirates that set out false Colours; when they come
near a Booty Religion is put under Deck" (*Political Thoughts and Reflections*, p. 221). Even the most marginal, least politically alert citizens,
the rabble, must be understood as part of the limiting, center-seeking
process of lawmaking. Had God intended to bar them, he would have

made them "Beasts, that by the Inferiority of their Nature they might the better submit to the Dominion of Mankind" (p. 223).

Halifaxian underclasses and outclasses are more inclined to legislate than to revolt. The unstable extremes of Halifax's world stay close to its artificial, stabilizing center. Consequently, the human world, however small and fragile, is broad enough to assimilate many of those extraneous forces that could otherwise destroy it.

SYSTEM AS DEVIATION

By differentiating the human world from God and nature, Halifax enlarges the problem of finding a foundation for judgment. How can a society judge an offender by standards that are inclusive and normative, but never absolute? What can one do about marginal influences like Catholics, who unbalance the ship of state but whose religion, as a religion, can neither be affirmed nor denied by the balancing, secularizing rhetoric that it helps to create?

To these questions Halifax offers some highly original answers. Rather than brood over the inability of a government to enforce its laws, he discovers legislative tendencies in even the most destabilizing influences. By thinking of government as a process and a mode, he makes it possible to think of the chance to respond to threatening influences as an extension, an opportunity for rather than an imperiling expenditure, of its powers. The making of policy, even against a threat, is the making of a procedure—a human "Creature." Threats maintain the activity, hence the identity, of government. The perennial challenge of Catholicism keeps the government perennially mobilized, judging, and defined. The most extreme threats facilitate the systematic use of extrasystematic sanctions, like prerogative or the public good, to enable the lawgiving process. Countering one destabilizing force by absorbing another, Halifax's political world takes advantage of disorderly influences to enlarge and stabilize itself, to ensure its own moral inertia.

Halifax rehabilitates deviation partly by replacing the rightly ordered with the rightly managed state. Rather than ask what his government is or what it represents, he asks what it does, especially what it does about specific threatening forces. Catholicism, for example, he recognizes as an ineradicable influence: "Popery is a Plant that may be mowed down, but the Root will still remain, and in spite of the Laws, it will sprout up and grow again" (*Trimmer*, p. 81). There is no use in arguing about what it is or where it goes wrong; the task is to control its influence by establishing disincentives. A wise—one might say a behaviorist—Catholic will see the "foolish ostentation of drawing inconveniences upon himself" (p. 85). Like Rochester's "hope and fear," political disincentives define clear practical boundaries for obscure religious ideas. The issue, however, is aesthetic as well as pragmatic; the question is not whether Catholics understand God; but whether their beliefs allow for a graceful display of political skills. Whatever religion may be, it can only be understood in terms of its enlarging moral and aesthetic effects: "*Religion* is a chearful thing, so far from being always at *Cuffs* with *Good Humour*, that it is inseparably united to it. Nothing unpleasant belongs to it, though the *Spiritual Cooks* have done their unskilful part to give an ill *Relish* to it. A wise *Epicure* would be *Religious* for the sake of *Pleasure*; Good Sense is the Foundation of both; and he is a *Bungler* who aimeth at true *Luxury*, but where they both are join'd" (*Advice to a Daughter*, p. 5). When religion influences human life, it does so first by aesthetic and then by moral means. Reinforcing "Good Sense," it serves as a system for the production of a pleasant virtue—as best evidenced by Halifax's cheerful indulgence in metaphor. "Get *Understanding*, and practise *Vertue*" (p. 7), Halifax tells his daughter. Understanding always outlines a pleasant program for its practical implementation; understanding of a big topic, like God, only yields a bigger program.

Deviation is essential to the Halifaxian program. Government is essentially a "doing," a process of organizing, and a "doing" requires a "done to." An organizing procedure must organize something, something that is not yet part of the system. The center of the human world not only is not fixed, but *must* vary with those extremes against which it is defined—and upon which it is performing its organizing acts. In Rochester, the human world is precisely centered between sharply defined contraries like the mind and the body, but in Halifax the center of this world drifts with variable factors. It would be quite consistent with Halifax's thought for Catholicism to become the defining mode in some world, with, say, Anglicanism as the liberal threat and Franciscanism as the conservative. Mediation between opposites is Rochester's theme as well as Halifax's, but Halifaxian opposites are more numerous, various, and malleable. An opposition of admirals and tarpaulins is not quite as rigid as one of mind and matter.

Halifax attempts to assimilate some (but not all) of these opposing influences, thus constantly redefining (and decentering) his centrist position. The mediating, assimilative human world displaces the rigidity of its components with the flexibility of art: "A Nation is best to be judged by the Government it is under at the time. Mankind is moulded to good or ill, according as the Power over it is well or ill directed. A Nation is a Mass of Dough, it is the Government that kneadeth it into Form" (*Political Thoughts and Reflections*, p. 220). This organizing, mediating process occurs in no fixed place. The kneading hands of the government carry out a mobile but cohering process. Though placeless itself, this process applies to particular places in general. There is *a* dough, some one context, not simply a generic dough for every use. By contrasting the physicality of metaphor with the generality of aphorism, Halifax stresses the systematic character of the particular. A single lump of dough exists only to be kneaded into a more systematic form. In the reciprocal process of "kneading," neither baker (the sovereign) nor dough (the people) alone yields a nation. The mutual action of royal authority and popular passion yields the nourishing bread of *a* but not *the* stable state. The character of the state may vary from loaf to loaf. Stable but not fixed, its flavor derives from the reciprocal action of forces that are always on the move.

That most destabilizing, most mobile of influences, doubt, has the only indubitable place in Halifax's system. By keeping reason mobilized, doubt shows that reason, too, can be understood not only as a faculty but also as a force, albeit a force for stability. Halifax, moreover, is a man of wit—he likes literary fashion—and doubt insures that government will change along with human tastes. Doubt-induced fluctuations insure that philosophy and mimetic art will vary with the variable relations between God, modish man, and experience. Doubt belongs in stable institutions, for doubt insures variability, hence long-term stability. Change, error, and uncertainty prove to be permanent influences on Halifax's dynamic human world. In dealing with dissenters, for example, Halifax allows the government a "prudential Latitude . . . as to the manner of prosecuting the Laws now in force against them" (*Trimmer*, p. 75). The applicability of generalizing laws to any one situation is dependably doubtful. Certain legal knowledge must acknowledge uncertainty, for it must be able to ask whether a law *must* be applied to a *contingent* situation. It must also allow that the act of application may be a destabilizing process: "In a corrupted Age the putting the World in order would breed Confusion" (*Miscellaneous Thoughts and Reflections*, p. 244). Doubt permits latitude in action; action generates doubt; together, doubt and action generate a negative sanction, liberty:

Our *Trimmer* owneth a Passion for Liberty, yet so restrained, that it doth not in the least impair or taint his Allegiance; he thinketh it hard for a Soul that doth not love Liberty ever to raise it self to another World; he taketh it to be the foundation of all vertue, and the only seasoning that giveth a relish to life, . . . all that the World can give without Liberty hath no Taste. . . . Since the reasonable desire of it ought not to be restrain'd, and that even the unreasonable desire of it cannot be entirely suppress'd, those who would take it away from a People possessed of it, are likely to fail in the attempting, or be very unquiet in the keeping it. [*Trimmer*, pp. 61-62]

Like certainty, liberty provides a freedom to act, at least so long as nothing too material gets in the way. Providing a "foundation of all vertue," this negative nexus of doubt and action opens into a positive moral space.

As a negating psychological action, doubt plays another important role in Halifax's thinking. It confirms the distinction of the doubting individual from the extending, enlarging, and affirming state. Doubt-born entities, like liberty and certainty, help to differentiate the individual from the totalizing system. In Rochester, by contrast, the human world emerged from an unremitting interplay between the personal and the external. Once Rochester withdrew his commitment to the act of explanation, the "tripartite" world collapsed. In Halifax, however, a human, negative, and yet quasi-objective sanction like "liberty" will persist even in the absence of the individual. Being only a negation, liberty can persist when the affirming individual withdraws. This capacity for *dis*continuity between a hypothetical government and those real persons who hypothesize it will be of great importance for Locke and others. For Halifax, it grants to explanatory art the ability to differentiate itself from destabilizing parties and, conversely, to protect those parties from assimilation into the stabilizing society. "To be too much *troubled* is a worse way of over-valuing the World than the being too much *pleased*" (*Moral Thoughts and Reflections*, p. 231); best to let a government run on its own. One of the most striking features of Halifax's thought is its tendency to reconcile competing parties by imposing a different solution from what either would advocate: "It appeareth that a *bounded Monarchy* is that kind of Government which will most probably prevail and continue in England"; considering the powers of oppression and revolution presently at play, "it must follow (as hath been hinted before) that every considerable Part ought to be so composed, as the better to conduce to the preserving the Harmony of the whole Constitution" (*New Model at Sea*, p. 175). Not only is government artificial, it is in the business of negating itself away from those real persons who form its constituency.

Never a timid reasoner, Halifax cultivates doubt in order to cultivate its counterpart, authority. Halifax, after all, builds a systematic doubt into human laws; why not remedy doubt (and complete the circuit) by constructing a systematic defense against a disunifying uncertainty—by invoking authority? Consider again the controversy over naval command: if a gentleman meets the requirements of his office, if therefore "he smelleth as much of *Pitch* and *Tar*, as those that were *Swadled* in *Sail-Cloath*; his having an *Escutcheon* will be so far from doing him harm, that it will set him upon the advantage Ground: It will draw a real Respect to his Quality when so supported, and give him an Influence and Authority infinitely superior to that which the *meer Sea-man* can ever pretend to" (*New Model at Sea*, p. 177). The very dubiousness of Halifax's ad hoc solutions seems to call for the invocation of supersystematic influences, like the aristocratic mystique, to make his expedients psychologically acceptable—to make them certain. The incompleteness of his solutions leads to the invoking of authority, not for its own sake, but for the sake of a balancing system in which authority is just another destabilizing force. Authority is not an alternative to, but an extension of, Halifax's reconciling mode.

Halifax regularly conjures up esoteric influences—powers that defy systematization, override rules, and otherwise save theories and procedures from getting locked up in themselves. Time and again he devises mysteries. He cuts holes through his system of government lest it obstruct its own organizing process: "There is a hidden Power in Government, which would be lost if it was defined, a certain Mystery" (*Trimmer*, p. 65). Or again: "When all is said, there is a Natural Reason of State, an undefinable thing, grounded upon the Common Good of Mankind, which is immortal, and in all Changes and Revolutions, still preserveth its Original Right of saving a Nation, when the Letter of the Law perhaps would destroy it" (p. 60). Rather than describe them theoretically, Halifax keeps such elusive influences in a kind of mystery world, a world just one step beyond hypothetical reasoning. By distancing the ground of theory from the clouds of mystery, he insures that stabilizing, explanatory discourse and real, destabilizing impulses will continue to bolt toward and energize one another. Yet mystery and explanation must remain close to one another; too far apart, and their authority, like their productive tension, dissipates. Maintaining this distance between mystery and explanation also entails the voluntary limitation of the explanatory impulse. In his root-and-branch metaphor, for example, Halifax signals his desire to keep the moral "juice" unseen. Exposing the sap means destroying the branch. Similarly, "*Lycurgus* might have sav'd himself the trouble of making Laws, if either he had been Immortal, or that he could have secur'd to Posterity, a succeeding Race of Princes like himself; his own Example was a better Law, than he could with all his skill tell how to make; such a Prince is a Living Law, that dictateth to his Subjects, . . . such a Magistrate is the Life and Soul of Justice, whereas the Law is but a Body and a dead one too, without his Influence to give it warmth and vigour" (pp. 54-55). A lucky state has a king who conceals an abundance of this invisible, undefinable vitality. Halifax would "perswade the King to retrench his own Greatness" (p. 101), to leave the laws alone but cultivate a regal character, a character through which his unseen will can energize these voluntarily alienated laws.

One good reason to exempt Halifax from a Marxist critique is his desire to *divide* the maker from the product and then to reassociate them through a personal, voluntary act—to applaud alienation as the precursor of private appropriation. Individual action of this kind is not limited to the elite; popular as well as sovereign influences may supercharge a government. From the "dough" of the people rises *Salus Populi*. Like royal prerogative, this "common good" can only work when kept at a moderate distance from law: "*Salus Populi* is an unwritten Law, yet that doth not hinder but that it is sometimes very visible; and as often as it is so, it supersedeth all other Laws which are subordinate Things compared" (*Political Thoughts and Reflections*, p. 210). To prevent the raising up of either principle, the common good or the reason of state, as some kind of absolute mandate, Halifax sets these imperatives in a complex, somewhat ironic relationship to the lawgiving process: "*Salus Populi* is the greatest of all Fundamentals, yet not altogether an immoveable one. It is a Fundamental for a Ship to ride at Anchor when it is in Port, but if a Storm cometh the Cable must be cut" (p. 212). Forces like "common good" or "prerogative" may stabilize our "ship" when it fails to trim properly through the cyclone of norm-producing forces. They must, however, deny their own finality or "immovability." Although extraordinary, these imperatives serve to reestablish normal procedures. They tend to reconceal themselves. Once again, the effect of the introduction of destabilizing, mysterious forces is the enlargement and stabilization of a system.

DEVIATION AS STABILITY

Terms like "reason of state" and "common good" allow Halifax to establish limits to the human world. By pointing toward absolute sanctions, these terms expand the boundaries of an artificial thing like language, for they suggest that language can invoke extralinguistic realities. These shorthand terms also suggest, of course, that real influences cannot be fully described by language. They mark as well as expand—or mark by expanding—the limits of explanatory discourse. Halifax's invocations of "living law," "reason of state," and "public good" don't really introduce transcendental powers into the human world; rather, they assert the persistence of this world despite the interference of these shadowy forces. At the end of his reflections on fundamentals, Halifax recurs to a tautology: "that *every Supream Power must be Arbitrary*" (*Political Thoughts and Reflections*, p. 214). Like Rochester in *Upon Nothing*, he pushes to the limits of discourse only to discover, in tautology, an "arbitrary" and limiting but potentially constitutive system of human conceptions. Explanation, nay, language itself identifies the boundary at which systematic definition and arbitrary power meet.

For Halifax, therefore, those mysterious forces that stand just beyond his explanatory discourse exert a limiting, defining pressure against the expanding human world. Halifax anchors his ship of state in that very instability to which his "trimming" is the purported answer. As a result, political systems are defined most clearly by deviant actions and events. Deviations throw into relief the assimilative, stabilizing powers of explanatory language. Irregularities elicit both an assertion of their exclusion from a given system and a counterassertion of their potential for assimilation into it. Together, these countervailing assertions maintain the boundaries of the human world.

Normative political systems can assimilate many of the occasions for invoking the "natural reason of state" or *Salus Populi*. A well-founded society can control deviation by making a system out of it. The clergy, for example, might ask for special prerogatives, but a tautologizing Halifax would support them "in their Lawful Rights, and in all the Power and Dignity that belongeth to them" (*Trimmer*, p. 72). Clergymen may preempt the law, but only on those occasions that the law allows. The violation expresses the rule. So in political theory and theology, even the most extreme absolutism is built out of the human "Creatures" of logic and rhetoric, and even religious mysteries vindicate philosophy by deviating from it: "*Religion* is exalted *Reason*, refin'd and sifted from the grosser parts of it" (*Advice to a Daughter*, p. 5). Devotion is "a steady course of good *Life*" (p. 5). Regularity and mystery fit hand in glove; theories run on the power of moral certainty.

Halifax is never a mystic. In his discussions of mystical sanctions, as in those of prerogative or common good, he aspires to engage these influences, to involve them in the intelligible human world, although he would do so without stripping them of their essential otherness and inexplicability. He would use epistemology to play up their historicity and objectivity. He would treat, say, "common good" as a particular, if unknowable, influence, which made a particular demand at some particular time and to which a satisfying, systematic response was made. Many of the ingredients in his elusive "English Juice," for example, have been recorded in the British constitution. This ever-emerging artifact has tracked the historical variations in the common understanding of "common good." It provides an outline of the past and an ad hoc guide to the future development and deployment of this imperative, whatever this imperative may actually *be*: "Our *Trimmer* therefore, as he thinketh the Laws are Jewels, so he believeth they are nowhere better set, than in the constitution of our *English* Government, if rightly understood, and carefully preserved" (*Trimmer*, p. 53). The last clause is the most important: it is not the skeleton of strictures, but the living process of understanding, that concerns Halifax. The ultimate artifact, the constitution does not so much *set* as provide a setting *for* the laws. It draws attention to the setting, to the understanding, responding, and explaining acts. As a record of inaccuracies, confusions, and irresolutions, the constitution portrays the acts of reconciliation and compromise as permanent, stable states of affairs. Halifax encourages princes to associate their preemptive prerogative with their regularizing laws:

There is a wantonness in great Power that Men are generally too apt to be corrupted with, and for that Reason, a wise Prince, to prevent the temptation arising from common frailty, would choose to Govern by Rules for his own Sake, as well as for his Peoples, since it only secureth him from Errors, and doth not lessen the real Authority, that a good Magistrate would care to be possess'd of: for if the Will of a Prince is contrary either to Reason it self, or to the universal Opinion of his Subjects, the Law by a kind restraint rescueth him from a disease that would undo him; if his will on the other side is reasonable or well directed, that Will immediately becometh a Law, and he is arbitrary by an easie and natural Consequence, without taking pains, or overturning the World for it. [*Trimmer*, pp. 55-56]

Law is a kind of setting for prerogative, a context in which an impulsive response to a threat can seem to be a stable rule. A prince should set up a system that will elicit his use of prerogative at those moments when both "Reason it self" and common good require it. These rare moments correspond exactly to those crisis moments when imperatives like *Salus Populi* may be invoked. It is in these emergency situations that divergent imperatives, from royal to popular will, respond most uniformly to real threats. Crisis situations permit Halifax to realize most fully the stability, coherence, agreement, and, paradoxically, engagement of his artificial world.

This surprising faith in the regularizing power of the crisis is reflected in Halifax's language. His commitment to the clever use of paradoxes, errors, and contradictions, his stretching of language by the inversion or denial of its usual meaning, parallels his affirmation of norms by their juxtaposition against crises and inexplicable forces. It is no accident that Halifax devotes many of his projects to trying to make sense out of a paradoxical term like "constitutional monarchy": "the exalting his own *Authority*, above his *Laws*, is like letting in his *Enemy* to surprise his *Guards*: The *Laws* are the only Guards he can be sure will never run away from him" (*Maxims of State*, p. 180); "We are by no means to imagine there is such an Antipathy between them, that the Prerogative, like a Basilisk, is to kill the Law, whenever it looks upon it" (*Political Thoughts and Reflections*, p. 222). Just as Halifax limits sovereignty with that very constitution that sovereignty authorizes, so Halifax defines and engages ideas with that language to which those ideas give meaning.

The crisis situation occupies a key position in Halifax's writings for yet another reason. Halifax's own approach to explanation is profoundly situational, and the crisis, an unusually compelling concurrence of circumstances, is the consummate situation. As an arrangement of factors, however inadvertent, the crisis evidences a kind of order. A crisis is an *identifiable* situation. Halifax, accordingly, uses the crisis as the ultimate test of his particularizing and organizing explanatory mode. Whether bringing order from an array of maxims or answering a particular problem, Halifax's thought always moves in this periphery-enlarging way, toward what could be described as "regional" or "departmental" systems. It promotes those explanatory and governmental systems that bring coherence to specific, specifically alarming parts of experience. Halifax will tolerate outright falsehood when it will stabilize some locally useful rule. In "the beginning of the world," at the founding of reality itself, there was "no Property." Like Locke, Halifax accepts this "Innovation introduced by Laws" lest the debunking of the concept of property disable that particular society that was built upon it (*Political Thoughts and Reflections*, p. 213). By isolating small regions of philosophy or experience over which clusters of rules hold universally, Halifax grants these rules a limited certainty even while recognizing their groundlessness. In the same way, heroic dramatists of the Restoration legislate theatrical "rules" that applied to a specific type of play, but that, in their sometimes spoofable mannerism, declare their inapplicability to anything else. The variegated teaching of the Anglican church earns respect only because it exerts an "indispensable Influence upon all Mankind" (*Trimmer*, p. 67), not because it is true in any context outside that of the human world. James can rule a limited, political world, even though he falters in his command of the church: "Our *Trimmer* approveth the Principles of our Church, that Dominion is not founded in Grace, and that our Obedience is to be given to a Popish King in other things, at the same time that our Compliance with his Religion is to be deny'd; yet he cannot but think it a very extraordinary thing if a Protestant Church should by voluntary Election, chuse a Papist for their Guardian" (p. 74). Belief itself is *in* something, in some local context. A matter of moral certainty, it veers away from generalizing, logical truth. Like the ever-unfounded Anglican church, it operates beneath a canopy of implicitly acknowledged errors. Parliament itself, the very center of the governing process, is a clearinghouse for local errors, and thereby also a factory for definitive local policies. Collectively, it constitutes the artificial image of the ideal free Englishman, an ideal that cannot extend beyond the locality of Britain. Individual members of Parliament cannot rise to a character that is, in fact, a historical situation, a local method for approaching the issues at hand: "If I should be ask'd, Who ought to be [elected to Parliament], my Answer must be, Chuse *Englishmen*; and when I have said that, to deal honestly, I will not undertake that they are easy to be found" (*Cautions for Choice of Members in Parliament*, p. 167). The ideal parliamentarian is the British parliamentary process: full of quirks when seen from abroad, unattainable by individuals, but committed to— certain of—the necessity of its policies.

Halifax is fond of the literary character because this genre enacts the stabilization of the individual deviant. This genre must always concern itself with local deviation—there can be no character of the perfectly average man—but it also portrays the reclamation of an eccentric into a system of conventions and stereotypes. Deviation, moreover, is a process; a deviant does deviant deeds. Schematizing a deviant in a literary character is a way of asserting that his or her deviant acts are, in fact, moving toward a normative, recognizable life-style. Like a crisis situation, he or she is assisting in the definition of a normal, if local, state of affairs. King Charles, stereotypical sovereign and stereotypical rake, is the best example:

The Figure of a King, is so comprehensive and exalted a thing, that it is a kind of degrading him to lodge that power separately in his own Natural Person, which can never be safely or naturally great, but where the People are so united to him as to be Flesh of his Flesh, and Bone of his Bone; for when he is reduc'd to the single definition of a man, he sinketh into so low a Character, that it is a temptation upon Mens Allegiance, and an impairing that veneration which is necessary to preserve their Duty to him; whereas a Prince who is so joined to his people that they seem to be his Limbs, rather than his Subjects . . . looketh so like the best Image we can frame to our selves of God Almighty, that men would have much ado not to fall down and worship him, and would be much more tempted to the Sin of Idolatry, than to that of Disobedience. [*Trimmer*, pp. 56-57]

Alas, King Charles falls short: "*Charles Stuart* would be bribed against the *King*; and in the Distinction, he leaned more to his natural Self, than his Character would allow" (*Charles II*, p. 202). As a result, Halifax must author a character of Charles, a character that portrays neither the beauty nor the beast, but the motion of the beast toward the beauty: "a King is to be such a distinct Creature from a Man, that their Thoughts are to be put in quite a differing Shape" (p. 204). A character, in other words, must *be authored*. Someone or some force must "put" the real person into the public persona. Pushing the deviant toward the system pushes authorial intention into the foreground—but only in a specific situation, namely, when the intention is to transform the deviant individual into the image of the public system. In styling himself as the Trimmer, Halifax proposes that this process may be self-initiated as well as imposed on someone.[6]

The genius of Halifax lies in his refusal to let the matter of systematicity rest in peace—as it might, say, in the case of failed "characters" like King Charles. Yes, he accepts the old saw that theory and practice, public character and private person, often disagree. It is, in any case, impossible to attain either virtue or order in a pure or general form; even so humble and so general an accomplishment as "Wisdom is only a comparative Quality, it will not bear a single Definition" (*Miscellaneous Thoughts and Reflections*, p. 255). Modesty and partiality are general states of affairs; more people, Halifax admits, try to earn their daily bread than to speculate on the constitution. Yet these local, proletarian deviations from the explanatory process tend to strengthen rather than to undermine the fortress of artifice. Even repugnant human experiences—say, for example, hunger—lead to the production of artificial phenomena, like a plan for getting food: "there is a Soul in that great body of the People, which may for a time be drowzy and unactive, but when the Leviathan is rouz'd, it moveth like an angry Creature" (*Trimmer*, p. 101). Ordinary experience, the status quo, is really the compromised, recumbent form of a vast collection of plans and potentialities.

The character is crucial to Halifax because it facilitates an important but paradoxical act, the consent to dormancy. The cultivation of one's own public character constitutes a voluntary resignation of the vigorous self to the stabilizing state. Turning oneself into a tooth in the jaw of a sleeping dragon preserves the fact of the individual's engagement with the human world, but it sets that commitment in the context of a transpersonal, artificial, and dormant system—a system that *is* as well as *is expressed in* the calming and stabilizing of conflicts, whether in metaphor or society. The laws seem to transcend those particular persons who made them because these persons voluntarily forget, downplay, abdicate, deny, or falsify their own destabilizing role in the production of the laws: "A Nation comes near to be Immortal" (*Trimmer*, p. 98), says Halifax, emphasizing with his paradoxical "near" the simultaneous linkage and difference of person and state, history and eternity. In disorderly theory, a nation is made and remade every minute by millions of citizens. In productively falsifying, practically theorized experience, everyone affirms that the laws endure beyond their makers, even after these makers, as it were, go to sleep.

The Halifaxian state, then, is a *work* of art, a stable product with an unstable, idiosyncratic origin. Like a work of art, Halifax's human world elicits a psychological commitment to an artificial production. It leads its audience into participation in a fiction, a fiction that gives a stabilizing form to the diversity of this audience: The "Natural Reason of State . . . carrieth a Power with it, that admitteth of no opposition, being supported by Nature, which inspireth an immediate consent at some Critical times into every individual Member" (*Trimmer*, p. 60). A good prince converts himself into one rendition of the mixed conceit of human knowledge, into an individual (and hence potentially destabilizing) "character" of the collected motion toward stability. The more extraordinary this character, whether the flippant Charles or the omnicompetent Trimmer, the greater the potential motion toward the still-greater fiction of collected stability. Near the conclusion of his *Character of a Trimmer*, Halifax gives this political and literary process an epistemological and even ontological twist:

Our *Trimmer* therefore inspired by this Divine Virtue, thinketh fit to conclude with these Assertions, That our Climate is a *Trimmer*, between that part of the World where men are Roasted, and the other where they are Frozen; That our Church is a *Trimmer* between the Phrenzy of Platonick Visions, and the Lethargick Ignorance of Popish Dreams; That our Laws are *Trimmers*, between the Excess of unbounded Power, and the Extravagance of Liberty not enough restrained; That true Virtue hath ever been thought a *Trimmer*, and to have its dwelling in the middle between two Extreams; That even God Almighty himself is divided between his two great Attributes, his Mercy and his Justice. [p. 103]

In Halifax's expanding, stabilizing human world, metaphor absorbs those premetaphoric influences that give rise to both literature and the explanatory mode. Nature and God themselves contribute to the trimming process. Nature and God traditionally provide objects for a mimetic art, but for Halifax they become the means of and the participants in an expressive but stabilizing explanatory discourse. Everything that can be talked about can be talked about as a means of explaining itself. The ever-flexible explanatory mode reinforces its own groundlessness as it absorbs both the divine and the natural foundations for philosophical explanation.

Halifax is perhaps more sincere than the "metaphysical" poets who influenced his prose, for he engages his conceits with things in the real world. Yet Halifax's exaggerated use of rhetorical trickery also exaggerates the distance between art and reality. Halifax allows that human knowledge harks back to those things and forces on which it is founded, but he fictionalizes the relation of the source to the product and speaks only ironically of the mechanism of production. Hurtling through an epistemological space, orbiting around its ontological foundations, the Halifaxian world enlarges the bounds of artifice but disallows that very sense of permanence that Halifax hoped to create. Halifax makes hypothetical knowledge absolute over the human world, but by systematically differentiating this world from reality, he risks the diminishing of that intense, Rochestrian sense of hope, fear, and conviction. As Aristotle said of the genius of tragedy, Halifax's world passed through many stages, came to its present, fully developed state, and stopped there.

CHAPTER THREE

DRYDEN
Incomprehensible Systems

The biggest obstacle to the understanding of John Dryden has always been the understanding of John Dryden. Writers at the very center of Restoration culture, I have argued, have been more inclined to use than to endorse theories and explanations. Rochester and Halifax, for example, never argue toward conclusions. Instead, they encircle their favorite topics with a cordon of hypothetical explanations. Throwing out postulate after postulate, balancing error against error, they define literary and philosophical centrality from an epistemological periphery. The study of Dryden, however, continues to be plagued by a desire to pin down what Dryden "is"—Catholic, Anglican, Tory, Trimmer, philosopher, scoundrel—when it might be more productive to ask how Dryden *uses* his ideas. Critics today, in other words, struggle against a neo-Romantic urge to rescue a "hypocritical" Dryden from the charge of insincerity. Louis Bredvold inadvertently started this rehabilitative program with his well-known attempt to portray Dryden as consistently fideistic.[1] A host of subsequent critics—Philip Harth, Robert McHenry, Thomas Fujimara, Michael Conlon, Elias Chiasson, Donald Benson, William Empson, and many others—have tried to improve on Bredvold by making Dryden into everything from an eclectic Anglican (a thesis troubled by the pesky fact of Dryden's conversion to Catholicism) to a man eager to please his wife. Recent criticism has made some headway against this impulse to orbit Dryden around a single point. Gerard Reedy, S.J., has underlined Dryden's "ambiguous," celebratory use of typology.[2] The Dryden of Ruth Salvaggio puts his reader at a distance from both sides of every question.[3] Yet even a monumental work like James Winn's biography grudgingly surrenders to the desire for a redeemed Dryden, a Dryden on a "search for religious truth"; even a careful handbook like David Hopkins's argues that Dryden "sincerely and honourably" accepted Stuart political theory.[4]

In response to these attempts to tenderize the toughest satirist of his age, I shall outline a reactionary, irregularizing approach to Dryden. I do not aim to belittle the great tradition of Dryden scholarship, nor do I hope to revive Sir Herbert Grierson's claim that Dryden believed in nothing but good verses.[5] I do want to suggest that the significance of Dryden abides in his refusal to "be" any one thing. Proceeding from my readings of Rochester and Halifax, I shall suggest that Dryden was interested more in belief—in the act of explaining and consenting—than in one or another set of beliefs. A citizen of the human world, Dryden cares more for multiplying and organizing explanatory systems than for selecting among them. He is even more concerned than are Rochester and Halifax with declaring the independence of the world of explanatory artifacts. In characterizing Dryden as the author of "incomprehensible" systems, I use a comical designation as literally as possible: to suggest that Dryden regards explanation as a process that cannot be captured by any one point of view, a process that, like the human world generally, is in the process of capturing other systems. Hence Dryden's none-too-modest belief that he can explain everything from drama to theology. I call my approach "reactionary" because it stresses Dryden's ingenious reactive use of destabilizing influences, whether movements like Socinianism or realities like God, to stabilize those very institutions that they threaten. I stress Dryden's opportunistic use of destabilizing, deviant parties as both topics of and consenting participants in an enlarging, self-regulating, and self-reifying satire. Moreover, I shall suggest that Dryden reacts against, rather than believes in, his own ideas, that, for example, he uses his own destabilizing outrage both to bring down opponents and to control the pretensions of his own philosophizing works.

In this way I hope to shed new light on the commonsense observation that Dryden characterizes his age. Specifically, my Dryden characterizes his era by "consolidating" the explanatory mode. Like Rochester and Halifax, he explains but doesn't tell the truth, including the truth about what he is doing. He outlines the mode of his time by surrounding its many fragmentary realizations with fragmentary explanations. Dryden, for example, can elicit philosophical meaning from his brutally funny confrontations with Shaftesbury, for the implosive pressure of these encounters crystallizes an array of conflicting contemporary ideas. By presenting the assimilation of deviation as an inevitable process, Dryden becomes an important figure in the intellectual history that leads up to Locke, for Locke also argues that everything in the world is inevitably known through a "comprehensive" system of common notions, like that established by a common language. Dryden lacks Locke's sense of the completeness of human knowledge, but he does present the human world as a method for assimilating everything.

Dryden is a big topic. I shall restrict my discussion to those well-known works in which the acts of explanation and judgment are so much in the foreground that they could be described as the topic. I shall, therefore, concentrate largely on the "satires" of the 1680s. In the process, however, I shall also show that a biting work like *The Medall* may be more constructive than critical—that it may be as problematic for the student of satire as a work like *Religio Laici or A Laymans Faith* can be. Consequently, I shall draw heavily on panegyrical inversions of satire, like *Annus Mirabilis: The Year of Wonders, 1666*, and on works concerned with the theory of aesthetic judgment, like *Of Dramatic Poesy: An Essay*. My argument will have four sections. In the first, I shall discuss Dryden's elusive, "incomprehensible" notion of explanation. I shall talk about the paradoxical way in which he treats the act of conciliatory explanation as both the antecedent of and the response to unstable situations. In my second section, I shall describe Dryden's presentation of his confrontational, often satiric philosophizing as the necessary condition of stability and quiet. In my third section, I shall talk about the inherently mysterious character of Dryden's explanatory acts, in particular their almost mystical capacity to regulate anything, including explanation itself. And in my final section, I shall discuss Dryden's effort to disconnect this increasingly mystical explanation from any potential ground, to treat philosophizing as a fully enfranchised, eminently expansionist counterpart to God, nature, and, in sum, reality.

SOLUTIONS AS IMPERATIVES: *HEROIQUE STANZAS*

Despite its reputation for radical vacillations, Dryden's intellectual life is a good deal more comfortable and consistent than Rochester's or Halifax's. The satirist and the statesman credit outside influences with the power to disrupt the human world, but the poet laureate assumes, even before a conflict happens, that explanatory language will resolve it. So worried is Halifax that he limits his discourse to preprocessed threats; he'll talk about the institution of democracy but keep silent about raw anarchy. Dryden is no soothsayer; he doesn't say which disputant or power will win; but he always assumes that the end of a dispute will be a systematic reconciliation of influences rather than an outright victory or defeat. Many critics have noticed that the resolution of conflicts is implicit in Dryden's language.[6] Dryden's couplets resolve contrasts through rhymed opposites and caesura-linked half lines.[7] Abstractions, periphrases, and a commitment to the representation of "general nature" imply that any clash among particulars will resolve in the production of some artificial image.[8] In Dryden's drama, says Anne Barbeau, the clash of particular persons gives way to the clash of ideas;[9] the battle of opposing parties is assimilated into the more homogenous language of philosophical debate. Donald Benson finds that Dryden's imagery directs attention away from rational truth and toward a "middle range" of ethical ideas—toward what I am calling a "human world."[10] In Dryden's writings, some well-defined form, system, or artifact not only does, but *must*, arise from head-on collisions.

Dryden's acute concern for history gives his rendition of the human world an air of durability. Recognizing that threatening forces predate the "crisis" moment, Dryden extends the historical dimension of the trimming process. He proposes solutions to the problems at hand, but he also suggests that solutions, like causes, antedate the problem. Consider one familiar passage:

> The Book thus put in every vulgar hand,
> Which each presum'd he best cou'd understand,
> The *Common Rule* was made the *common Prey*;
> And at the mercy of the *Rabble* lay.
> The tender Page with horney Fists was gaul'd;
> And he was gifted most that loudest baul'd.[11]

Dryden postulates not only a rule but also its emphatic commonness. Common usage, long-standing linguistic habit, requires that the adjective "common" precede the noun "Rule." Common habit and Dryden's singularly insistent outrage converge in an easy (and apparently inevitable) turn of phrase. The rule, which appears as the climax of this abbreviated history of common usage, gains the power to condemn those common people from whom, presumably, it was derived. Benson and Conlon have accordingly argued that Dryden likes to talk about "lending" a prefabricated order to an experience that seems to await its fulfillment.[12]

Heroique Stanzas sets the pace for Dryden's career. It argues that one particularly important, particularly militant "form"—Cromwell's heroic life, or, more to the point, Dryden's attempt to elicit a justifying form from that checkered biography—not only may be at odds with its mundane object, but may use the tension between form and object to energize rather than to undermine its conciliatory powers. Dryden's choice of the Gondibert stanza serves two purposes: first, it heightens his moralizing distortion of experience by deploying a self-consciously "heroic" form; second, it controls the heroic project by calling attention to a pretentious, modern form, a form that has elicited satire almost from the day of its invention. The choice of Davenant's measure subtly demonstrates the assertive *and* stabilizing power of rhetoric. It supports a major moralizing project, but it also controls that project through its countervailing power to draw laughter.[13]

In Davenant's hands, the Gondibert stanza jams epic ambitions into short quatrains; In Dryden's hands, it compresses high ideals and bad examples into a series of assertions about the management of history. Both myth and fact, fable and history, Dryden's unrelentingly heroic poem forces Cromwell to live through a transmutative process in which raw experience and inner genius are compressed into artificial laws. This most hypothetical of poems teeters between Cromwell's possible faults and possible virtues:

> He, private, mark'd the faults of others sway,
> And set as *Sea-mark's* for himself to shun;
> Not like rash *Monarch's* who their youth betray
> By Acts their Age too late would wish undone.
>
> And yet *Dominion* was not his Designe,
> We owe that blessing not to him but Heaven,
> Which to faire Acts unsought rewards did joyn,
> Rewards that lesse to him than us were given. [ll. 33-40]

Poised between sins that he avoided and a "Dominion" that he didn't want but was forced to exercise anyway, the heroic Cromwell rises out of a process of mediation, a balancing of the negative features of his biography, that story that is the historical reality of his life. The poem, similarly, ends with a call for secular peace, a call that has little to do with its martial hero. Macroscopically, the poem balances and complicates literary mimesis itself, for it weighs Cromwell the literary character, the seemingly inimitable source of moral truth, against Cromwell the man, who would have done well to imitate the role model that he posthumously validates. Setting the passive, historical Cromwell against the hero who arises from the poem, Dryden builds a faith in the schematizing process of his poem while he erodes confidence in a passive, empirical approach to history.

Collaterally, *Heroique Stanzas* indicts fixed, objective standards of judgment. Dryden gives his already historically alert audience reason to believe that the real Cromwell can no more withstand objective evaluation than he can live up to the lionizing Gondibert stanza. The word "war" and the imagery that goes with it perforate the poem, calling into question Cromwell's capacities as protector of Britain's safety and security. Yet, despite this aroma of ambiguity, the poem savors of seriousness and straightforwardness. Dryden makes no clear commitment to irony, nor does the poem leave the reader laughing, smiling, or even sneering. *Heroique Stanzas* ends up glorifying not Cromwell but the evaluative process. The story of Cromwell provides an occasion for putting obviously flawed things into a form that elicits a favorable judgment. A panegyric assumes that every reader agrees on the excellence of its subject; Dryden enlarges the panegyric process by making his reader enjoy the act of judging Cromwell favorably. He makes it comfortable to consent to the consensus opinion, to depreciate evidence, and to adapt personal opinions to rhetorical schemes.

By surrounding Cromwell with the evaluative processes, Dryden ends up glorifying Cromwell's hypocrisy. He must emphasize Cromwell's skill at producing rather than being his character. When Cromwell is praised, it is for his ability to convert his experience into an occasion for self-schematization and self-definition. The "Confident of Nature," he "from all tempers . . . could service draw." He can organize indifferent natural influences, like the humors, so that they seem to produce his character. The *source* of "a *Fame* so truly *Circular*" (l. 18), he casts an irregular reputation into a geometrically defined, "circular" format. Cromwell converts real "tempers" into directed processes, processes to which other moral agents can respond and through which, therefore, a collected character may be constructed. While Dryden's panegyrical passages celebrate the building of a character, his attacks on people or ideas almost always target abortive attempts at self-definition. The "Jews" in *Absalom and Achitophel*, for example, are criticized less for rejecting authority than for failing to define their own law (ll. 45-56).

A self-defining character, then, ought to complete the circuit of ontology and epistemology by inserting his or her artificial character—or the process of its formation—between theory and experience:

> For from all tempers he could service draw;
> The worth of each with its alloy he knew;
> And as the *Confident* of *Nature* saw
> How she Complexions did divide and brew.

Or he their single vertues did survay
By *intuition* in his own large brest,
Where all the rich *Idea's* of them lay,
That were the rule and measure to the rest. [*Heroique Stanzas*, ll. 97-104]

As the "Confident of Nature," Cromwell differentiates himself from
but nevertheless dialogues with the objective world. As himself, obviously, he knows and can manipulate the "rich Idea's" in his "brest."
By intervening between nature and ideas, he creates useful "rules"
and "measures." It is important to note, however, that this interces-
sion is eventuated, if not completed, before the fact, by Dryden's
reconciling discourse. The structured opposition of mental and physical phenomena, for example, is never allowed to become polarized.
Terms like "complexions" compress the mind-body dichotomy, for
they can apply to mental states or to physical substances. Self-
definition is a paradigmatic process for Dryden, for it capitalizes on
Dryden's own dependable unreliability. By defining a discourse of
limited, regulated dualities, Dryden pretends to commit himself to
and carry out a process of reconciliation that has, in some sense,
already been completed by his inherently reconciling language.[14]

IMPERATIVES AS QUIET: *ANNUS MIRABILIS*

Dryden's lifelong habit of denying, absorbing, enlarging, and transforming evidence shows that his ideas will upset any category into
which they are placed. It is easy, for example, to discover a utilitarian
strain in Dryden's celebratory poems:

O truly Royal! who behold the Law,
    And rule of being is your Makers mind,
And thence, like Limbecks, rich Idea's draw,
    To fit the levell'd use of humane kind. [*Annus Mirabilis*, ll. 661-64]

One can easily reduce God the "Maker" to an appliance store from
which heroes like King Charles can buy political vacuum cleaners.
An appliance store, however, can be a problematic organization. As
the new historicists have been quick to point out, its splendor can
conceal the countless processes that led to the production of its in-
ventory. This stanza, after all, is about need, about "use." It describes
the stabilization and orderly application, to somewhat less orderly
problems, of apparently preprocessed "Idea's," ideas that the ruthless
Cromwell turns into unchallengeable laws and oppressive strategies.
Dryden pretends, in his panegyric mode, that a selection of war-torn

"Idea's" can be drawn directly, in new condition, from the spotless, stable shelves of this celestial Zayre's. This passage avoids the reality, but glories in the systematizing, of *Salus Populi*.

Dryden is a master of metaphors, similes, and stories in which forceful but stabilizing applications seem to culminate and displace a suppressed history of conflict. *Annus Mirabilis*, for example, ascends generically from a narrative about catastrophic events to a moralizing apostrophe to human knowledge. The sea of historical battle and the stormy sky of prophecy meet in a stabilizing image of propulsion, of progress toward a stable shore beyond a defining horizon:

> And, while this fam'd Emporium we prepare,
>   The *British* Ocean shall such triumphs boast,
> That those who now disdain our Trade to share,
>   Shall rob like Pyrats on our wealthy Coast
> . . . .
> Thus to the Eastern wealth through storms we go;
>   But now, the Cape once doubled, fear no more:
> A constant Trade-wind will securely blow
>   And gently lay us on the spicy shore. [ll. 1205-1216]

History leads up to increasingly elaborate systems for managing history—or at least to another well-disposed appliance "Emporium." The conclusion to history includes the rhetorical application of an extreme practice, piracy, to the stabilizing system of trade. The story is the same in theology as in politics. The surprising, "skeptical" resolution to *Religio Laici* proclaims that "quiet," now a somewhat noisy imperative, may absorb, conceal, and suppress those balancing forces from which it has been abstracted:

> That private Reason 'tis more Just to curb,
> Than by Disputes the publick Peace disturb.
> For points obscure are of small use to learn:
> But *Common quiet* is *Mankind's concern*. [ll. 447-50]

Like the Trimmer's vessel, Dryden's activated stability rides over the tidal wave of truth but drifts with the progressive currents of social norms. Unlike the Trimmer's vessel, Dryden's boat is piloted by the majority of society, not just a few moderate men. Halifax's Trimmer steers through and is defined by many powerful forces, but Dryden's collected Trimmer ends up steering and defining those minority influences that surround his central position. *Annus Mirabilis*, after all, is about the reconstruction, in prophetic poetry, of a city that has been demolished by all-too-real influences, a city that, like Dryden's hollow crystal pyramid (l. 1121), will come to enclose these fiery forces.

The inevitability of "quiet," systematic stability, is most clearly demonstrated by the history of that great source of instability, the individual citizen. *Heroique Stanzas* and *Annus Mirabilis* both portray militant heroes who, even in the midst of their guerrilla activities, are directing their thoughts toward quiet. Self-definition amounts to self-direction; self-direction, in Dryden's reconciling world, always aims at the formation of a stable system. Dryden's poems, especially panegyrical exercises like *Annus Mirabilis*, abound with what could be called "reverse personifications." Complex, artificial constructs, like patterns for the good society, replace personalities, rather than vice versa. In Bunyan, for example, "Christian" stands in for a body of beliefs; in Dryden, a body of beliefs stands in for, say, King Charles. In "To Sir Robert Howard," a panegyric is interrupted at dead center with the announcement "A sober Prince's Government is best," so that Howard the man, the personification of virtue, is metaphorically absorbed into a much larger scheme of social values. David Vieth notes that *The Medall* portrays a king who is quickly schematized into a balance of forces.[15] A cavalcade of similes placed in the center of *Astraea Redux* attaches King Charles's attributes to society in general rather than to the King's person. In the "King's Prayer" in *Annus Mirabilis*—another infusion of conventionalizing, moralizing motifs into the center of a historical narrative—Dryden systematically varies his and his reader's perspective on Charles, alternating between the king who implements God's ideas and the king who must convince us that his thoughts are being implemented by his people's history:

O God, said he, thou Patron of my days,
   Guide of my youth in exile and distress!
Who me unfriended, brought'st by wondrous ways   [King as ward of God]
   The Kingdom of my Fathers to possess:

Be thou my Judge, with what unwearied care
   I since have labour'd for my People's good: [King as participant in
To bind the bruises of a Civil War,   commonwealth]
   And stop the issues of their wasting bloud.

Thou, who hast taught me to forgive the ill,
   And recompense, as friends, the good misled;
If mercy be a Precept of thy will,   [King as ward of God]
   Return that mercy on thy Servant's head.

Or, if my heedless Youth has stept astray,   [King as scapegoat for
   Too soon forgetful of thy gracious hand: commonwealth]

On me alone thy just displeasure lay,
But take thy judgment from this mourning Land. [ll. 1045-60]

One result of this alternation, which persists for several more stanzas, is to confuse the assignment of responsibility—to God, Charles, or the people—for the people's "woes."[16] By confusing the relative locations of essences and qualities, by declining to ask whether Charles embodies government or government drags along the body of Charles, Dryden mobilizes and manipulates the boundaries between the real person and the social system. He can imply that the apparently destabilizing individual is really, knowingly or not, moving toward participation in the "Common quiet."

This inevitable motion from the noisy individual to the collected quiet can explain some puzzling aspects of Dryden's later poems. For one, it can help to make sense out of the preemptive conclusions to Dryden's later satires. The proclamations with which "David" starkly asserts the end of the revolution in *Absalom and Achitophel* (ll. 939-1025) should be understood *as* assertions, as explanatory *and* proclamatory acts by which the unsteady David asserts the unity of his individual character with his character as the personification of a nation. David's self-justifying proclamations are devices by which he explains his own motion into his extended role as the whole political system.[17] Without risking a greeting card sentimentality, we might say that he explains what it feels like to be a stereotyped overachiever, a man who became king. The motion toward quiet and the mechanism of reverse personification can also elucidate Dryden's dislike for certain philosophical commonplaces. In *Religio Laici*, the same Dryden who loves to talk about experience, who visits shipyards, and who isn't above a pastoral poem, decides to trash the argument from design (ll. 12-22). Metonymy won't work; in Dryden's world of reverse personifications, a search through experience won't make God into a personification of the world, for God-the-person must find some way to assert, like David, that He is personified by his complex creatures— the universe and the state.[18]

Dryden's verse characters and characterizing panegyrics chart a course for certainty. They depict the motion of the unquiet, unstable, and unknowable individual toward full participation in a familiar, knowable context, the common quiet. Dryden's characters demonstrate that anything that can be talked about must move toward a knowable, conventional form—much as David's proclamatory comments, at the end of *Absalom and Achitophel*, put him and his fatherly feelings into the familiar form of a paternalistic monarch, of a great communicator and professional proclaimer (see l. 942). Dryden's attention to character, his interest in disclosing that most unknowable of things, the individual mind, points up that he can't be classified as a skeptic.[19] Telling the story of an individual, a character or panegyric is a kind of explanation, an explanatory history of the progress from psychological, motivational factors to their disclosure in some public context.

The example of *Annus Mirabilis*—the story of the inevitable motion of noisy parties toward an organized but aggressive "Common quiet"—informs most of Dryden's work. Consider, for example, the case of Achitophel. "Great Wits are sure to Madness near ally'd / And thin Partitions do their Bounds divide" (*Absalom and Achitophel*, ll. 163-64), says Dryden of Achitophel; "Restless, unfixt in Principles and Place" (l. 154), Achitophel's character, his instability, paradoxically explains why Achitophel fails to attain a character, why he fails to schematize himself into a model for a coherent social program. Achitophel's literary character explains two similar processes: the process by which the inevitable conventionality of character and its representation publicly discloses a private mind, even one that cannot otherwise disclose itself, and the process by which such inevitably intelligible characters reinforce the common quiet. Unwillingly cut and pasted into a character, Achitophel inevitably builds his demonic kingdom on conventional principles:

> If you as Champion of the publique Good,
> Add to their Arms a Chief of Royal Blood;
> What may not *Israel* hope, and what Applause
> Might such a General gain by such a Cause?
> Not barren Praise alone, that Gaudy Flower,
> Fair only to the sight, but solid Power:
> And Nobler is a limited Command,
> Giv'n by the Love of all your Native Land,
> Than a Successive Title, Long, and Dark,
> Drawn from the Mouldy Rolls of *Noah's* Ark. [ll. 293-302]

Achitophel affirms the conventional role of "Royal Blood" and "Mouldy" titles in supporting "solid Power"; in so affirming, he discloses his own confused consent to monarchy. Likewise Zimri, who does "every thing by starts, and nothing long" (l. 548), regularly defects from his own political programs. He unsuspectingly defines his character (via Dryden) through his negativity, as someone "always in the wrong."[20] The fallen Absalom defines himself by his inversion of (but also desire for) the graces of an arbitrary, systematic civil code ("Behold a Banisht man, for your dear cause / Expos'd a prey to Arbitrary laws!" ll. 700-701). And, in *Religio Laici*, "*anxious Thoughts* in *endless Circles* roul" (l. 36); like Cromwell's ambiguous "fame," chaos (as more than a few recent mathematicians have shown) inevitably takes on the most conventional of forms.

SYSTEMATIC QUIET AS SYSTEMATIC MYSTERY

Dryden is a man of procedures. His favorite device, the character, is a procedure for affiliating the unknowable individual with the lucid world of conventions, customs, and other explanatory and regulatory devices, for making one person appear as the keystone in an arch of stereotypes. Literary procedures such as the literary character are forms of confrontation *and* belief, for they always demand that readers not only see and believe in but also assert the congruence between single parties or anecdotal events and the general, conventional forms that represent them. Dryden believes that he can make the evidence disclose what Zimri is, even though Zimri himself won't do so on his own. He remarks in his *Life of Plutarch* that "mathematical certainty" varies inversely with "ethical certainty,"[21] that data and belief confute one another—yet, even here, Dryden has a rule, an inverse ratio, to relate them. Explanation is therefore a partly mysterious affair, a process involving an assertive, often groundless, and occasionally antievidentiary belief: "Poesie must resemble Natural Truth, but it must *be* Ethical" (*Defense of the Essay*, p. 120). Scripture itself can disclose little information without a boost from a mysterious, charismatic "living law."[22] He may be no great admirer of the French, but Dryden believes that their neo-Aristotelian "rules" of drama "represent the reduction of nature and the moral perception of nature into method and ultimately depend on the unerring intuitive faculty"[23]—a dependence on a mysterious faculty, intuition, which should not be underestimated.

Dryden's philosophizing program is broader than either Rochester's or Halifax's, for it has two foci. Dryden presents the systematizing process as both the *response to* and the manageable, explicable, and public *form of* mysterious influences. Put in the terms of the perennial debate over Dryden's religion, Dryden's self-regulating program is both Catholic and Anglican, both fideist and probabilist. Like Halifax, he limits every explanatory act by pitting it against some inexplicable, mysterious power, but he also tries to annex that mysterious power into the explanatory human world. He treats mystery as the foundation and motivation, as well as the boundary, of explanatory discourse. In his *Of Dramatic Poesy: An Essay*, for example, Dryden praises the academic skepticism of the Royal Society, suggesting that the immediate, inexplicable experience of an orderly dialogue will prove as instructive as the opinions of the participants.[24] In the *Defense of the Essay*, similarly, Dryden presents the issues in the debate, but leaves the impulsive act of decision to the reader. In the *Sylvae*, Dryden gives all critical ideas the best possible English translation, expecting that a systematic presentation of the possibilities will elicit an act of judgment. *Religio Laici* makes a similar systematic run through the varieties of skepticism, thus suggesting that voluntary organizing action can elicit a systematic character from the most antisystematic body of philosophical lore.[25]

The Medall is an essential part of Dryden's philosophizing program. As a satire supporting Royalism, this poem exposes the aggressive tendencies of the "Common quiet." As a satiric clash of ideologies rather than, say, a one-sided satire on the vices, it tests the ability of an aggressive norm to define and regulate itself as well as to vanquish competing forces. Dryden, it could be said, tests not for validity but for ability; while Halifax derives a normative system of values by balancing whatever forces are on the loose, Dryden assumes that mediating, regulating action is itself a positive force. The author of *The Medall* would "abhor the thought of Arbitrary Power"; mediation is itself a position that can only be compromised so far. Dryden would consolidate "the laws under which we were born" into a book ready to "transmit to our Posterity" (p. 39).[26] Writing and transmission, of course, are expressive rather than regulatory or deliberative acts. Yet they serve to increase the inertia of Dryden's aggressively moderate position. The elegant regularity of the laws—including the dependability of their transmission—drives out the destabilizing, deregulating questions concerning their origin and legitimacy (what was their status before "we were born"?). The poem as a whole attacks any and all theories, whether Filmerian or Shaftesburian, that threaten to overturn an artificial, regulating system by tying it to some unregulated absolute. Shaftesbury

> preaches to the Crowd, that Pow'r is lent,
> But not convey'd to Kingly Government;
> That Claimes successive bear no binding force;
> That Coronation Oaths are things of course;
> Maintains the Multitude can never err;
> And sets the People in the Papal Chair. [ll. 82-87]

People and Pope fuse in one huge, threatening, and disorderly mass; constitutional monarchy moves to differentiate, regulate, and hence subordinate these influences.

The Medall lauds that king who will aggressively balance competing opinions. Kings should assert their differentiating and limiting power by breaking absolute sanctions into modest, balancing influences. Dryden again enlarges on Rochester and Halifax; governments support a social scale, a Rochestrian fulcrum, that has been "cast" "at last / In equal Balances" (ll. 117-18), the "at last" suggesting an enduring, broad-based equilibrium. Near the center of The Medall, Dryden remarks, "That Kings can do no wrong we must believe" (l. 135). The ordinary citizen probably disagrees with some kingly policy, but that citizen has an opportunity, in the act of consent, both to participate in and differentiate him or herself from the government.[27] By affirming that monarchy should regulate his or her interests, the citizen cooperates in the government's attempt to recognize his or her influence. "Government" amounts to a program for harmonizing disagreements, including that between individual and state; a systematic miracle, it draws order from chaotic situations and commitment from cantankerous parties. Not only can government do no wrong, it *requires* some irregular situation through which to implement its rectifying power. A citizen who *must* believe seems to be under some constraint, probably being tempted not to go along with the program so cheerfully. The disordered satiric situation becomes, if not the mirror image of, at least the precondition to, a forceful regulating system. Moreover, any good government, like the "hypocritical" Dryden, must be able to agree with almost anything, to an appropriate degree.

The real problem with the villains in The Medall is not their pigheadedness or their volatility, as critics usually hold, but their failure to be aggressive enough, to affirm that multiplicity *will* conform to a unifying ideology:

> Almighty Crowd, thou shorten'st all dispute;
> Pow'r is thy Essence; Wit thy Attribute!
> Nor Faith nor Reason make thee at a stay,
> Thou leapest o'r all eternal truths, in thy *Pindarique* way! [ll. 91-94]

The insurgents tolerate no energizing, dramatic tension between ideological rule and unorganized experience. They try to preclude rather than absorb opposition. It is Dryden who must impose the conflicting "Pindarique" form—a form of violation and conflict—on Shaftesbury's career. Dryden, after all, hypothesizes that once a "nature" is admitted, a rule for its correct imitation must come into being (*Defense of the Essay*, p. 122), even if that "nature" is a study in disorder and inimitability. So for government: if a challenge arises, a state must lengthen "dispute" to accommodate it.

The Shaftesbury example makes clear that Dryden regards language itself as the ultimate explanatory process. As kingship weighs and transforms revolt, so rhetoric balances and defines anomalous ideas. Language can never become wholly idiosyncratic, for it presupposes a widely diffused logical, grammatical, and cultural system. Its systematicity is miraculous: it always lends order, even when order seems impossible; it does so arbitrarily, for the only other alternative is silence; and it tolerates no opposition, for one can only alter its meaning within strict limits. Achitophel, for example, cannot talk about power without either mentioning royalty or seeming to speak ironically. Just as Dryden's reverse personifications draw the self toward its literary and social role, so language, like the kings mentioned in *The Medall*, "can do no wrong" (*The Medall*, ll. 135); every sentence must theorize that a thing, person, or event can be put in an expressible form: "But when Action or Persons are to be describ'd, when any such Image is to be set before us, how bold, how masterly are the strokes of *Virgil!* we see the objects he represents us with in their native figures, in their proper motions; but we so see them, as our own eyes could never have beheld them so beautiful in themselves" (*Annus Mirabilis*, p. 54). Virgil wins out over Ovid because of his capacity to get beyond personal experience, to reconcile the inexplicable, radical *objectivity* of objects with their miraculous, artificial representation in language, language that is, in Virgil's case, both wholly conventional and wholly original.

In its manifold irony and complicated allegory, *Absalom and Achitophel*, the predecessor of *The Medall*, can be seen as an extended, incantatory attempt to transmute verbally a chaotic political situation into the public image of providence. The critical debate over the status of Dryden's typology—does he take the association of Charles with David seriously? what does it mean?[28]—is itself a function of the complex, formative character of Dryden's language. Language makes things intelligible through an assertive, fundamentally mysterious act of organization. It allows the understanding of things, but it resolves understanding itself into an unknowable, extralinguistic gesture. Language naturally supports an allegory that characterizes a natural person, like Charles Stuart, by complicating and even supernaturalizing the understanding of him. Language thus makes and remakes the character of Charles.[29] The portrait starts in the Davidic kingdom, at the dawn of political history, in an era close to the miraculous advent of language:

> In pious times, e'r Priest-craft did begin,
> Before *Polygamy* was made a sin;

> When man, on many, multiply'd his kind,
> E'r one to one was, cursedly, confin'd:
> When Nature prompted, and no law deny'd
> Promiscuous use of Concubine and Bride;
> Then *Israel's* Monarch . . . [ll. 1-7]

The poem then continues to construct Charles, his history, and the language to describe him. In the process, it constructs all the ambiguities, uncertainties, associations, and limiting devices that language has accumulated throughout its history. Taking advantage of the preemptive as well as the descriptive powers of language, Dryden not only constructs but also literally deconstructs his characters. He tries to talk his opponents out of existence, the best example being his disassembling de-characterizing of Shaftesbury in *The Medall*. Dryden's portraits become more comprehensive and more lengthy as they exorcise more complicated, more obdurate things. In *The Medall*, hard, terse language erodes hardened persons presented in brief characters. In *Religio Laici*, Dryden's explanatory, "Legislative" language—"Plain and Natural, and yet Majestic" (p. 109)—takes on naughty philosophical systems as well as evil persons. By *The Hind and the Panther*, Dryden's "characters" engulf religious institutions as well as philosophical systems and plain bad folks, as the enormous portrait of Bishop Burnet, the "Buzzard" of Anglicanism, will show (3.1141-1304).

Like Halifax, Dryden judges all systems, but especially the system of language, by a systematic means, propriety. "I have never yet seen the description of any Naval Fight in the proper terms which are us'd at Sea," he comments in *Annus Mirabilis* (p. 51); the excellence of language is measured by the appropriateness of its application. It is not the "what" but the "how" of marine life, the proper way of describing big-corn powder or pitchy planks, that interests Dryden. Propriety thus involves differentiation, but it also entails systematic engagement. There is one coherent dialect-system that applies to one situation, no matter how singular that dialect or that situation may be. More flexible than even Halifax's "state," Dryden's language not only responds to but also surrounds the most marginal things and influences. The Marcel Duchamp of his time, Dryden can enclose the junk of the dock in the frame of culture.

Dryden does distinguish the form from the content of a work, but this distinction itself is enclosed within a discussion of the use of language—what we now call the "compositional process":

The composition of all Poems is or ought to be of wit, and wit in the Poet, or wit writing, (if you will give me leave to use a School distinction) is no other than the faculty of imagination in the writer, which, like a nimble Spaniel, beats over and ranges through the field of Memory, till it springs the Quarry it hunted after; or, without metaphor, which searches over all the memory for the species or Idea's of those things which it designs to represent. Wit written, is that which is well defin'd, the happy result of thought, or product of that imagination. [*Annus Mirabilis*, p. 53]

Dryden's discussions of the relation of form to content, ideas to representations, boil down to plans for compressing the two into a comprehensive system of poetic production. Dryden confronts the "things" of his brave new poetic world by allying them with preexisting, regulating plans for their representation. His "Idea's" are "*of*" (my emphasis) things that he "designs to represent" (p. 53).

> Amidst whole heaps of Spices lights a Ball,
>   And now their Odours arm'd against them flie:
> Some preciously by shatter'd Porc'lain fall,
>   And some by Aromatick splinters die. [*Annus Mirabilis*, ll. 113-16]

Here is experience; Dryden claims to present history as it happens. Here is artifice, for most of the objects at play—balls, porcelain—are artifacts. And here is intellectual abstraction, for the stanza culminates in a conceit. The "wit" of this stanza resides in Dryden's capacity to catch disparate influences in the act of suddenly converging into the conventional forms of poetic discourse. Like Halifax, Dryden canonizes his shards of wit in conceits reminiscent of the "metaphysical" poets. It is this very unexpectedness, this miraculousness, of such explosively self-organizing events that underwrites the regulating, systematizing power of Dryden's language.

The perennial question of the relation of tenor to vehicle in *Absalom and Achitophel* is therefore misguided. Dryden's aggressive but reconciling polemic renders tenor and vehicle one. *Absalom and Achitophel* begins with the most humorously violent of catachreses. It greases up "David" with God's annointing: to balance this initial, humorously justifying act, the poem must end with an angrily comic prophecy, with the seriocomic bolting of divine order into the secular world. As the beginning is comic but not easily dismissed, so the conclusion is deadly serious but hopelessly comic. It summarizes a story about the compression of comedy and tragedy, divine authority and experiential deviancy, into the fragile, tragicomic discourse of kingship. Through his freewheeling use of both "metaphysical" conceits and miraculous turns, Dryden tries to enlarge the range of the human world, to allow miracle and system to surround and absorb one another. So it is with politics: "For who can be secure of private

Right, / If Sovereign sway may be dissolv'd by might?" (ll. 779-80). The poetic politician must push supersystematic forces, like "Sovereign sway" or military "might," into a secondary position—to a line that only explicates that artificial "private right" in which, in the first line, they are compressed. Authority and duress follow from, and are limited by, individual liberty, a comprehensive sanction that, paradoxically, is defined *within* the political system. "Private right" provides a complete, regulating system in miniature; it reconciles absolute authority with democracy by limiting authority to the smallest of jurisdictions, the individual life. And so with miracles themselves, "though they *prove* not, they *Confirm* the Cause, / When what is *Taught* agrees with *Natures Laws*" (*Religio Laici*, ll. 150-51). Authority, "what is *Taught*," and experience, "*Natures Laws*," form a miniature system; together, they follow after miracles, which (as Hume would later explain) can only be identified as miracles when set in the context of customary expectations. Plays, Dryden comments, legislate an "analogy or resemblance of fiction to truth" in which "consists the excellency of the Play" (*Defense of the Essay*, pp. 126-27). The "excellency" of explanatory theories thus consists for Dryden in their capacity to "comprehend," at least rhetorically, a logically antecedent and objectively powerful array of influences—to annex the miraculous into the systematic.

ABDICATING INFINITY

Ever comprehensive, Dryden is ever ambiguous. Comprehending mysteries, he domesticates them; affiliating the human world with its mysterious counterparts, he gives this artificial world the self-grounding capacities of an "arbitrary" divinity. Dryden is in the process of abdicating his claim on infinity, of grounding explanation on its own inevitability. At the same time, he takes advantage of this groundlessness to promote the indefinite expansion of his systematizing world. This motion toward an unrepentant groundlessness is acted out in *Religio Laici*, a poem that is both explanatory and satirical. A work whose title foretells a reconciliation, it accommodates what Winn would like to call the "search for religious truth" to a limiting, self-regulating discourse. The groundwork for this poem, as for many of Dryden's works, was laid in Dryden's early poems of praise. Taking place through proclamatory gestures, Dryden's abdication of the infinite retrieves more than it surrenders:

> Then, we upon our Globes last verge shall go,
> And view the Ocean leaning on the sky:

> From thence our rolling Neighbours we shall know,
> And on the Lunar world securely pry. [*Annus Mirabilis*, ll. 653-56]

The catamaran of science and commerce, like the trimming ship of the human world, follows a hyperbolical path toward an infinity that it can never expect to reach. By sailing continuously, however, Dryden's ship sails into a kind of moral infinity, for it defines a steady program for indefinitely extended action. Throughout this "Digression Concerning Shipping and Navigation," "Nature's Hand-maid, Art" allegorizes the *process* of progress, a process in which art progressively expands out from and around reality. Like suburbanizing cities, this progress "makes one City of the Universe"; it expands indefinitely while remaining theoretically bounded, finite, and emphatically distinct from unincorporated areas.

The progress of a Drydenian state is not necessarily a march into a secular society, but it is a march from a society that depends on either a revealed religion or a single theology to a society that enacts a continuing miracle: the systematic practice of moral imperatives and the development of a consistent *mode* of worship. "Revelation being thus Eclipsed to almost all Mankind, the light of Nature as the next in Dignity was substituted," explains the commonplace-loving Dryden (*Religio Laici*, p. 100). As Earl Miner has said, Dryden's definition of right reason has two goals: to differentiate the human mode of thinking from its divine counterpart and to free the former from unreasonable expectations.[30] An austere definition of right reason improves the relationship between God and man by keeping them out of one another's way.

Dryden's discussion of the salvation of the heathens illustrates this process of productive limitation.[31] Dryden announces that the damnation of those who have never known of God is inconsistent with God's infinite mercy. It "has always been my *thought*, that Heathens, who never did, nor without Miracle cou'd hear of the name of Christ were yet in a possibility of Salvation" (*Religio Laici*, p. 99). As this discussion continues, the "God" discussed slips further behind the discussing "I" and "my." This "I" reifies itself through a political metaphor, a comparison of savages with those under a "Bill of Exclusion." Divine imperatives dwindle into the opinions of Dryden, these opinions then generating an expansive metaphor, a metaphor by which the spiritual condition of foreigners and savages may be understood within the context created by domestic political debate. Always appearing within political metaphors, Dryden's God is always on the edge of being sliced away by Ockham's razor:

If the Gentiles, (Whom no Law inspir'd,)
By Nature did what was by *Law requir'd;*
They, who the written Rule had never known,
Were to themselves both Rule and Law alone.
[*Religio Laici*, ll. 200-203]

Yet Dryden refuses to serve any one ideology, even a harmless agnosticism. He has his cake and eats it too; a "rule" appropriate for a given state—for the "Common quiet"—implies the sanctioning influence but not the oppressive presence of God. Refusing to get caught in the dialectic of secular and sacred, he turns the "venerable Hooker" inside out. He brings to the foreground the systematizing act of dividing the universe; he puts in the background the fact of its division into disconnected real parts. By opening the possibility of an ordained separation between human thought and divine affairs, he opens the possibility of an infallible but humanized church, a self-limiting religion that secures God's blessing on Dryden's abdication of the infinite, on what is tantamount to the relinquishing of any claim to a divine (or any other absolute) foundation for human knowledge. In the opening address of *Religio Laici*, the dwindling divine beacon quivers into a new wavelength of light. Reasoning like that of Rochester's "formal band and board" (*Satyr against Reason and Mankind*, l. 46) must give up its pretentions to divinity. Yet all is not lost, for infinite thought passes over into expanding and directive but limited and regulated human reasoning:

Dim as the borrow'd beams of Moon and Stars
To *lonely, weary, wandring* Travellers,
Is *Reason* to the *Soul*: And as on high,
Those rowling Fires *discover* but the Sky
Not light us *here*; so *Reason's* glimmering Ray
Was lent, not to *assure* our *doubtfull* way,
But *guide* us upward to a *better Day*.
And as those nightly Tapers disappear
When Day's bright Lord ascends our Hemisphere;
So pale grows *Reason* at *Religions* sight;
So *dyes*, and so *dissolves* in *Supernatural Light*. [ll. 1-11]

Passing down from God to soul, then up again to moral guide, reason changes from an organ of rational knowledge to a directing power. Dryden's expanding program for maintaining good order takes precedence over the preservation of a decaying truth.

Dryden's human world is rather like a bubble. It can expand indefinitely without losing its defining shape, although the further it expands, the more extenuated and fragile it becomes. In the big questions of philosophy, the proper duty of explanation is to identify and enhance those formative processes that lead *to* or substitute *for* an answer: "There is some thing above us, some Principle of *motion*, our Reason can apprehend, though it cannot discover what it is, by its own Vertue" (*Religio Laici*, p. 100); "Let us be content at least, to know God, by his own Methods" (p. 101). Dryden, as philosophizer, is anything but original in these assertions. His aim may well be to bore the reader with these old hat, neo-Aristotelian injunctions, to use them as part of a ploy to get the exasperated reader to "comprehend" them with a still more formative, more modern, and more forceful precept, clarity: "Whatsoever is obscure is concluded not necessary to be known" (p. 102). Dryden talks about the formal clarity of theories, not the Cartesian clarity of perceptions; he is less interested in clearing up *what* is known than in explaining (and using) what, in the context of the human world, it is *necessary* to know.

This kind of ethical clarity can counteract, if not overcome, insurmountable problems like the textual instability of the Bible:

> More Safe, and much more modest 'tis, to say
> *God wou'd not leave Mankind without a way*:
> And that the *Scriptures*, though not *every where*
> Free from Corruption, or intire, or clear,
> Are uncorrupt, sufficient, clear, intire,
> In *all* things which our needfull *Faith* require.
> [*Religio Laici*, ll. 295-300]

Dryden agrees with Father Simon that Scripture is a mess. The moral "way," on the other hand, leads to those texts that make the strongest claims on the reader, in which "clear" means "convincing" and intellectual trouble gives way to moral systematicity and aesthetic coherence. Dryden looks for a church that is primarily an ethical procedure, a church that promotes "Common quiet" (*Religio Laici*, l. 450), especially when that "quiet" both distances and co-opts, both legislates and tables, deep mysteries.[32] Reconstructing its deconstructed Scriptures, Dryden's church exploits its emphatic difference from God to enlarge its moral mandate, to extend the organizing human world without infringing on God's prerogative or tripping over his biblical text: "Good life be now my task: my doubts are done, / (What more could fright my faith, than Three in One?)" (*The Hind and the Panther* 1.78-79). The surrendering of any claim to supernatural knowledge, the turning away from frightening mysteries, encourages the open-ended practice of a religious *mode* of life.

The equilibrium of Dryden's expanding world is maintained both by internal and external pressures. The "Common quiet" exemplified by the church expands against pressure from both natural and political forces and from divine "frights." Like Halifax, Dryden would use the autonomy of this artificial world as an explanation for its engagement with its counterparts:

> Our Temp'rate Isle will no extremes sustain,
> Of pop'lar Sway, or Arbitrary Reign:
> But slides between them both into the best;
> Secure in freedom, in a Monarch blest.
> And though the Clymate, vex't with various Winds,
> Works through our yielding Bodies, on our Minds,
> The wholsome Tempest purges what it breeds;
> To recommend the Calmness that succeeds. [*The Medall*, ll. 248-55]

Weather, of course, is only a metaphor, yet Dryden uses metaphors to relate real forces to artificial "Ideas." Meteorology and politics are quite different, but both evidence systematicity; systems, as systems, can be engaged with one another, through metaphor if through nothing else. Once again, the reality, the climate, follows the political metaphor. This process of rhetorical assimilation must be kept in balance by some one dominant system or metaphor, lest the moral world "burst its Bag" (l. 296) under the uneven pressure of diverse influences. Pressures from the most destabilizing influences may be absorbed so long as they can be made to balance one another. Dryden's believer is a trimmer with an anchor, a sailor who can rest at the center of the disputative sea and who can affirm the miraculous permanence of his anchorage because the currents at play always counteract one another.

Dryden's most remarkable act of comprehension—and the best explanation for his conversion to Catholicism—is his paradoxical attempt to engage the human world with its end, to confine the real and the absolute in his limiting program of explanation. Hypotheses, after all, aim to explain *things*; does not an explanatory mode that multiplies and balances but that never proves its theories end up frustrating itself? "How answ'ring to its end a church is made, / Whose pow'r is but to counsell and persuade?" (*The Hind and the Panther* 1.491-92). "As long as words a diff'rent sense will bear, / And each may be his own Interpreter, / Our ai'ry faith will no foundation find" (1.462-64). What can one make of a religion that prohibits a destabilizing evangelism?[33] The "panther" of the Anglican church remains a spotted animal because she conceives of herself as a disengaged product of extrainstitutional forces. Her life remains a continual balancing between distant truths, a series of ad hoc, ever-varying, Rochestrian compromises. The hind, Dryden's English version of Catholicism, pays more heed to a more positive tradition, to a collection of prefabricated explanations and reconciliations rather like those ready-made laws under which, Dryden says, "we were born." Tradition has produced the religious equivalent of the Halifaxian constitution, a record of decisions that has systematically extended the boundaries of right and wrong:

> 'Tis said with ease, but never can be prov'd
> The church her old foundation has remov'd,
> And built new doctrines on unstable sands:
> Judge that ye winds and rains; you prov'd her, yet she stands.
> Those ancient doctrines charg'd on her for new,
> Shew when, and how, and from what hands they grew.
> We claim no pow'r when Heresies grow bold
> To coin new faith, but still declare the old.
> How else cou'd that obscene disease be purg'd
> When controverted texts are vainly urg'd?
> To prove tradition new, there's somewhat more
> Requir'd, than saying, 'twas not us'd before. [2.587-98]

Dryden's Catholic church seems to have a reserve of novelty and applicability. It accumulates more and more applications of its flexible mandate. Its durability rests on a foundation, its antiquity, which, in fact, points up the arbitrariness and unprovability of that authority. To "declare" proves more important than to "prove" the faith, especially in a world with such flexible definitions as those Dryden applies to important terms like "new." Indeed, Dryden doesn't categorically deny that some practices are new. Rather, he uses his ignorance of "from what hands they grew" to point up the miraculous convergence of innovations—deviations—on a conventional system of beliefs. Rather than move off its central foundation each time a new revelation descends or a new challenge arises, the church canonizes its own erratic and erring career, asserting that its history of absorbing any old threat proves that it will systematically assimilate any new threat. A stable system for organizing and explaining all future events, the Catholic church provides an example of an institution that prefers certainty to legitimacy:

> I then affirm that this unfailing guide
> In Pope and gen'ral councils must reside;

Both lawfull, both combin'd, what one decrees
By numerous votes, the other ratifies:
On this undoubted sense the church relies.
[*The Hind and the Panther* 2.80-85]

It is this undoubtedness, this power to elicit consent, that impresses Dryden the most. Indeed, the psychology of consent described here could be characterized as a complete system, a system rising from Dryden's positive affirmation and culminating with the doubly negative, quasi-objective undoubtedness, the moral certainty, of the church's mandate.

On a larger scale, equal pressures from the disparate parties of Pope and council promote the equal, concentric expansion of this model of the comprehensive, secular *and* religious, state. Any questions that might arise—even, say, questions relating to the nature of God—could eventually be confined by this constructive (and constructing) discourse of explanations. Wholeheartedly secular, Dryden's visionary church defines the full range of dispute, then cheerfully declares that it has outlined a program for answering all questions. It assumes that its theories, as instruments of mediation, will mark out that range of knowledge within which the "search for religious truth," as Winn calls it, must take place. Dryden's limiting explanatory discourse encircles the whole of intellectual history, from the days of King David to the emergence, in the later seventeenth century, of the expanding "human world." Culminating in a visionary, allegorical, and imperialistic traditionalism, Dryden's writing cooperates in a programmatic exploration of the whole institution of human knowledge, an exploration that was to be carried out more fully by John Locke.

PART II

Confrontation with Certainty

CHAPTER FOUR

LOCKE

Analogies of Conflict

The writings of Rochester, Halifax, and Dryden offer complexity rather than conclusions. Relishing the act of explanation, these writers confront, complicate, and circumnavigate truth. Through song, satire, treatise, and maxim, they "philosophize"; they examine points of view but conclude by concluding nothing. Rochester, Halifax, and Dryden advance a rhetoric of comprehension, a discourse in which "human creatures"—laws, conventions, theories—can displace, encompass, and substitute for "truth." Theirs is a discourse which redirects destabilizing forces, a discourse in which, for example, a fiery dispute can fuel the mediating engine of the church.

The cost for so expansive a program is, surprisingly, a certain passivity. Dryden and his colleagues tend to think of mediation as a response to and a reactive counterattack on more aggressive threats. "Trimming," promoting the "Common quiet," is certainly not the loudest of performances. For writers working before John Locke, the fun of explanation often results from the defiant juxtaposing, inverting, and complicating of prefabricated theories that someone else believes to be true. Halifax, for example, smirks that some men regard fundamentals as "Peg[s] of Iron" (*Political Thoughts and Reflections*, p. 209); he delights in hitting those Scholastical nails on the head. This devil-may-care bashing of truth is an essential ingredient of his philosophizing rhetoric. Truth, or, more precisely, the reaction against the failure to attain truth, is a motivating, if unsolvable, problem for the rakish intellectuals of the Restoration era.

Locke and his successors, however, take a more entrepreneurial approach to the "human world." As a younger (and less conservative) post-Restoration intellectual, Locke, too, delights in scholar bashing.

Nevertheless, the novelty of his work (and its relevance to later authors) lies less in its many attacks on a hidebound philosophical tradition than in its attempt to place the whole question of truth in parentheses. Locke is not unique in his supposed empiricism; many of his contemporaries examined experience. He is of signal importance, however, for his presentation of human knowledge as a device for comprehending everything, including those contrasts, contradictions, truths, errors, and theories from which Rochestrian, Halifaxian, and Drydenian philosophizing begins.

Scholarship on Locke has always fallen into three distinct categories: the evaluation of Locke's political thinking, as by Richard Cox, John Dunn, Gordon Schochet, John Tully, Neal Wood, Geraint Parry, Leo Strauss, C.B. MacPherson, and others; the contemplation of Locke's epistemology, as by I.C. Tipton, John Mackie, John Yolton, Jonathan Bennett, Willis Doney, Anthony Flew, Robert Armstrong, and their colleagues; and the presentation of Locke as an influence on later literature, as by Ernest Tuveson, Rosalie Colie, Ricardo Quintana, and thousands of eighteenth-century scholars. I have profited from the work of all of these writers, but I want to argue against compartmentalizing Locke. Locke himself, I shall suggest, calls for a more inclusive approach and a more resilient explanatory discourse. My own term, "human world," describes nothing so much as that open-ended, compromising, and often irregular "system" advanced by this adventurous philosopher. It is, I think, a mistake to expect Locke, as does Mackie, to define specific philosophical problems. One ought to look to Locke to define a system like Halifax's, a system for the resolution of problems, for the organization of competing pieces of evidence, and for the practical implementation of fragmentary bits of advice. Part of my project will be to show that Locke's epistemology is fundamentally ethical. In practice and conception, Locke's epistemology centers on issues of power. Its goal is the production of a systematic but social "sense" from disorderly experience. Locke's social theory, likewise, is never crudely political. Neither pre-Marxist nor precapitalist, neither Whig nor Tory, Locke is the sort of ideologue who provides a recipe for all possible forms of government and who argues only for the necessity of a commitment to some one of them. His politics is epistemological; it lets one know how to formulate and explains why one may believe in some one government or some one ideology.

This chapter will present a Locke who, despite his Whiggery, continues the project started by less radical writers like Dryden, Rochester, and Halifax: the project of extending, enlarging, and also comprehending the world of explanatory discourse. This chapter will also present, however, a Locke who completely regrades the artificial terrain of the human world. Rochester and his peers may regard explanatory discourse as a means of confronting outrageous situations, but Locke treats confrontation as the foundation of explanation and the explanatory mode. Like Dryden, Locke anticipates a solution to every conflict; moving beyond Dryden, he uses his reconciling discourse to define and displace the conflict itself.

I shall hope to silence the familiar refrain about how Locke's writing is some kind of paean to subjectivity. Locke's thinking is a celebration of public conflict and its public resolution in a public discourse. His philosophy is not an ontology in subjectivist disguise. It is not a form of or precursor to solipsism, Romanticism, Marxism, or any other specific answer to problems in philosophy. Locke's thought *is* a commitment of ontology to a discursive world in which ontology may be explained and comprehended. The Lockean world may have a place for topics like God, nature, and mind, but its character abides in what Locke calls "relations." Its framework is the stuff of interactions, mediations, and processes; its substance is an aggressively public system of human laws, artifacts, and procedures. Locke, I shall argue, not only stabilizes but asserts the priority of a world of artifice. As Dryden would say, Locke's human world "lends" intelligibility to its real origins. For Locke, the relation of evidence to explanatory discourse ceases to be a one-way affair; his human world and its real counterparts parallel, lead to, and sometimes collide with one another.

In the first section of this chapter, I shall draw attention to the role of conflict in Locke's epistemology. Arguing against the notion that Locke wants words to correspond with things, I shall show how Locke engages knowledge in the reconstruction of those things and forces on which both language and epistemology depend. In my second section, I shall talk about Locke's views on identity. Locke uses the notion of "identity" to undercut its literal meaning—to suggest that identity is a means for annexing many influences into a single political and epistemological construct. In the third section, I shall describe Locke's use of "coherence" and of "coherent" systems to fabricate, a posteriori, purportedly a priori grounds and tools for understanding the world. I shall present a Locke whose concretizing philosophy "lends" credibility—believability—to fictional worlds. In my last section, I shall describe Locke's use of a legal metaphor, the contract, to characterize a self-contained philosophy, a philosophy that proposes as well as follows its own models for comprehending experience.

No account of Locke could be more misleading than the cliché presentation of this writer as the champion of "ideas" and the founder of a "pre-Romantic" subjectivity. First, Locke is not an ontologist. His ideas are not stable "things," nor are they "pictures" of an external reality, nor are they the contents of an individual mind.[1] The notion that Lockean ideas are "signs" that correspond to "things" is a gross oversimplification. Second, Locke's project, like the ideas in it, puts social before epistemological purposes. Locke is more inclined to argue for a moderate and useful common sense than for a self-edifying knowledge.[2] Locke wants to escape, not reinforce, subjectivity; he wants to talk about social processes, not philosophical ruminations. Aiming to "to enquire into the Original, Certainty, and Extent of humane Knowledge; together, with the Grounds and Degrees of Belief, Opinion, and Assent," Locke deals with knowledge in its collected, "humane" character and begins his analysis with the grounds of consent.[3] Consent, the featured action in Locke's political thought, is not only relevant to but *is* the making of a commonwealth. Our "Portion and Degree of Knowledge" serves "the Conveniences of Life, and the Information of Vertue." Utility and virtue depend on a *"moral Knowledge,"* which is "as *capable of real Certainty*, as Mathematicks" (*Essay*, 4.4.7).

For a writer like Dryden, mathematical and moral certainty are inversely related, but the ever-comprehensive Locke regards them as correlates of one another. Mathematical knowledge attains certainty by abstracting itself away from experience and individuals; its counterpart, moral knowledge, reconciles these two parties: "Our Observation employ'd either about *external, sensible Objects; or about the internal Operation of our Minds, perceived and reflected on by our selves, is that, which supplies our Understandings with all the materials of thinking.* These two are the Fountains of Knowledge, from whence all the *Ideas* we have, or can naturally have, do spring" (2.2.2). Thinking, for Locke, is never a simple or solitary business. It involves a number of processes and entities, not all of them limited to the individual mind. Ideas cannot be wholly manufactured by the mind, although "thinking" can work *on* ideas, and "Observation" can "furnish" them. Like "Understanding," "Observation," which is not the same as "thinking," applies to yet a fourth item, the "materials of thinking."[4] Ideas enjoy a measure of independence from all these independent processes. The opening paragraphs of the second book of the *Essay* make it clear that, despite his reputation for empiricism, Locke regards manipulative thinking as a more productive part of the cognitive process than either "subjective" ideas or passive observation.

Locke's epistemology has, therefore, a public face. Dedicated to the solicitation of belief in a general human knowledge, it values outward-directed psychological processes like belief and consent. Locke appreciates experience more for its publicity and its forcefulness, for its ability to elicit belief in its externality, than for its status as objective experience per se: "Perception [of an external object] is so distinct, that few of his [the percipient's] *Ideas* are more distinguishable from one another. And therefore he hath certain knowledge . . . that actual seeing hath a Cause without" (4.11.5). Instead of knowing experience, percipients know that they must affirm the presence of a likely cause, an external force, behind their perceptions. A strong, clear perception leads percipients to postulate relations of influence between their minds and the objects of their perceptions.[5] This relation, moreover, is not known *in* an experience, but as a kind of immediate, reflexive explanation *of* an experience. "Human knowledge" centers on higher-order, quasi-explanatory "ideas"—on ideas like "intensity" and "clarity," ideas that arise from and measure the tensions inherent in the subject-object relation.[6] For Locke, then, knowledge becomes at least partly a matter of technique. Knowledge is as much a matter of the procedure for its entry into the mind as it is a thing found in the mind or available in the world. Knowledge can only become knowledge when it explains how to turn passive data into forceful belief.

Locke wants his reader to understand that esoteric ideas like "intensity" are fully participating members in the society of ideas. They don't belong in some metaphysical world or in the brain of some lunatic. Force, belief, and relations are essential parts of Locke's system, a system that, in turn, systematizes and comprehends not just one but many types of ideas. Complex, subjective ideas—like, say, the idea of the psychological experience of judging—fit just as well in the omnivorous category of "ideas" as do, say, ideas of colors or tastes. God, Locke declares, deals with the *idea* of a soul (a real thing) and the *idea* of a triangle (a set of relations) within a single, aggregative category, "ideas." Human percipients perceive relations, whether something as simple as "left" or "right" or something as complex as a moral attitude, through the same "ideas" through which they perceive colors or smells.[7]

If anything stands at a distance in Locke, it is experience itself. Lockean knowledge has a peculiarly comprehensive quality, for Locke dissociates it from anything that savors of simple objectivity, raw subjectivity, or, worse, unsociability. Material and spiritual substances, for example, remain utterly unknowable (*Essay*, 2.23.23-27). Lockean knowledge is always unstable, for its component ideas are always being related to other ideas, yet it is also relentlessly stable, for it is always relating itself to and balancing itself against a destabilizing reality. Cognition itself reflects this mixture of dynamism and organization and evidences this tendency to move toward a medial ground between the mind and the world. The act of perception yields not knowledge, but "an assurance that *deserves the name of Knowledge*" (4.11.3). The "actual receiving of *Ideas* from without"—the act of receiving—makes demands on as well as informs the perceiver. This "receiving" presents the idea of a finished thing to the percipient, but it also commits that percipient to a belief-inducing process. Perceptions both contain and explicate the destabilizing idea of withoutness; they involve the subject in a progress toward objectivity.

Lockean ideas include rather than represent or correspond to things. They don't disclose, but they do postulate, control, and involve the percipient with "things" and "powers." From the inclusive power of ideas there can be no escape, for "power" is at the root of "ideas," including the idea of the perceiving self. Even "simple" ideas, Locke announces, include the ideas of their transmission and reception— the idea of "power." Ideas become the by-products—the precipitates—of a reaction between perceiving and perception-producing powers. Locke defines "Qualities," the sensible attributes of things, as "the Power to produce any *Idea* in our mind" (*Essay*, 2.8.8). When "observation" and "objects" interact, they produce "ideas." Knowledge is the more-or-less stable product of a confrontation between the percipient's power to perceive and the object's power to produce a perception. Power and outwardness—sociable encounters with other influential things—are basic ingredients in any ideas, whether ideas are thought of as representations of objects or as subjective states. Indeed, Locke preempts the dichotomy of subject and object by treating ideas as the nexus of the interplay between the two. Locke's showpiece argument against innate ideas, likewise, rests on the claim that to speak of an idea that is not being thought, that is not in the process of being presented *by* something *to* a mind, is contradictory:[8] "*Idea* . . . [is] that Term, which, I think, serves best to stand for Whatsoever is the Object of the Understanding when a Man thinks" (1.1.8); "To ask, *at what time a Man has first any* Ideas, is to ask, when he begins to perceive; having *Ideas*, and Perception being the same thing"

(2.1.9). Locke has a genius for co-opting the most refractory influences. The discovery of a microscopic world, for example, might seem to suggest that knowledge may extend beyond the range of perceptual powers (2.23.11). Locke replies that the perception of this tiny world does, in fact, result from the extraordinarily vigorous interplay of perceiving and producing powers. These powers have simply been amplified by appliances; when the power of the microscope is increased, more ideas are perforce produced.

The interplay of powers is a paradigm for Locke's thinking. As the example of the microscope shows, interplaying powers could produce an unlimited number of worlds, systems, and perceptions. The "interplay of powers" paradigm emphasizes the artificial, human character of experience. It presents experience as an inevitable progress toward a common, artificial, and organized knowledge. The development of the legal concept of property, for example, parallels the development of an idea in perception. In the initial condition, the "state of nature," people had certain property-producing powers, while the earth had the power to become property. The earth was "common to all men," "yet every man has a property in his own person," in his labor:[9] "Whatsoever then he removes out of the State that Nature hath provided, and left it in, he hath mixed his *Labour* with, and joined to it something that is his own, and thereby makes it his *Property*. It being by him removed from the common state Nature placed it in, it hath by this *labour* something annexed to it, that excludes the common right of other Men" (*Second Treatise*, sec. 27). The exchange of powers between laborer and nature generates a "thing," "property," which "exists" only in an artificial social system. This "something" is eventually "multiplied" into "positive laws to determine property."[10] As in the case of the microscope, the application of more and more powers leads to the empowering of a more and more extensive, more and more artificial, system of legal (and of epistemological) relations. "The power that every individual gave the society, when he entered into it, can never revert to the individual again, so long as the society lasts," no more than an idea can revert to those natural and mental forces that made it. The acquisition of a system of legal relations parallels the acquisition of the systematic knowledge of "relations": both are stories about the assimilating, systematizing, socializing, and explaining of power.

IDENTITY AND COMPLICATION: SIMPLICITY AS SOCIETY

Locke's catchall category, "ideas," has a way of disintegrating into an array of conflicting perceptual and political powers. Confronting the vitality of his own discourse, Locke faces the major problem of ex- plaining the inevitability of order. Why do some ideas fall into certain patterns? Why does the hit-or-miss interaction of perception-related powers produce such remarkably uniform results? How can we rec- oncile productive powers with those passive ideas through which they are presented? In the Castor and Pollux allegory (*Essay*, 2.1.12), Locke talks about the power of the "soul" to assert its authority over the interplay of its ideas; but what is a soul and what exactly does it assert?

Problems like these bring the question of identity to the center of Locke's attention. Locke's philosophical project is, after all, an at- tempt to compress everything in the perceived universe into one big container, one magical identity, "ideas," even while affirming the extraordinary heterogeneity of experience. When Locke talks about "identity," he refers to (and incorporates) two quite different things. First, "identity" may refer simply to those similar features that allow diverse phenomena to fall under one heading. Dr. Johnson, for ex- ample, growls that any one blade of grass is identical to any other. Second, "identity" may refer to an assertive act through which dis- similar ideas are annexed into a complex idea of some thing or person. The identity "Shaftesbury," for example, might annex compassion, discipline, and connoisseurship. The first type of identity is passive and collective, while the second type is aggressive and differentiating. For Locke, the task is to identify the two types—to combine, as Dry- den did in describing the "common Rule," common usage with vig- orous consent.

The question of identity is therefore far-reaching. Locke deals with the dissonance between representative ideas and productive powers by reevaluating the identity of ideas themselves. Any idea, he concludes, is inclusive, complex, and systematic. Every idea be- longs to some identity, some other "thing," while every thing ap- propriates several ideas. Those things in which ideas are found always support several types of idea. There are no fewer than three types of "powers" or "qualities" in every object: those that constitute the real nature of the object ("primary qualities"), those that generate the effect of the object on the subject ("secondary qualities"), and those that underlie the influence of objects upon one another or, alterna- tively, affect relations among ideas (tertiary qualities) (*Essay*, 2.8.23). Locke's use of his terms varies, but it is clear that these three categories are intended as at least a first step toward a taxonomy of all possible ideas. Although no ranking is overtly declared, the last category, ter- tiary qualities, interests Locke the most, for it potentially covers most of what Sprat and Cowley would classify as human creatures—those laws, theories, and artifacts that, for Locke, are ultimately constructed from ideas in experience and the relations between them. Locke notes that Molyneux's blind man emeritus, for example, cannot, at the moment of his remedy, know the relation between visual and tactile ideas. He can't connect the feeling of a ball to its appearance. Unable "with certainty to say, which was the Globe, and which the Cube" (2.9.8), this recently remedied ophthalmic patient may see all the primary and secondary qualities he wants, but none of these will do him a bit of good until he learns about tertiary qualities, until he learns to see not only the diverse, representational ideas, but also the identity-forming, system-building, relational ones. Molyneux's patient needs to devise linking ideas—to assert, when he cannot see, that all his ideas participate in some master plan, that they participate in a single system with a knowable identity.

The faculties of the individual—including the individual poet—play an important part in perception, but not because Locke is a lover of individuality. Many faculties in many people means many tools for producing relations and relating identities. Through "several acts of its own," one mind may unite, compare, and abstract ideas (*Essay*, 2.12.1). It may, for example, make the idea of "one entire thing" by relating diverse ideas. These workings of wit are far more than amusing moves in a literary game. Locke is doing more than explaining how poets imagine the idea of a chimera. The resulting relational ideas, *as* ideas, posit a relation between themselves and those powers that produced them—the same sort of relation as that between lower-order, more "natural" ideas and their real and cognitive origins. The production of a new set of relational ideas helps to identify an object, but it also postulates the existence of another identity, its producer or discoverer.

Locke's epistemology could therefore be described as the explanatory mode in reverse. Instead of explaining outside influences, Locke's discourse allows an outside influence, a "person," to explain and identify himself or herself as the producer or discoverer of relations among ideas: "Another Faculty, we may take notice of in our Minds, is that of *Discerning* and distinguishing between the several *Ideas* it has. . . . On this faculty on Distinguishing one thing from another, depends the *evidence and certainty* of several, even very general Propositions" (*Essay* 2.11.1). Certainty, a psychological commodity, is identified through its manifestation, the act of surely differentiating, clearly identifying, and confidently relating sets of ideas. Locke reifies individual taste and judgment in a public system of relations; personal pleasure, for example, arrives at the end of a paragraph that charts the extension of the mind into a system of moral relations:[11] "The infinite Wise Author . . . Having also given a power to our Minds, in several Instances, to chuse, amongst its *Ideas*, which it will think on, and to pursue the enquiry of this or that Subject with consideration and attention, to excite us to these Actions of thinking and motion, that we are capable of, has been pleased to join to several Thoughts, and several Sensations, a *perception of Delight*" (2.7.3). Without the opportunity to differentiate itself from and to act its way through this moral system, identity, life itself, would pass away in a "lazy lethargick Dream." Percipients who can't "perceive" this system should learn to judge it into existence, to assent to its validity when "certain Knowledge" is "not to be had," even if such a strategy might evidence "Laziness, Unskilfulness, or Haste" (4.14.3).

Like his discussions of "power," Locke's discussion of the taxonomy of ideas leads to the conclusion that no idea, not even that of identity, is truly "simple." Whatever it may be, identity must be known through a complex of relational ideas: "Any idea that we have, whencesoever we have it, contains in it all the properties it has, which are nothing but relations it has to other ideas."[12] Every idea includes the ideas of existence, of unity, of power, of succession, and, as a result, of its relation to other ideas (*Essay*, 2.7.7-10). An "idea" is a producing, a predicating of relations to itself. "Identity" itself is an idea; it, too, is a method for multiplying itself.

Human, "personal" identity is the consummate example of such systematizing simplicity. Ideas of the mind and of the body contribute to the formation of personal identity, yet "nothing but a participation of the same continued life" (2.27.6) can make an identity. The relating of many things to a single, organizing life constitutes a "person": "This Organization . . . is that individual life, which existing constantly . . . it has that Identity" (2.27.4). Locke tries to simplify this overriding principle of organization by treating it as a single idea, but there is no getting around the fact that ideas are given to complicating tendencies. And so with memory: "Memory, signifies no more but this, that the Mind has a Power, in many cases, to revive Perceptions, which it has once had, with this additional Perception annexed to them, that it has had them before" (2.10.2). The definition—the identity—of memory amounts to the power to add the idea of memory to other ideas. Human identity, likewise, is a program for adding that most important and most emphatically relational idea, moral responsibility, to other ideas. Every idea that *is* an idea must be connected, in someone's mind, with an accompanying moral idea, "ownership" or responsibility.[13] The idea of ownership points up the systematicity of identity, for it has no other job in life than tagging along with and mediating between "identities" and those many ideas that they appropriate.

The inevitable complexity of ideas carries profound implications for a poet like Pope, a poet who uses fragments of experience—vignettes, characters, rural scenes—to invoke a vast range of moral ideas. It is the character of a Lockean identity to take on and to produce more and more meaning. Periphrasis, the foremost device of eighteenth-century verse, loses its absurdity when understood as a means of clarifying and even producing relations—and as a means of defining, differentiating, and engaging the poet's personal identity.

COHERENCE AND COMPLETENESS: GROUNDING A DISCOURSE

The "*Ideas* in our Minds, being only so many Perceptions, or Appearances there, none of them are *false*" (*Essay*, 2.32.3), including the relational ideas. Locke doesn't really need to worry about truth, for his all-inclusive system of relations among ideas includes the relation of true propositions to verifying observations. Locke's job is finding some way to turn propositional truth into apparent truth:

For these several Appearances, being designed to be the Marks, whereby we are to know, and distinguish Things, which we have to do with; our *Ideas* do as well serve us to that purpose, and are as real distinguishing Characters, whether they be only constant Effects, or else exact Resemblances of something in the things themselves; the reality lying in that steady correspondence, they have with the distinct Constitutions of real Beings. But whether they answer to those Constitutions, as to Causes, or Patterns, it matters not; it suffices, that they are constantly produced by them. And thus our simple *Ideas* are all real and true, because they answer and agree to those Powers of Things, which produce them in our Minds. [2.30.2]

Truth can appear in experience because experience, like truth, is ultimately understood through its coherence, through the relating and the fitting of the truth-seeking mind to the truth-supporting world. Truth itself is little more than the consistent, systematic relating of mental propositions to evidences. Differences of opinion among percipients only emphasize the verifying power of relations. The epistemological distance between opinions makes room for a relation between them and for charting that relation onto the self-verifying system of relations among ideas. Differences of opinion, moreover, point up the marvelous way in which a diverse society can use deviation to expand the "common sense" system for organizing diverse things. "Some of our *Ideas* have a natural Correspondence and Connexion with one another" (2.33.5), but *all* ideas, Locke continues, enjoy a customary association (or dissociation) with one another. This customary association may result from chance, but more often it is learned through what we nowadays call "socialization."

Locke thus works in two directions at once: like Dryden, he uses political and epistemological deviation as a means of playing up the artificiality of the human world, but he also assumes that a well-organized society will act as a ground of explanation—that it will generate a conventional body of explanatory lore, that it will, in short, regulate the minds of its members. No one, for example, has the chance to perceive everything first hand. Society must provide some system for disseminating a purportedly "empirical" experience. "Empiricism" needs to find some way to relate "experience" to its audience, to go public with a corporate view of life.[14] Coherent *"Probabilities* rise so near to *Certainty*, that they govern our Thoughts as absolutely, and influence our Actions as fully, as the most evident demonstration" (*Essay*, 4.16.6). Locke values testimony by the regularity with which it is communicated, not by its proximity to experience.[15] A second-hand report by a reliable, articulate author is better than an eyewitness testimony from a dimwit. Likewise in more theoretical concerns: an argument based on comparisons might be more useful or persuasive, in some circumstances, than a logical or scientific proof. *"Analogy* in these matters is the only help we have, and 'tis from that alone we draw all our grounds of Probability. Thus observing that the bare rubbing of two Bodies violently upon one another, produces heat, and very often fire it self, we have reason to think that what we call Heat and Fire, consists in a violent agitation of the imperceptible minute parts of burning matter" (4.16.12). The violence of the metaphor is not without force, for Lockean knowledge can be aggressive. It is in the business of validating itself, of producing and then perceiving such credible analogies. To observe that white is not black or that a circle is not a triangle is first to assert that whatever powers might cause these differing ideas must also differ, and then to claim that the differing actions of those powers have been observed!

It is in the nature of an observation that anyone might make it. Locke's analogies assert their validity and visibility across the whole of the public domain: " 'Tis on this *Intuition*, that depends all the Certainty and Evidence of all our Knowledge, which Certainty every one finds to be so great, that he cannot imagine, and therefore not require a greater" (*Essay*, 4.2.1). Reasoning by analogy, which Locke

calls "demonstrative reasoning," is a way of filling in the gaps between related ideas. Interposing ideas borrowed from other parts of
experience, it *makes* relations visible to the public at large. Swift's
Houyhnhnms exemplify this Lockean society; they have no need of
discursive reasoning because they can see, thanks to the coherence
of their society, all the relations among ideas. Locke states: "*Knowledge*
then seems to me to be nothing but the *perception of the connexion and
agreement, or disagreement and repugnancy of any of our Ideas*. In this
alone it consists. Where this Perception is, there is Knowledge, and
where it is not, there, though we may fancy, guess, or believe, yet
we always come short of Knowledge" (4.1.2). Critics tend to play up
Locke's interest in either the coherence or the visibility of truth, but
Locke refuses to distinguish the two. In his complex world, appearances, truth, and the grounding of one in the other cannot be separated. A matter of implementing itself in experience, propositional
truth is naturalized by being publicized. Moral truth is a special class
of propositional language in which actions serve as signs.[16]

Coherence and consistency, the good ordering of relations, replace correspondence to the objective facts as the test of an explanatory system. Locke would rather talk about "nominal essence" (the
artificial relating of ideas into the definitive identity of a "thing") than
look for real essences (the real nature of a thing) because "real essence" is "so *wholly useless*, and unserviceable to any part of our
Knowledge, that that alone were sufficient, to make us lay it by"
(*Essay*, 3.3.17). By relating disparate ideas, nominal essences allow
order, or at least the motion toward order, to dominate the sheer
perception of experience. Once again, Locke is particularly fond of
ideas relating to ethical matters. Any idea pertaining to ethics will
include the idea of action; it will play up the schematizing over the
simple seeing of natural experience. A thousand disjointed incidents
contribute to the abstract idea of drunkenness; a million to the idea
of "the good"; by implication, someone or some society must act to
relate all these component ideas.

The most legislative of ideas are the "mixed modes." Mixed modes
are both the most complex and most artificial of ideas; made only by
the mind, they combine not only several ideas, but several *kinds* and
varieties of ideas (*Essays*, 2.22.1-2). Mixed modes "are not looked upon
to be characteristical Marks of any real Being" (2.22.1). Moreover, they
can define identities without any direct input from experience. The
"Man who first framed the *Idea* of *Hypocrisy*" had no hypocrite before
his eyes, but "framed that *Idea* in his Mind, without having any such

pattern to fashion it by" (2.22.2). By disclosing the distance between human knowledge and experience, mixed modes disclose the autonomy and adequacy of human knowledge.

Locke, of course, claims that the only adequate idea is one that accurately represents its archetype (*Essay*, 2.31-32). Unfortunately, the "archetypes" for most Lockean ideas are powers rather than things.[17] The archetype of "white" is the power to produce the idea of white. How can one "represent" a power? Mixed modes get around this difficulty, for they both *represent* and *are represented*. Mixed modes incorporate the idea of representing into their representations; they represent representing. Presentation replaces representation as the space between idea and archetype vanishes: "For these abstract *Ideas*, being the Workmanship of the Mind, and not referred to the real Existence of Things, there is no supposition of any thing signified by that Name, but barely that complex *Idea*, the Mind it self has formed, which is all it would have express'd by it; and is that, on which all the properties of the *Species* depend, and from which alone they all flow: and so in these the *real* and *nominal Essence* is the same" (3.5.14). As its own archetype, a mixed mode represents itself. Legislating themselves into existence, mixed modes close the space between epistemological systems and moral implementations, for mixed modes are both patterns for and acts of arranging ideas. Garden variety experiences, what one might call poorly mixed modes, are at best inadequate analogies of these artificing archetypes. Interestingly, the act of literary criticism, in a Lockean universe, is less than arbitrary and more than subjective; a text, however deconstructed, is one of those complex modes that insists on presenting themselves completely and coherently.

Dryden considers language the ultimate explanatory device; Locke considers language the ultimate mixed mode. Languages and mixed modes share a common archetype, the act of arranging ideas. Mixed modes amount to the act of naming and producing human creatures. A mixed mode resolves what appears as a defined idea into a representing, differentiating, and finally comprehending act of definition. When a Lockean government invokes the sanction of *Salus Populi*, it invokes more of a defining than a defined imperative. Like mixed modes, such arbitrary sanctions act to purify, to pare down, and then to expand the arbitrary definition of government. In dismissing Parliament, Locke says, Charles did not set up a new order, but "restored the old and true one" and "rectified the disorders, which succession of time had insensibly, as well as inevitably introduced" (*Second Treatise*, sec. 158).[18] The thorough explication of any definition, especially that of a mixed mode, will, however, yield (and elicit belief in) a whole system of collateral propositions. Explaining "property," for example, involves declaring that the theft of property is an instance of injustice (*Essay*, 4.3.18). In the case of mixed modes, these collateral propositions are known with the same certainty as the mixed mode itself. As the products of analyses of mixed modes, they derive from an idea so coherent that it grounds, presents, and represents both itself and every collateral idea accompanying it. In the case of that biggest of mixed modes, "society," the problem of consent to collateral propositions all but vanishes. The idea of society contains the idea of consent, whether to taxation or to eminent domain (*Second Treatise*, sec. 140); it both requires levies and requires that those levies be conjoined with popular approval. Consent to a social system entails systematic consent to all its components: "This legislative is not only *the supreme power* of the Common-wealth, but sacred and unalterable in the hands where the community have once placed it" (sec. 134). Once established, a society cannot be defined in any other way, no more than a mixed mode can alter its defining nominal essence.

As the ultimate mixed mode, the idea of language justifies the application of language to virtually any "human creature"—ethical reasoning, explanation, poetry, and prose. Language is nothing but an explaining, an extension of itself to more and more things. Some forms of language are closer to the aboriginal mixed modes than are others.[19] Witty literature, for example, is more dangerous than judgmental criticism, for it can exploit its close relation to language to yoke together inconsistent ideas (*Essay*, 2.11.2). Never too Whiggish, Locke tacitly consents to a hierarchy in epistemology. Simple "qualities" occupy the lowest stations, deferring, in order, to identified things, to complex ideas, and finally to mixed modes. Language, likewise, ascends from generally descriptive adjectives, to names, to abstractions, and finally to terms for mixed modes. The parallel between words and ideas tightens as Locke ascends the ladder of artificiality and complexity. General names are formed in the same way as general ideas, with the advantage that the general names "save the labour of enumerating the several simple *Ideas*" that make up general ideas (3.3.10). Language and ideas finally overlap in mixed modes. Locke treats both the individual word and the individual idea as routes to their foundation—a foundation not in ordinary experience, but in an elite mixed mode, language. By accelerating the ascent from particular to modal ideas, language converts fragmented knowledge into a systematic common sense: "*Substances are determined into* Sorts, *or* Species" by *"the nominal Essence"* (3.6.7). Language is a method by which the arrangement of ideas in the individual mind can be checked against the "determination" imposed by a public language:[20] "For all Things, that had the Texture of a *Violet*, producing constantly the *Idea*, which he called *Blue*; and those which had the Texture of a Marigold, producing constantly the *Idea*, which he as constantly called *Yellow*, whatever those Appearances were in his Mind; he would be able as regularly to distinguish Things for his Use by those appearances, and understand, and signify those distinctions, marked by the names *Blue* and *Yellow*, as if the Appearances, or *Ideas* in his Mind, received from those two Flowers, were exactly the same, with the *Ideas*, in other Men's Minds" (2.32.15).

Like the real contents of nature, the real contents of the individual mind are intelligible only when they relate to this larger linguistic system. Dryden and Halifax affirm that deviation must define itself with regard to the established system; Locke adds that the deviant mind can only explain itself to itself in the context of this comprehending linguistic process. When an individual gives a name to an idea, he or she must use a word; in so doing, he or she must relate that idea, say the idea of a particular marigold, to the social, "nominal" conception of this flower. Words "in their primary signification" may apply to ideas in the speaker's mind, but "Men learn Names, and use them in Talk with others, only that they may be understood: which is then only done, when by Use or Consent, the Sound I make by the Organs of Speech, excites in another Man's Mind, who hears it, the *Idea* I apply to it in mine, when I speak it" (*Essay*, 3.3.3). Like Rochester, Locke regards talk about language as a matter of action and a process of excitation. "Use," "explanation," and "consent" might as well be synonymous. Like Dryden, Locke grants to language the power to initiate the formation of that esoteric "common sense" that is the stuff of the artificial human world. "Sounds," after a long period of conventional use, may "readily excite certain *Ideas*, as if the Objects themselves, which are apt to produce them, did actually affect the senses" (3.2.6). What has enjoyed longer use as a means of exciting a sense of transcendental reality, of epistemological groundedness, than a sound, "nature"?

CONTRACT OF CERTAINTY: RULES FOR PRODUCING KNOWLEDGE

Whether directed toward politics or epistemology, Locke's explanatory discourse grounds itself on systematicity rather than on the more usual foundations of God, nature, or axioms. God is not part of "present Business" (*Essay*, 2.21.2); the physical world hides behind ideas. However "progressive" he might be, Locke accepts all the classical and humanist limitations on human knowledge, although he turns the humanist tradition inside out by justifying those limits in terms of the groundlessness of the human world: "I think I may conclude, that *Morality* is *the proper Science, and Business of Mankind in general*" (4.12.11). The proper study of mankind is man. Knowledge arises from those habitual acts of organization that represent a societywide assertion of coherence among ideas. Civil society, in turn, derives from an arbitrary, self-defining action: "Where-ever therefore any number of Men are so united into one Society, as to quit every one his Executive Power of the Law of Nature, and resign it to the publick, there and there only is a *Political, or Civil Society. . . . And this puts Men* out of a State of Nature *into* that of a *Commonwealth*" (*Second Treatise*, sec. 89). Locke's society is more than a leviathan. It is more than the sum of differing opinions. It is an independent world that, like a mixed mode, perfectly matches and consistently implements its archetype: the power to make formative rules.

In Locke's thinking, "God," "mind," "nature," "the good," and "the beautiful" give up their bifurcated roles as foundations and targets of explanation. Instead, they become products of the explanatory process. Ideas of divine or natural law, for example, derive from an explication of artificially produced mixed modes. To know God one needs to explicate the laws of the good society. Neither God nor nature, for example, has "originally a private Dominion" (*Second Treatise*, sec. 26). Dominion, even God's, cannot exist until someone invents the artificial idea of "property." Everything known is known through ideas; as products, ideas are artificial; things artificial lead to artificing powers; and artificing powers, for the ever-ethical Locke, have no meaning outside of the production of artifacts.[21]

The consummate example of Locke's use of groundless systems to produce and comprehend particular "things" is the example of property. Like ideas, real property acquires value only when it participates in a network of artificial relations.[22] Nothing prevents a denizen of the American woods from claiming title to thousands of virgin acres (*Second Treatise*, sec. 48). Yet this "property" acquires value only when it is sanctioned by a more comprehensive social contract. Once the Indian joins a society, the miniature contract by which he appropriated the forest can be affiliated with, differentiated from, and appraised in relation to other similar contracts. As a right to exclude other claimants, property entails the social idea of "right" and the social reality of competitors. A contract is linguistic; it requires readers; property is not truly property unless it is surrounded by a society of proprietors and deeds. Alexander Pope's aggressively artificial *Windsor-Forest*—a poem that draws on elaborate literary and historical traditions but that, like Locke's Indian, allegedly dwells in a wild-wood—comes closer to Locke's systematic idea of "real property" than does an ordinary woodlot.

The idea of a comprehensive contract, a general procedure for reconciling, organizing, and absorbing interests, surrounds most of Locke's thinking. Locke's work on social theory, after all, antedates his work on epistemology. Both his epistemology and his politics evidence his desire to make particular persons into the unseen center (and perhaps the captives) of a comprehending human world. Never one for sentiment, Locke thinks of the marriage contract, for example, as a means of surrounding a cloudy idea, that of the personalities of the newlyweds, with a clearer idea, that of their social function, re-production. Marriage has little to do with the parties involved; it treats them as the consenting parties *to* an agreement to procreate (*Second Treatise*, secs. 78-83). A "person," likewise, is less of a thing than a contractual entity, a fiction by which an aggressive mind claims own-ership over a set of perceptions: "It is a Forensick Term appropriating Actions and their Merit; and so belongs only to intelligent Agents capable of a Law, and Happiness and Misery" (*Essay*, 2.27.26); "In this *personal Identity* is founded all the Right and Justice of Reward and Punishment" (2.27.18). For Locke, human government and hu-man knowledge both amount to contracts in which generative forces acquiesce to more systematic and thenceforward more primary prod-ucts, the "idea" and the "state." Locke's world of human knowledge is an array of such acts of assertive acquiescence. The perceiving pow-ers of individuals interact with the perception-producing powers of objects, with the result that ideas *are produced*. Once ideas are pro-duced, most individuals tacitly agree to act in a way consonant with their perceptions and to expect that other people will acquiesce in doing the same. Likewise, people must be born into some social set-ting; like it or not, they *are assumed* to acquiesce to its laws unless they expressly deny them.

Contracts are devices for regulating and controlling violence. They balance self-aggrandizing desires against obstinate facts and against one another. Following Locke's example and reasoning back from metaphors to reality, we can conclude that Locke's contractual world abounds with assertive acts. An "identity," the most basic item in Locke's epistemology, is a device for turning "things" into "owned things"—into metonymies for the assertion of ownership. Political identity, likewise, rises on the shaking platform of political action. A citizen is identified by the doing of actions that imply an "express Promise or Compact" (*Second Treatise*, sec. 122). Commentators have missed the miraculous, epistemologically supported teleology of Locke's human world. In Locke's contractual universe, violence seldom merits fear. The only forces that can even come to our attention are those that appear in ideas—those that, as a result, must be known through orderly systems of relations. One can only know a dangerous commodity like liberty when it is defined by some context and when it enables one to do constructive things: *"Liberty is not an Idea belonging to Volition, or preferring. . . .* Wherever restraint comes to check that Power, or compulsion takes away that Indifferency of Ability on either side to act, or to forbear acting, there *liberty,* and our Notion of it, presently ceases" (*Essay*, 2.21.10). Revolutionary impulses can only make themselves known by constructing a system. New societies arise through "men withdrawing themselves, and their obedience, from the jurisdiction they were born under . . . and setting up new governments in other places"; rebellion seems to imply reconstruction, resettlement, or the reestablishment of society. Anyone is "at liberty what Government he will put himself under" by either finding or making a new state (*Second Treatise*, sec. 118). To describe Locke's happy teleology is to paraphrase (and invert) Dryden's comments on imitation: when a new force comes into the world, it must provide a conventional rule for its understanding. Halifax's nation may be a "Mass of Dough," but Locke's is a cake mix that comes out perfect every time.

Locke's world could be described as a world of foregone agreements. Tacit, inevitable agreements both stabilize the human world and form the idea of its relation to God and nature. Foregone conclusions underwrite a complete, systematic lexicon of knowledge. Regulating itself, knowledge always admits its subordination to a larger system of knowledge. Knowledge, whether political or natural, may extend no further than its contractual character, its status as a limited compromise between competing powers, will permit. A "king," for example, is a legal entity, replete with contractual limitations. He *is* the contract among men, a living expression of the right to enforce (and the restraints on) the collected will. A king may be overthrown if he oversteps his contractual right, but a revolution must be bloodless, for it may affect only the king's legal, never his real, person (*Second Treatise*, secs. 205-06, 233-35). Conflict is minimized because everyone tacitly agrees that its happy conclusion is a foregone one.

The "assurance of the Existence of Things without us, is sufficient to direct us in the attaining the Good and avoiding the Evil, which is caused by them"; the assurance is as sufficient *"as our Condition needs"* (*Essay*, 4.11.8). In "our Condition," within the world of artificial explanation, it is "assurance" that underwrites "Things." The "experience" championed by Locke is, indeed, a special commodity. It reminds one of Rochester's "sensual" poems, for it diverts sense-data into a paradoxically immediate, systematically moral and aesthetic evaluation of sense information. Locke compresses immediate sense-data and detached judgment into the highly processed but immediately perceived ideas of "Pleasure and Pain; i.e. Happiness or Misery." The natural truth of "φυϑικη" and the critical truth of "ϭημειωτικη" should contribute to "πρακτικη," "not bare Speculation, and the Knowledge of Truth, but Right, and a Conduct suitable to it" (4.21.2-4).

A coherent system of knowledge, in other words, must be truly comprehensive. Like sense experience, explanatory discourse must, first, predict the future, and, second, allow itself to get out of the way of that more intense and more immediate sense of certainty that it inspires. Hence Locke says of proofs once worked out but now forgotten: "In his adherence to a Truth, where the Demonstration, by which it was first known, is forgot, though a Man may be thought rather to believe his Memory, than really to know, and this way of entertaining a Truth seem'd formerly to me like something between Opinion and Knowledge, a sort of Assurance which exceeds bare Belief, for that relies on the Testimony of another; Yet upon a due examination I find it comes not short of perfect certainty, and is in effect true Knowledge" (*Essay*, 4.1.9). A proof is merely a device, a procedure, by which reasoners may find their way through steps in a proof to a highly wrought but also highly immediate sense of certainty. The end of knowledge is the production of an original and originative sense of conviction, of belief in a larger system. Reasoning brings about the public, linguistic reconstruction of an immediate feeling of certainty. If forgetting a proof encourages this process, then proofs ought to be forgotten.

Locke's "human knowledge" thus offers a complex of rules for the systematic construction of impulsive certainty. Like Dryden's expanding world, Locke's flexible rules must cover all future applications:

All the Discourses of Mathematicians about the squaring of a Circle, conick Sections, or any other part of Mathematicks, *concern not* the *Existence* of any of those Figures: but their Demonstrations, which depend on their *Ideas*, are the same, whether there be any Square or Circle existing in the World, or no. In the same Manner, the Truth and Certainty of *moral* Discourses abstracts from the Lives of Men, and the Existence of those Vertues in the World, whereof they treat: nor are *Tully's* Offices less true, because there is no Body in the World that exactly practises his Rules, and lives up to that pattern of a vertuous Man, which he has given us, and which existed no where, when he writ, but in *Idea*. [*Essay*, 4.4.8]

Abstracting "from the Lives of Men," Tully's moral discourses fit with the abstracting (but never abstract) language of Locke's epistemology. As a process of abstraction, Tully's writings provide a map from the incoherent individual case to the formative mixed-modal idea. The comparison of Tully to mathematics is more than gratuitous, for Locke takes the same approach to mathematical as he does to moral models. The "idea of infinity" consists only of a procedure for removing limits from other ideas. It cannot bring us "one jot" nearer to a real infinity (2.17.3). A program rather than a sign, "infinity" names a procedure for moving away from particulars. It has no "content"; like Dryden's ship and like Tully's discourses, it leads only toward the paradoxical destination of more progress. "*Our Idea of Infinity* being, as I think, an *endless growing Idea*," it programs a "*supposed endless Progression of the Mind, over what repeated Ideas* of Space it pleases" (2.17.7). The fact that no one could ever carry out this program—that no one could ever "have" this idea—explains its centrality to Locke's program.[23] "Infinity" exemplifies Locke's plan to downplay the "real" referents and possessors of ideas. "Infinity" is the kind of idea that quickly expands into context, that manifests itself through the collateral, organizing actions of an expansionist society.

Locke's project completes those of Rochester, Dryden, and Halifax. Like those authors, his explanatory discourse is a discourse of denial, a discourse that distances itself from an inferior object world. Locke's system becomes self-sustaining through constructive negativity. Dryden may try to stabilize the future of some specific institution, like the church, by denying its authority in some specific, dangerous subjects, but Locke raises denial to new levels of comprehension. He relies on the negativity of his program, on its motion away from particular, presystematic realities, to imply that these same influences must play a role in his system of knowledge by *not* being known in it. More speculative than his empiricist credentials might suggest, Locke uses the system of human knowledge to postulate, verify, and even demand the influence of those facts and forces from which it is differentiating itself. Without these factors, obviously, there could be no process of differentiation. Obscure entities like the soul should be illuminated systematically but negatively. The inhabitant of a "*dark Room*" (*Essay*, 2.11.17), the "soul" is an undefined, anonymous screen on which a more systematic entity—an identity—is projected. The projecting of knowledge posits the existence of a screen, but the projections also deny, conceal, and distract attention from their target. There are probably a few cretins who attend the movies in order to admire the workmanship of the screen, but most viewers watch the images and attend to their role in the story. The enlarging idea of infinity works in the same way. It "retroactively" postulates and then negates the idea of that real infinity from which it is differentiating itself. Certainty itself, "a firm Assent of the Mind" (4.17.24), demands the presence but denies the knowledge of a believing agent. Certainty compensates for ignorance, but it destroys that doubt that creates the need for certainty in the first place. "Assurance" implies but also limits the roles of an assured, believing "soul."

Words like "mind," "God," and "nature" attain any meaning that they may have as a result of their exclusion from Locke's system. Locke's system is so negative, so much a procedure and so little a reality, that it questions its own systematicity. Breaking itself into three interacting subsystems—logic, ethics, and semiotics—Locke's human world creates three quite distinct sciences. Yet all these areas of knowledge can be subsumed in one highly synthetic, mixed-modal category, "Objects of our Understanding." There is no natural or rational way to get from the ethical creature of politics to the real man of physics or from the soul of theology to the poetic man of the arts. Yet Locke's plan to detail a "human" knowledge suggests that the plurality of disciplines demands the formation of an overarching system, a human world. This world, in turn, demands some identity, some Halifaxian "living law," to exemplify it. Caught up in the rhetoric of empiricism, Locke would represent everything, even general concepts, as particular "ideas." Yet Locke also pulls away from a particularizing faith in experience, toward a complex and unresolved program for converting sense into system. This critical exchange of sense for system and system for sense would accelerate in an unexpected way in the writings of Locke's self-styled critic and satirist, Jonathan Swift.

CHAPTER FIVE

SWIFT

Residual Conflicts and Casual Systems

Locke's role in the development of the human world could be summed up in one phrase: "coherence and consistency." For Locke, the crowning achievement of empiricism is the development of a language that is internally coherent but that permits its users to think, act, and believe in a way consistent with "common" notions about the world. Lockean "empiricism" wages a truly civil war, a war in which a social explanation of experience bloodlessly overthrows the ever-violent world of "objects" and "things." Given Locke's desire to set epistemology on a moral basis, it is odd that Jonathan Swift should be caricatured as the premier critic of both Locke and the empiricist movement that Locke has come to represent. Swift, the cliché argument goes, may well have had eclectic tastes, but he could never quite overcome the nostalgic antiquarianism of his one-time patron, Sir William Temple. Disgusted with the virtuosi, suspicious of Cartesian metaphysics, frightened of Lockean subjectivity, and outraged at bodies of all kinds, this ultraconservative Swift indicts anyone who relies too heavily on either empirical evidence or modern wit. Swift, this argument concludes, may have had friends in many factions, but "by temperament" he remained "a Tory, inclined to pessimism, to a distrust of innovation, and to a nostalgic attachment to the values (including the political values) of the past"—certainly not someone sympathetic to the revisionist "essays" of the great Whig philosopher.[1]

In this chapter I shall attempt to show that Swift's major writings constitute a ratification of Locke's thinking rather than a satire on it. I don't want to claim that Swift's writings are some sort of allegory of Locke's theories. More than a product of a "background," Swift, like Locke, doesn't trifle with endorsing or rejecting particular philosophers. He deals with the foundations of belief, and he does so in a decidedly Lockean way. The fact that Swift favors an elusive mode like satire is no obstacle to treating him as a philosopher, or at least what I have called a "philosophizer." Swift's beguiling language, whether the language of irony, satire, burlesque, parody, travesty, or polemic, is a key part of his reformist project for empowering Locke's mediating language. His perplexing discourse directs attention away from the meanings of words to their role in a system of meaning; it forces that linkage of denotative meanings with belief-inducing values for which Locke could only argue. Part of the problem with the understanding of Swift's attitude toward Lockean "human knowledge" is a faulty belief that a satirist may have no sympathy for his butts. But, as I have shown in my chapter on Halifax, the assimilation of deviance may be an essential function of this most judgmental of literary modes.

Swift's is a revisionist program, a brutal assault on any vestige of philosophical naturalism, realism, or Scholasticism in Locke's or anyone else's thinking. Angry at Locke's failure to be fully Lockean, Swift uses the aggressively artificial language of literature to drive out incoherences in Locke's system. Locke, for example, suggests that morally neutral "primary qualities" inhere in as well as represent judgeable "objects," but Swift dislikes vestigial notions about physical things. He prefers a "clothes philosophy"—or, rather, a clothes epistemology—in which commonsense, moralizing judgments about "things" appear right up front, in the visible superficies of experience. Swift revamps Lockean linguistics, for his words, things, and judgments merge together rather than merely refer to one another. In Swift's texts, primary, secondary, tertiary, and mixed-modal ideas are all at play in one grand, if disorienting, literary process. Swift sees an inconsistency between ideas that only represent things and ideas that engage themselves in a complex of morally significant relationships. What Swift presents is a more coherent, more compact, more dominant, and more useful human world. He offers a world of relations, a world in which acts of reconciliation, organization, and explanation have all but overwhelmed those "real" experiences to which they were supposedly responding. This is not to say that Swift can't see reality when it hits him in the face; rather, it is to suggest that Swift tries to show bad or powerful things as *nothing but* influences that lead to a reconciling rhetoric. Swift encourages the application *of* knowledge *to* experience; his stable, autonomous human world looks even more like a civil warrior than did Locke's.

By setting Swift in the tradition of Halifax and Locke, I want to accomplish a number of secondary and tertiary tasks. First, I want to bring out the fusion of social, literary, and philosophical concerns in Swift's writing. Mine is not an essay on Swift's political affairs, but it does attempt to recognize Swift's critique of distinctions between literature, philosophy, and their civil applications. *Gulliver's Travels* is, after all, a collection of ethnographic surveys in which a variety of "human" activities are recorded. Second, I want to avoid sanitizing Swift. Many critics like to explain away Swift's nastiness by portraying him as the kind wizard behind the curtain of the "persona." Swift, however, is never afraid to take responsibility for himself. Like Locke, he has no trouble with the idea that stabilizing acts of judgment may derive from angry impulses. Nor does Swift need to be consistent with himself (and hence at odds with his spokesmen). Swift sees himself as a little commonwealth, a coordinating of conflicting views. It is the tenderheartedness of our era that wants to segregate Swift from those outrageous views and uncomfortable attitudes that are, in fact, his most powerful weapons. From *The Mechanical Operation of the Spirit* to "The Day of Judgement," Swift's writing is all about the "progress" from uncivil, idiosyncratic impulses to delightful, believable, and publicly understood social conventions.[2] John Traugott has called for the redemption of a demonic Swift, a Swift full of anger, burning with indignation, and ablaze with outrage, from those post-Sherburnian angels who would dowse him in a "background" or suffocate him in a persona.[3] By heeding Traugott's call, I hope to reply to those moderns, like David Nokes, who would not even permit the "persona" theory to be questioned![4] Third, and finally, I want to work against the view that we can understand Swift as the advocate of one or another opinion, and argue instead that we should pay attention to the manner in which he assimilates opinions into his explanatory discourse.[5] Collaterally, I shall show that Swift, in his critique of Lockean, empirical, and similarly avant-garde reductionist philosophies, was not so much rejecting a particular point of view as exposing the ambivalent attitude toward experience implicit in these allegedly sense-prizing but actually mode-valorizing movements. Swift was bringing out, satirically exaggerating, and, in the last and the most comprehensive analysis, embracing that flexibility and variability that had come to characterize a worldview favoring acts of cognition and processes of consent over "true" propositions.

My discussion will have four parts. In the first, I shall present a Swift who relishes the arbitrary character of human knowledge. I shall discuss Swift's projects to denaturalize and to play up the groundlessness of explanatory discourse, to treat the grounding of philosophy as a kind of valuable but laughable, satirized but prized free play. In my second section, I shall talk about Swift's presentation of systematicity as the managing partner in the contract of knowledge. Swift, I shall claim, takes his own satire seriously; he uses the flawed, inadequate character of particular things as a model for the construction of a specialized, limited, and intellectually domineering human world. In my third segment, I shall describe Swift's interest in what could be called "implied" form: the inevitability of belief in an inevitably stable system of the world. Finally, I shall argue that Swift presents a world in which everything is not only explained but perceived as an open-ended process of explanation. The very inexplicability of critically over-evaluated places like Houyhnhnmland makes them good foundations for and incitements to an unending process of explaining. Swift, I shall conclude, is an author who, like Locke, turns experience into a self-sustaining process of self-justifying explanation.

In this chapter, I shall concentrate on Swift's two best-known works, *A Tale of a Tub* and *Gulliver's Travels*. For this contraction of Swift's canon I offer four defenses: first, the bigness of the subject; second, the repeated selection of these works, by critics, as representative of Swift's writing; third, their placement at the beginning and end of Swift's career as a narrative satirist; and, fourth, their shared relation to William Temple, and hence to a critique of traditional philosophical paradigms.[6]

PHILOSOPHY AS ARBITRATION: PURGING RESIDUES OF REALISM

The angry rhetoric and the exaggerated imagery of Swift's writings make it difficult to take Swift's ideas seriously. Despite his popular reputation as a reductionist, Swift does everything that he possibly can to play up the mannerism and eccentricity and to play down the realism and rationality of his art. Who would expect to meet Peter, Martin, and Jack at MacDonald's? Who *could* meet, anywhere, the heroine of "The Progress of Beauty," who disintegrates before the end of her poem? Is there anyone in the profession who has been drenched by a flood of turnip tops? The usual explanation for Swift's grotesquerie, that his characters are not characters but concepts, that they personify, allegorize, or otherwise stand for assorted abstractions, is unsatisfactory. Do the Struldbruggs really personify old age? Does Virgil, in *The Battle of the Books*, really represent the heroic poet, or even some attitude of Swift's toward him? The answer to all of these questions is "no." There is a quotient of terror and incomprehensibility in these and many other of Swift's characters, which resists their simple resolution into historical prototypes or their traditional allegorization into symbols for this or that theme or issue. Yet a gnostic or an ironic reading of Swift will not work either. Swift is always alluding to classical literary ideals. He leads his reader to suppose that he is instructing as well as delighting, that he is conveying information, and that his works and characters mean something. But what sort of data does he transmit? What *is* information about the inability to transmit information?

The answers to these questions are nonanswers, or perhaps post-answers. Swift is more concerned with what happens after a question is answered than with any particular response to it. Always ready to point up the arbitrary basis of knowledge, Swift wants to go past particular issues, to make more meaning rather than less. Literature and language serve as means of multiplying interpretations, not as means for defending specific opinions.[7] Swiftian characters and events, therefore, draw attention away from a their supposed allegorical meaning and toward a more complex, more adequate, and more self-verifying discourse. The three brothers of *A Tale of a Tub*, for example, act as allegorical figures, individual persons, and personifications. Language produces all of these conventional constructs—allegory, identity, personification—but no one of these constructs may fully describe the literally meaningful system that made them. Working in several literary modes at once, the brothers serve as the multiple foci of a multiplying literary system. Like Lockean objects, their essences *are* their appearances, for their appearances depend on and redirect attention to those categories that define them.

Critics should therefore be chary of categorically reducing Swift's more outrageous passages to irony, or satire, or shock: "They held the Universe to be a large *Suit of Cloaths*, which *invests* every Thing; That the Earth is *invested* by the Air; the Air is *invested* by the Stars, and the Stars are *invested* by the *Primum Mobile*."[8] This famous "clothes philosophy" passage is more than a spoof on Scholastic philosophy or a nasty bite at human nature. It is, of course, a naughty project, but it is also a half-serious demonstration that any experience can be classified according to just about any coherent system—or, alternatively, that the act of classification can create a literary experience. Dryden, I have argued, excelled at reverse personification, the replacing of persons by abstractions. Swift goes further, allowing a taxonomic system to invest a figure (or a nonfigure) with meaning. It is of great importance for a post-Lockean like Swift that this "meaning" is superficial, that it is to be found on the surface of ideas. Locke, after all, suggested that the taxonomy of ideas is itself a complex of ideas, that it could, with effort, be seen, or at least broken up into perceivable ideas. Swift's "clothes philosophy" extrapolates from the mode-loving Locke, for it presents experience as both a vehicle for and the image of its own explanation. The "clothes philosophy" passage is no fluke; this same fusion of explaining with perceiving is at work in many other areas of Swift's thought. Swift argues, for example, that kings must always be kings de jure and de facto; one cannot identify someone as a king without consenting to and experiencing his kingly offices. Whoever looks and acts like a king is a king, and vice versa; a king *is* a suit of clothes, but that suit presents a whole political system.[9]

The commonsensical Locke would always assume that, say, real fire and real water will never mix, but Swift wants to purge empiricism of its attachment to realism. Swift searches for that Lockean promised land, a world wholly intelligible as ideas—a world in which simple ideas and mixed modes (as well as everything in between) belong in one common category: " 'Tis manifest, what might Advantages Fiction has over Truth; and the Reason is just at our Elbow; because Imagination can build nobler sciences, and produce more wonderful Revolutions than Fortune or Nature . . . the Debate meerly lies between *Things past*, and *Things conceived*; and so the Question is only this; Whether Things that have Place in the *Imagination*, may not as properly be said to *Exist*, as those which are seated in the *Memory*" (*Tale of a Tub*, p. 108). This passage deals with a psychological concern, obtaining happiness, but it also suggests that the identity of ideas is determined largely by their status *as* ideas and by the system in which they are placed. An idea is from the past because it has been ideated and because it participates in memory; memory, in turn, creates the idea of a past. It is quite possible to read this and similar passages as instances of Swiftian irony. Yet Swift is living this irony, as he is living Locke. His definition of happiness as a *"perpetual Possession of being well Deceived"* (*Tale of a Tub*, p. 108) his bleak picture of human experience, and his repeated attempts to drown experience in a deluge of interpretation all combine to suggest that he takes his assertions more than half seriously.[10]

In trying to reconcile "things" with "things conceived," Swift follows three Lockean strategies: first, he shifts attention from knowledge itself to its orderly arrangement and its power to elicit belief; second, he locates the question of belief *within* the system of knowledge; and, third, he implies that identity, as an artificial system of ideas, depends on productively arbitrary actions. The "Digression on Madness" in the *Tale* (pp. 102-14) carries this last strategy to the extreme, for it suggests that a calm sanity may prove less systematic than a vigorously productive madness. In its self-conscious character as a digression, "On Madness" identifies itself as part of a system of genres. It also identifies the genre of the "tale" per se by explaining and defining its own character as a deviation. It postulates the genre from which it varies. The sane part of the work becomes little more than an alternative to the crazy part. Insanity systematizes and conventionalizes; it throws into relief the systematic character of an ambling and directionless but sanely presented story. Like the history of Jack, Martin, and Peter, sanity and sane literature derive their conventional forms from "custom"—that is, from habitual, potentially insane acts of assertion. Once again, literature is no privileged field. In the *Mechanical Operation of the Spirit*, Swift points out that the very foundation of normalcy, the conventional practices of organized religion, are only the result of the repeated, systematic implementation of local peculiarities: "This was the Original of the *Scythian Long-heads*, and thus did Custom, from being a Second Nature proceed to a first" (p. 175).

Swiftian knowledge is more negative than positive. It deflects attention from things to relations and relatings. Swift's "red" is "something not blue" or "something related to orange." Although critics may differentiate Swift from his persona, Swift uses his apparent distance from his spokesmen to play up his relation to and engagement with his textual counterparts. Swift may not really want to cannibalize children, but his assembling of unlikely ideas is a way of negatively identifying himself, of relating himself to his *Modest Proposal*. Through the persona, Swift can act as the unknown force that holds together the identities of his stories and his character; he can experience vicariously the consent to an outrageous political system.

If identity is a system of relations, Swift asks, how does this system relate to something not in the system, like the person who "appropriates" an identity? Do naturally perceived ideas add up to an idea of human nature, or is there some other force involved? Can a system of relations invoke a consenting action? "My Master had found a strange Animal in the Field, about the bigness of a *Splacknuck*, but exactly shaped in every Part like a human Creature; which it likewise imitated in all its actions; seemed to speak in a little Language of its own, had already learned several Words of theirs, went erect upon two Legs, was tame and gentle, would come when it was called, do whatever it was bid, had the finest Limbs in the World, and a Complexion fairer than a Nobleman's Daughter of three Years old" (*Gulliver's Travels*, pp. 79-80).[11] As for Locke, the "nominal essence" *man* is formed by grouping together its component ideas. Yet the elemental ideas in this group will not, unaided, add up to "human nature." To obtain an identity for "man" that is consistent with commonsense notions, Swift implies the operation of some arbitrary power, some systematizing but groundless force.[12] Something distinguishes Gulliver from his possible alter identity as clockwork. Swift's reader and critic are enlisted in the operations of this power, for they could very well agree with the king's opinion that Gulliver is a piece of clever machinery, were it not for the overwhelming impulse, rising from common sense, to affirm that Gulliver is more than he seems to be. A consistent identity must be *made* consistent; the greater the distance between the coherent identity and the cohering power, between persona and author, the greater (or at least the more forceful) the implied participation of the cohering power.

Swift, then, sees an advantage in the limitation of human knowledge. Small systems, states, and areas of knowledge are easy for some arbitrary force to make consistent. Coherence and consistency are, by definition, complete conditions; "partial coherence" makes no sense. In Swift's decrepit world, this kind of complete coherence can occur only in small systems, societies, or worlds. Swift's characteristic juxtaposition of formal coherence against fragmented settings plays up the role of big, arbitrary, and unidentified forces in the making of the limited human world. It also helps to explain why Swift can keep on satirizing the same old human limitations with such remarkable virulence—as he does, for example, in his progress poems, where the targets of his satire often decay before the end of the poem, or in his verses on his own death, where satire seems to persist even in the absence of the satirist. Satire keeps itself going by trying, over and over, to correct particular problems in the vain hope of achieving total moral coherence in a severely limited setting. As is suggested by Swift's post-Gulliverian satire on the island of his own personhood, *Verses on the Death of Dr. Swift*, human identity is one of these small systems. An assertive declaration of its own limits, "identity" tries to make a whole out of pieces; as a result, self-satire, Maynard Mack aside, becomes a possibility, and Gulliver's and Swift's angry satire on their own small problems—say, for example, Gulliver's persistent need to go to the toilet at awkward times—begins to make sense.[13]

To understand Swift's complex attitude toward coherence, limitation, identity, empiricism, and satire is to understand his nagging sympathy for many of the limited human worlds that he and Gulliver visit as well as the insistently even tone of Swift's prose. The Lilliputians, for example, refute Gulliver's explanation of his birth. They substitute an absurd theory about his stellar origins (*Gulliver's Travels*, p. 33). Swift's reader may laugh at this attempt to oust common sense with arbitrary system, but Swift maintains a deadpan face. Empirically describing this event in the same evenhanded way he describes everything else, he draws no contrast between what his captors think and what is true, for he recognizes that the Lilliputian's hypothesis is marvelously consistent with their limited experience. It justifies an effective, complete, and consistent plan of action for dealing with the very real problem of a giant. Arbitrary but coherent, the theory compares with those arbitrary but necessary mixed-modes that regulate human thinking in Locke's epistemology. In the same way, Swift's almost manic prose soon passes for an often monotonous discourse of description, even for journalism; a tense, obsessively direct, and aggressive idiom, it lacks that contrast with its subject, assorted evils and outrages, that usually characterizes the high satire of low offenses. Swift's language sets rather than reports the standard of normalcy for Swift's fictional worlds; it defines the limits of places like those in Gulliver's travel narratives, places that exist only in words, and, at that, words of a peculiarly hard-hitting variety.

Maurice Quinlan has warned that Swift despises "projectors" more for the incoherence of their projects than for their errors. Errors are, after all, common to humanity.[14] Projectors, for example, ruin Lagado by imposing schemes inconsistent with its limited agrarian economy (*Gulliver's Travels*, p. 161). Of all the lands that he portrays, Swift evidences the least sympathy for Laputa, where Cartesian thinking systematically conflicts with practice:[15] "I have not seen a more clumsy, awkward, and unhandy People, nor so slow and perplexed in their Conceptions upon all other Subjects, except those of Mathematicks and Musick. They are very bad Reasoners, and vehemently given to Opposition, unless they happen to be of the right Opinion, which is seldom their Case" (p. 147). The Laputans' problem is that their thinking is too consistent to be consistent. It lacks that elusive flexibility, that arbitrary, creative power, that allows Locke's mixed modes to organize limited, irregular segments of experience.[16] Like Locke, Swift looks for knowledge that is infinite in a negative way, which, being incomplete, allows for the continuous production of a vocabulary of actions, reactions, and explanations. They live in the unlimited world of mathematics, yet their ideas, which no one admires, remain local to their culture. The Laputans themselves become inconsistent with their own zeal for consistency; their use of "flappers" to keep themselves alert suggests that their thinking is too rigid to support even consciousness.[17] Totalizing, Laputan thinking cannot take advantage of its own limitations to throw into relief a system-manipulating power like the individual mind or the authorial personality. It depends on, but it cannot produce, consciousness.

Swift's quasi-classical talk about nature—his preferring, say, of the bee over the spider in *The Battle of the Books*—should be understood in its modern and post-Lockean as well as in its classical sense. "Nature," for Swift, is a compromise, a mixing of an ultracoherent human knowledge with a still-cohering, ever-limiting experience. Gulliver's voyages, for example, are travel narratives, but they offer very little in the way of the description of geographical, zoological, or other factual details. Seldom one for reporting natural wonders, Gulliver regales the reader with a list of those habitual actions, choices, and beliefs that constitute the human response to experience, that make up one limited but coherent culture. The natural history of Lilliput or Houyhnhnmland is less important than the description of the arbitrary choices that these societies make, than their devising, as Locke might say, some consistent mode for understanding the world.

EXPLANATION AS DOMINATION: RECLAIMING REALISM

Swift styles himself the self-assured defender of common sense, yet, when all is said and done, his writings still evince a frantic quality that defies any particular explication. The last sentence of *Gulliver's Travels*, for example, reads like a good-natured Shriner's plea to help the infirm and improve society. Yet in it Swift manages to insert a great deal of what could be called "limnal" discourse—words like "unsupportable," "Yahoo," "absurd," or "tincture," which refer to things on the very edge of intelligibility and describability.[18] Urgent, outraged, and even frenzied, Swift's writings reflect his tacit, Lockean admission that knowledge is de facto engaged—that knowledge *is* the process of forming systems, relations, and, thence, values and ideologies. Nothing in Swift's world can remain neutral; everything, every word, either implies or provokes an act of judgment.

Although Swift is no Shaftesburian, his world, like the third Earl's, is ready to leap into (or out of) form. Explanation is a matter of power and domination; specific types of discourse always follow the lead of the dominant, mixed-modal ideas of a given society. The Houyhnhnms, for example, think of nothing so much as simplicity and economy; as a result, their day-to-day language becomes a lean, efficient system:[19] "Their Language doth not abound in Variety of Words, because their Wants and Passions are fewer than among us" (*Gulliver's Travels*, p. 226). Only in a dysfunctional world, such as that of the Laputans, do cultural systems, like ordinary language, conflict with the culture's ideological core. While on Laputa, Gulliver fails to derive an etymology of the name of this nation, thus failing to "identify" Laputan society and suggesting that Laputan culture is not fully amalgamated: "I could never learn the true Etymology. *Lap* in the old obsolete Language signifieth *High*, and *Untuh* a *Governor*; from which they say by Corruption was derived *Laputa* from *Lapuntuh*. But I do not approve of this Derivation, which seems to be a little strained" (p. 146). In the same way, the Lagadoans' machine for the automatic production of language literally spins us away from the organizing genius behind literature and into a whirlpool of signs and signifieds (p. 168). Yet it, too, ultimately follows the centrifugal lead of a de-centered Lagadoan culture.

Like Locke, Swift wants to distinguish while relating human knowledge and the contents of the individual mind. He wants the more artificial, more public of the two, knowledge, to dominate the process of reconciliation. Gulliver, after all, spends most of his time adrift on the sea of common human (mis)conceptions, moving from one arbitrary social arrangement to another. He is always going to—and always inadvertently stopping at—one place or another; like it or not, he is de facto always dropping anchor, always trying to assimilate himself into some more comprehensive social system. As a mosaic of persons (including Swift) and experiences, "Gulliver" is an act, an identifying process who is always appropriating not only ideas but whole cultures. A relativist with a difference, he turns himself into a ground for his own judgments by identifying himself with society after society. Gulliver's story as a whole transforms the grounds of judgment into a perpetual, systematic, and self-grounding process of searching. Gulliver, after all, covers the whole world of evidence—from the small to the big—and of philosophical approaches—from the enthusiastic to the ultrarational. As a result, he comes to epitomize Swift's satire, a satire that goes beyond (and encompasses) any one standard of judgment.

Always adapting to some new set of social mores, Swift's satire makes it impossible to get hold of any one dominating foundation for judgment, yet it keeps its reader on the go, always in search of one—always, as it were, being dominated and directed by an ideal that never appears. As the most enduring feature of Swift's work, this endless search becomes a kind of self-supporting, all-powerful process. It drags Gulliver and his judging reader into not one but several public settings. Swift's reader always knows that a satire is taking place, but the all-important question, the relation between satire, its foundations, and its targets, remains always in the foreground because this relation is always in the process of formation. The Houyhnhnms, for example, blast Gulliver for the imperfect adaptation of his body to the duties of a rational creature (*Gulliver's Travels*, p. 226). "Perfections of Nature," they base their satirical attack on a standard of judgment that is consistent with their ideal understanding of nature. But Gulliver, many critics have observed, can hurl the same abuse at the Houyhnhnms. As one well-known incident shows, nothing could be less suited to threading a needle than a horse's hoof. For both parties, the implied general rule "Tools should match tasks" remains intact, yet this general rule remains incomplete, for it waits to be related to both particular experiences and general cultural modes.

Swift specializes in dramatic situations in which some person or some influence must produce literary relations—who is the butt? who is the satirist? what is the standard?—but in which the identity of that influence is only implied and is never finished with its task. The thread-and-needle scene may imply that there is a judge, but it only foments judgment, never suggesting what the judgment is going to be. The *Tale of a Tub*'s concluding "Experiment very frequent among Modern Authors; which is, to *write upon Nothing*" (p. 133), is a similar case. Here we have the sheer form of a conclusion. Related to nothing, not even to the book that it concludes, it becomes inconsistent with its character as a conclusion to the rest of the book. The format of the book makes the individual reader expect a conclusion, yet the conclusion, by refusing to finish the book, forces the reader to keep looking for the story-conclusion relation. Swift may rail at the modern "Humor of multiplying" chapter divisions (p. 43), but his enormous satire on preliminaries to books directs attention, first, to the act of organization and, second, to the fact that relations tend to establish power structures, that they make some things and ideas dominant over others. Why or by what means does one section of the book become preliminary to the other? Like it or not, the reader gets involved in the production of and consent to some ad hoc ground for differentiating, judging, and relating the various components in Swift's writings. Swift so heavily emphasizes the process of completion that the works themselves are never finished off. His readers are forced to recognize either an unknown or an impromptu standard of judgment, a standard that they recognize to be arbitrary because they themselves are involved in producing it.

Swift's highly visible campaign for common sense tends to conceal the miraculously teleological, highly arbitrary character of his thinking. For Swift, things have a way of suddenly taking on moral, philosophical, and ideological meaning. They usually do so both automatically and unexpectedly. A poem about cosmetics can instantly take on large didactic duties or assume cosmological proportions. Human thinking is teeming with signs of its aggressively purposive, arbitrary character. Domination and submission, teleology and obedience, suffuse the human world. Extraordinary powers work just below (and often right at) the surface of experience. Whether in solemn tracts like *On the Trinity* or narrative satires like *Gulliver's Travels*, Swift tries to show that many mysteries, miracles, and madnesses are casually admitted, inevitably implied, and splendidly organized in the most ordinary ideas:[20] "The King, although he be as learned a Person as any in his Dominions and had been educated in the Study of Philosophy, and particularly Mathematicks; yet when he observed my Shape exactly, and saw me walk erect, before I began to speak, conceived I might be a piece of Clock-work, (which is in that Country arrived to a very great Perfection) contrived by some ingenious Artist. But, when he heard my Voice, and found what I delivered to be regular and rational, he could not conceal his Astonishment" (*Gulliver's Travels*, p. 87). The centerpiece of a closed, conventionalized world, man qua thing is an unaccountable miracle, an astonishing force within a system. The knowledge built on such a prodigy is equally miraculous; man himself is a floating island buoyed aloft by powers more mysterious than magnetism. A mechanical man might well be made to talk, but talking is the foremost example of turning things (sounds) into identities (words) that serve a purpose. There can be no appeal beyond Gulliver's words; words are the point at which evidence, in this case sounds, and miracles, here an arbitrary act of linguistic organization, come together. Through his act of self-explanation, Gulliver points up both the self-sufficiency and the unlimited flexibility of the human world. Built on miracles, human knowledge must elicit the quasi-providentialist belief that all sorts of things will somehow contribute to its sudden, "astonishing" formation.

To understand Swift's conception of the arbitrarily absolute is to understand that mixture of heroism and outrage that informs his satire. Why is Swift always so upset over small issues? Because infinite anger and triviality reinforce one another. Savage indignation and the kind of joke that undercuts "The Day of Judgement" are necessarily conjoined. Together, big and small, infinite and insignificant, seem to point up their own extremity, and thus to invoke a mediating but equally arbitrary discourse. Exaggerations seem to ask to be cut down to size and set in order. The reader of Swift's poems feels a certain sense of astonishment when either scatological talk or melancholy reflections somehow lead back to the same old satire, to the judgment of human, social concerns. "The Progress of Beauty," for example, assures its reader that it has adapted its horrifying story of decay to a more regular form, that it will repeat the same old tale with each new moon, rather like *The Reader's Digest*. This same process works outside the venue of satire. The legislature in Swift's *The Church of England Man*, for example, is "absolute" because it prescribes only the forms of conduct, forms that dependably apply to irregular cases as these cases come regularly along, one after another. As in Locke, even infinitely wise judges must manifest their self-sufficiency through an unending series of small judgments of particular cases.

Works like *Gulliver's Travels* or *A Tale of a Tub* can therefore be seen as an extension of Lockean thinking. A gradual enlargement of the human world until it includes even complex modes like "satire," the *Tale*, for example, seems to satirize Locke because it keeps applying Swift's infinite outrage to more and more outrageous cases. Alternating between an allegory of church history and a satire of human learning, the *Tale* reaches out, in successive thrusts, toward more and more marginal incidents and concerns, ranging from a simple will to the outer limits of Bedlam, from, as it were, the secular scripture of Northrop Frye to the papers blotting up the intellectual diarrhea of lunatics. For Locke, this repeated application of grandly fictitious, mixed-modal ideas eventually leads away from particular things and toward a more programmatic, more domineering process. Lockean "infinity," for example, leads away from both individual numbers and real infinity, organizing instead an unending process of counting. For Swift, mixed-modal ideas like coherence, justice, or beauty are always on the move away from, or in the act of transforming, their exemplifications. An abstraction like "the economy" can turn Gulliver into a showroom dummy, a hangar for the collected work of a hundred craftsmen. Similarly, Swift can turn complex, negative abstractions like "folly" into positive regulating ideas by arguing that all men may be categorized not as people but as fools.[21]

Experience itself has a way, for Swift, of extrapolating and negating itself into schematized parables. Through a process both comical and miraculous, life is "immediately mythologiz'd." Parable displaces irregular experience with a more regular representation in literary language:

This Parable was immediately mythologiz'd: the *Whale* was interpreted to be *Hobbes's Leviathan*, which tosses and plays with all other Schemes of Religion and Government, whereof a great many are hollow, and dry, and empty, and noisy, and wooden, and given to Rotation. This is the *Leviathan* from whence the terrible Wits of our Age are said to borrow their Weapons. The *Ship* in danger, is easily understood to be its old Antitype the *Commonwealth*. But, how to analyze the *Tub*, was a Matter of difficulty; when after long Enquiry and Debate, the literal Meaning was preserved: And it was decreed, that in order to prevent these *Leviathans* from tossing and sporting with the *Commonwealth*, (which of it self is too apt to *fluctuate*) they should be diverted from that Game by a *Tale of a Tub*. [*Tale of a Tub*, pp. 24-25]

What starts as a journalistic report becomes a parable; this parable, in turn, becomes a means of converting its literal meaning into a systematic allegory of something else. The content of this passage is exhausted as the colloquial meanings of words surrender to a clarifying—and often oddly sensible—interpretation. Swift is no deconstructionist; his point is that meaning is so much a part of the human system that it is inescapable, that referential words will inevitably lead to engaged, moral, and domineering significations. The Houyhnhnms, for example, aspire toward a super-human—or super-equine— society guided by "unerring Rules" (*Gulliver's Travels*, p. 261), to a politics that not only regulates, but *is* regulation, that not only means something, but *is* meaning.[22] Like Swift's cetacean hermeneutic, the systematizing mode of the Houyhnhnms *makes* more "common" sense than the critic looking for irony wants to allow.

Whether in politics, ontology, theology, ethics, or literature, Swift takes every opportunity to underline the difference between the human world and its "real" counterparts. But he does so only in order to transform "sense" into "common sense," to assert that experience *is* explanation, and to show the miraculous conversion of experience into a valuable moral order. In politics, the human world cannot disclose the true nature of good government because good government has no nature. Good government *is* the transforming of available, "equally lawfull" forms of government into some—any appropriate— specific means of producing order (*Church of England Man*, p. 17).[23] In theology and ontology, theoretical opinions are little more than hypothetical identities, tolerable when they contribute to an agreeable order or otherwise mark out the proper relations among citizens (pp. 5-6). Ideas exist to be turned into sets and patterns. In ethics, "Moral Honesty" is inferred from observable patterns of behavior (*On the Testimony of Conscience*, p. 152). Behavior, once seen, becomes an evaluated system of behavior. What people call "Moral Honesty" reveals little about the real condition, the goodness or badness, of the soul; yet, for practical purposes, the pattern of behavior is all that can be known, and it is fortunate that it "consists" with the interests of the wicked and selfish to seem, and so, *de facto*, to be "Honest." And, in literature, the world itself ends up being dominated by complex attitudes built from simple ideas.

Gulliver's Travels is the best example. Swift sets up apparently impassable physical barriers around the places that he visits, but this impassability turns out to be more a matter of social will than an issue of geography. Dominant, totalizing cultural ideals displace that experience from which they were abstracted, just as they do in Locke. The peninsular Brobdingnagians are "wholly excluded from any commerce with the Rest of the World"; there is, however, little to stop them from building a ship and sailing away. A geography of perception, their shore seems to block out both the rest of the world, even though it stands wide open to it. The Brobdingnagians amplify the limiting, comprehending character of their setting but suppress its alternate meaning, its openness. Swift drives home the point by having Gulliver come and go, however awkwardly, from this allegedly blockaded land. The Brobdingnagians' perspective on the world "will ever produce many *Prejudices*, and a certain *Narrowness of Thinking*" from which "the politer Countries of *Europe* are wholly exempted" (p. 117); yet the saving grace of European nations is only their engagement in a more complex world, where they have less direct control over the relations between natural and moral geography.

Swift, then, is once again more Lockean than Locke. While the Lockean system of knowledge is laboriously worked out through the millions of encounters between things and persons, the Swiftian picture of the world develops almost automatically, as part of the casual experience of daily life. Conventionalized appearances and meaningful systems arise everywhere, in life as well as in literature. Locke wants to connect knowledge and judgment with experience and to get away from ancient authority; for Swift, experience *is* judgment, and authority resides in the central ideas of a culture. For Locke, language codifies a common notion of reality over which individuals have very little power. For Swift, any language used to challenge this conventional conception of nature is going to end up reinforcing that same conception. "*Reason* alone is sufficient to govern a *Rational* Creature" (*Gulliver's Travels*, p. 243), the Houyhnhnms advise. The Houyhnhnms claim to have developed a life-style so rational that it transcends conventions, customs, contexts, systems, and places. Yet the only place where one finds perfectly rational creatures is on an island like Houyhnhnmland—a land where a dominating, perfectly uniform notion of reality all but obliterates that idea of variety, complexity, and individuality on which the idea of a "rational creature" is founded.[24] Gulliver has a means of visiting islands, bounded but wide open places, places where sharply defined shorelines make it easy to see nothing but boundaries and even easier to appropriate these confined worlds into a dominant cultural ideal. In each of his adventures, Gulliver finds it difficult to satirize cultures in which he is gradually assimilated. The island of Swift's own discourse, likewise, makes it impossible for Gulliver to be completely disengaged from his domineering, commentating creator. Castaway, "Gulliver" is a way of merging the public spokesman and the private author—a way of bounding Swift's own character into a controlled context and a way of escaping Swift's personality by placing it in a distant public place and plotting it on a global map of human nature.

EXPLANATION AS NARRATIVE: IMPLYING AN ORDERLY ENDING

Swift's writing reconciles two distinct motions: a satiric, destructive motion from a highly synthetic common sense toward highly deviant particulars, and a comprehending, constructive motion from raw particulars toward that formative, artificial, and sometimes satirical discourse through which they must be explained. The first motion, the satiric, needs little explanation; the second, more constructive movement, is less often commentated. An understanding of this second motion helps to explain Swift's zeal for narrative satire. As a motion toward explanation, this progress from the particular to the synthetic tells a story. Having undercut most of the possible foundations for judgment, eroded the credibility of experience, and exposed the limitations of private wit, Swift needs to make up some kind of story to explain how he gets from raw deviations to a system in which these deviations may be judged to be deviations.

The preliminaries to *A Tale of a Tub*, for example, serve as preludes to and progresses toward judgment. They train the reader to accept a judgmental satire even while they satirize the pretension to judge. "There generally runs an Irony through the Thread of the whole Book, which Men of Tast will observe and distinguish" (p. 4); working their way through a series of incidents, the format, tone, and mode of this tale together convince readers that some basis for judgment, some reason for categorizing the piece as an instance of irony, is being constructed. "An Irony," a mixed-modal abstraction, explains more about the book than any of the statements in it. Accordingly, the rhythmic alternation of narrative and digression—which breaks down only after its amplification into a digression on digressions—implies that Swift is fabricating literary relations among disconnected events. The calm, even tone in which Swift recounts the catastrophic stories of Peter and Jack is Swift's way of explaining that the story is about making stories, about assimilating the most extraordinary events into the easy, intelligible format of the book:[25] "I have chosen to relate this worthy Matter in all its Circumstances, because it gave a principal Occasion to the great and famous *Rupture*, which happened about the same time among these Brethren, and was never afterwards made up" (*Tale of a Tub*, p. 74). So calm a presentation of the most calamitous event in Western history can only exist in a kind of no-man's-land between the outraged author and the reader, who, as part of the history described, is one of the victims of these events. Swift and his audience look on in wonder at the fact that this denarratizing "Rupture" can derupture into a coherent story.

The persona that Swift assumes, likewise, is less of a literary character than an implied, narrative synthesis of incomplete points of view. Swift's persona elicits a directive, narrative coherence from the astonished, satiric reactions of both himself and his reader to a disordered world. Reactions are relations; appearing over time and in some context, they establish affective links between persons and events. They underwrite a story. Like Locke, Swift treats his and our unfolding reaction to experience as the groundwork of a more comprehensive, more human presentation of experience. He progresses from a two-part, reactive conversation between Swift and the reader into a dominating monologue by his narrator.

This same process may work within Swift's stories. Gulliver produces his own character by synthesizing and presenting, in one coherent form, several possible reactions to experience. In one spontaneous act, for example, he joins the aggression of the Yahoos with the reasoning of the Houyhnhnms: "I drew my Hanger, and gave him a good Blow with the flat Side of it; for I durst not strike him with the Edge, fearing the Inhabitants might be provoked against me. . . . I ran to the Body of a Tree, and leaning my Back against it, kept them off, by waving my Hanger" (*Gulliver's Travels*, p. 208). Swift's satirical literature works in the same way as Gulliver does. It synthesizes a moderately aggressive, constructive course of conduct from a series of bad examples. At the end of Gulliver's story, for example, Gulliver's degeneration into an unresolved combination of rationality and bestiality seems to eventuate in the appearance of a more integrated, mediating character like Don Pedro.[26] As a result, the story must conclude in a nonconclusion. Ending in the synthesis of endings, it leaves us in the act of finalizing our opinions about Gulliver's odd desire to act like a horse. It leaves us to continue the satire, to draw conclusive judgments, rather than spurring us on to some ready-made happy conclusion.

The fact that most ordinary persons neither know nor want to know anything of Swift's esoteric "common sense" is no indictment of Swift's project. Swift is the first to admit that human knowledge is more often an approaching than an attaining. In Swift's ironic world, knowledge and order are emerging everywhere, but, being processes rather than things, they are nowhere in particular to be seen. The elusive character of human knowledge necessitates the telling of stories about the approximating to or the veering away from it. Laying the groundwork for the midcentury novel, *Gulliver's Travels* associates human identity with the story of its formation. The Houyhnhnms are "at a Loss how it should come to pass, that the *Law* which was intended for *every* Man's Preservation, should be any Man's Ruin" because their own law is perfectly exemplified in every single mind (p. 232).

Human law, on the other hand, is an organizing process. It applies to everyone but is fully exemplified in no one: "The Mind of Man is, at first, (if you will pardon the Expression) like a *Tabula rasa*; or like Wax, which while it is soft, is capable of any Impression, until Time hath hardened it" (*Critical Essay upon the Faculties of the Mind*, p. 250). The tablet of the mind cannot write itself into alignment with those collected, human rules for the direction of the mind that have emerged from centuries of abstraction. While copying their father's will, Martin and Jack evidence no bad intentions, yet they nevertheless start down Peter's path of distortion and abuse (*Tale of a Tub*, p. 75). Granted, these allegorical characters are more than individuals. Yet they still remain partial and imperfect in comparison to those pure processes, those sheer, organizing imperatives, that make up the undecipherable "Will." Martin and Jack *must* act out a story; they cannot simply *follow* pure principles, but, instead, must deviate from, return to, and reconstruct them. Even when they peek at the will over their shoulders, distortion still creeps in:

They both immediately entred upon this great Work, looking sometimes on their Coats, and sometimes on the *Will*. *Martin* laid the first Hand; at one twitch brought off a large Handful of *Points* . . . For the rest, where he observed the Embroidery to be workt so close, as not to be got away without damaging the Cloth . . . he concluded the wisest Course was to let it remain, resolving in no Case whatsoever, that the Substance of the Stuff would suffer

Injury . . . But his Brother *Jack*, whose Adventures will be so extraordinary, as to furnish a great Part in the Remainder of this Discourse; entred upon the Matter with other Thoughts, and a quite different Spirit. [pp. 85-86]

Each brother *must* choose between integrity of form and integrity of content, and therefore *must* deviate from the law. Martin and Jack cannot be parties to a "satire" in the traditional sense of the term. They may participate in a constructive, critical reordering of experience, but they cannot simply lay down judgments from the mountaintop. Were every prince to command seven scholars to comment on the *Tale*, Swift quips, "whatever Difference" would "be found in the several Conjectures, they will be all, without the least Distortion, manifestly deduceable from the Text" (p. 118), for exactly the same reason that Peter, Martin, and Jack can all deduce their ideas from the will. A moral mandate *must* multiply its exemplifications; indeed, laws, *as* laws, are *not* exemplifications. Any use of the law must be a distortion of it. Conversely, Swift suggests, any experience at all, no matter how bizarre, must be exemplifying (or distorting) some general rule, if only a pseudorule like that critical nonguide for the production of a nonstory exemplified by the "Nothing" in which the *Tale* concludes. Like it or not, everything in Swift's world must be in the act of telling an erratic tale, a tale less of its deconstruction than of its motion toward intelligibility.

EXPLANATION AS RELAXATION:
COMMON ACCESS TO COMMON SENSE

Swift raises Locke's principal dilemma to its highest pitch. How, Locke asks, do complex ideas, like justice, fit in with their simpler, less perfect counterparts? How, the author of *The Mechanical Operation of the Spirit* queries, can the ecstasies of Quakers be explained in terms of sexual desire (p. 189)? How can the most exquisite forms of madness be understood by an ordinary, sane observer? And how can a collected, normative understanding of the world be made accessible to the ordinary—and ordinarily defective—person?

Swift, in other words, is looking for the middle ground of epistemology. Modal ideas like "justice" are too big and complex for a mediating human world. A truly modal, truly comprehensive, and truly human idea should be more consistent with the universally limited condition of man. Far from being a *vir bonus* who growls at the flaws of humanity, Swift assimilates inadequacy into his post-Lockean, revisionist satire. He satirizes the pretension to satirize while also stressing the satirist's participation in the construction of positive role models and "certain" explanations. There is, for example, nothing odd about Swift's using deeply ironic tracts, like his *Modest Proposal*, for political purposes. Satiric tracts are essentially civil; they curb any effort to understand or make use of hugely complex ideas like "authority." They show how to replace such ideas with an entertaining and perhaps edifying artifact built from the more limited materials of political incompetence. While Locke would have us rule our lives by abstracting laws from millions of experiences, Swift settles for laws, rules, systems, and imperatives abstracted from however many bits of evidence he can find. A rule drawn from a few examples may hold over a limited universe. Yes, Gulliver is often ridiculous, but his behavior can also be taken seriously. It is the best that he can manage, "on shifts," in a world where the idea of going to the toilet must be included in the ultra-complex idea of heroism.

Swift's accommodation of Locke should not be seen simply as an adaptation of Locke to a more naturalistic or more realistic or even more empirical view. Swift's attempt to account for real-life conditions is a way of emphasizing the artificiality of knowledge and of the human world, a strategy for revealing the antiempirical bias inherent in and the cultural positivism necessitated by empiricism. The perfect knowledge of one world may vary with that of another; Gulliver may be absolutely right, in our world, to consider the giant Brobdingnagians coarse (*Gulliver's Travels*, p. 91), even though this same judgment would be wrong in the land of the giants. Swiftian reasoning is not a single mechanism leading to a single end, but a succession of compromises, abstractions, and distortions. The politic Lilliputians inadvertently set a fine example of this relentlessly confident, constructively distorting empiricism when they stay the execution of Gulliver for reasons of public hygiene. The Lilliputians may advance theoretical arguments for and against capital punishment, but the most abstract rule that can mesh with (and ennoble) the present situation concerns practical needs.[27] We should not be too quick, likewise, to condemn Gulliver just because he wants to live the life of a rational horse. Swift wants to *relate* ordinary people to a general "common sense." Common sense must belong to some particular commonwealth; if that commonwealth is made up of horses, well, then, it's time for an equine revision of commonsensical "human" knowledge and for a knowledgeable, humanizing revision of equinity. Perhaps "human" itself is a mixed-modal term, a way of organizing experience and of making "Mans Creatures" out of undifferentiated, non-species-specific information.

For Swift, then, few things are more artificial, more aggressive, and yet more accessible than are moderation and mediation. It is, at least, a far shorter step from the state of nature to a world of moderately artificial laws than from raw experience to a mixed mode like "justice." One reason that Swift distrusts "Conscience" as a moral guide is its tendency to interfere with common beliefs or moderate rules of public behavior (*On the Testimony of Conscience*, pp. 150-51).[28] In Swift's writing, moderate abstractions are better at explaining experience than are full-scale mixed modes: "Upon the whole, the Behavior of these Animals was so orderly and rational, so acute and judicious, that I at last concluded, they must needs be Magicians, who had thus metamorphosed themselves upon some Design" (*Gulliver's Travels*, p. 210). Gulliver explains what he sees by enlarging particular appearances into patterns of "Behavior." The horses are probably but not definitely members of the moderately-sized category "Magicians." Yet he doesn't mistake this limited pattern for a final or even general truth.

Our judgment of Gulliver should be equally moderate. Gulliver's conclusion, that the Houyhnhnms are magicians, may be inadequate, but his ascription of magical powers to these miraculous beasts is not wholly in error. Gulliver, after all, gradually changes "Magician" to "rational animal" as his acquaintance with more and more appearances yields a better hypothesis. But he never calls the civil horses "men," nor, as we know, will he define man as a rational animal. He identifies things in a limited way, through categories yet to be perfected. The Houyhnhnms also construct their idea of Gulliver's identity by working up a highly localized format, the pattern of his behavior: "They looked upon it as a Prodigy, that a brute Animal should discover such Marks of a rational Creature" (*Gulliver's Travels*, p. 218). Gulliver becomes an unusual, limited system for reconciling Yahoo with Houyhnhnm. In the same way, Swift's program for the advancement of religion begins with a literal reformation of particular manners and appearances, a local regimen from which, presumably, the emergence of a generally pious society would follow (*Project for the Advancement of Religion*, pp. 56-57).

"Manners" and "appearances," in Swift's post-Lockean nomenclature, imply "processes of abstraction." Objects inevitably imply patterns of behavior. An appearance conjures up ideas of those actions that led up to its production and of those mental processes by which it is perceived. As the story of Gulliver demonstrates, everything is perceived in some pattern, in some context; there is no simple idea, nor is there any idea that is not the result of organizing actions. Organizing action is at once the source, end, and test of Swift's human world. In *Thoughts on Religion*, Swift suggests that reason and experience might encourage suicidal thoughts (p. 263). The passions, on the other hand, engage the melancholy reasoner in the process of making life appear to be good, orderly, and attractive. A religious system should, he continues, promote a certain constructive disorder; it should organize but also stimulate the passions, and should deal with whole truths only after it has created an ad hoc moral system: "It seems a Principle in human Nature to incline one Way more than another" (*Church of England Man*, p. 1). The best church both recognizes and rejects experience. It devises a system by which to organize and harness the moral power of this recurrent irregularity.

Society ought to be arranged on practical rather than rational principles; it ought to be set up so as to permit freedom of conscience but to minimize the friction between private persons and public contexts, to create an environment in which the political self can restrain the private self and in which ideologies do not continually clash with one another (*Thoughts on Religion*, p. 263). A government need not look beyond itself for legitimacy, for those people who consent to a social contract *are* the social system. Their behavior plays out, in local contexts, its governing, mixed-modal principles. The Struldbruggs, those grotesque polycentenarians from *Gulliver's Travels* (pp. 195-98), strangle on the boundary lines of existence because they live beyond the reach of this limiting, self-defining system. Arriving, in their great age, at a point beyond our conventional ideas of human identity, the Struldbruggs are literally defined out of the human world. Gulliver himself ceases to be human when he voids that part of the social contract that establishes the normative character of human behavior: "By conversing with the *Houyhnhnms*, and looking upon them with Delight, I fell to imitate their Gait and Gesture, which is now grown into a Habit; and my Friends often tell me in a blunt Way, that *I trot like a Horse*; which, however, I take for a great Compliment: Neither shall I disown, that in speaking I am apt to fall into the Voice and Manner of the *Houyhnhnms*, and hear my self ridiculed on that Account without the least Mortification" (p. 262-63). Treating Houyhnhnm behavior as a "thing" to be imitated, Gulliver can't mediate between general principles and particular actions. Turning a mode of life and a method of philosophy into a set of gestures, he fails to imitate that moderate, flexible, and human understanding of which the Houyhnhnms are masters.

For Swift, then, empirical experience merges with its literary and philosophical representations. For Locke, ideas represent mediation.

They reveal the interplay of perception-related powers, but they also terminate this interplay with a finished idea. Swift wonders whether such final representations might participate more fully in the development of human knowledge. Could knowledge influence its mental and physical antecedents? Might literature act on as well as present experience? Could human knowledge, which, for Locke, culminates all cognitive actions, also generate those actions? "The Captain, a wise Man" who rescues Gulliver, evidences a "very good *human* Understanding" (*Gulliver's Travels*, p. 272). Gulliver speaks contemptuously of Don Pedro, yet Gulliver is, in this scene, in the process of making a fool of himself, while Swift is using an unmistakably Lockean term to complement the captain. In the case of Don Pedro, "Human understanding" drives that very "Behavior" from which, as Swift's first meeting with the Houyhnhnms shows, human knowledge can also be abstracted. The flexible "Understanding" by which Don Pedro conducts his life brings about as well as explains his good behavior. His actions ground the evaluation of his actions.

A good deal of critical mileage has been run over Swift's description of Houyhnhnm reason, a reason so similar to the "intuitive" reason described by Locke:[29] "As these noble *Houyhnhnms* are endowed by Nature with a general Disposition to all Virtues, and have no Conceptions or Ideas of what is evil in a rational Creature; so their grand Maxim is, to cultivate *Reason*, and to be wholly governed by it. Neither is *Reason* among them a Point problematical as with us, where Men can argue with Plausability on both Sides of a Question; but strikes you with immediate Conviction; as it must needs do where it is not mingled, obscured, or discoloured by Passion and Interest" (*Gulliver's Travels*, p. 251). Houyhnhnm reason is concerned with appearances, with their management, and with its own management, its "cultivation." Whether or not the Houyhnhnms themselves live up to their ideal, their reasoning only works when it engages itself with and works through ideas and experiences. Don Pedro, for that matter, could pass as a Houyhnhnm, for his behavior is "wholly governed by" his reflexive moral reasoning. The high-flying (or perhaps globe-trotting) Gulliver is drawn out of his equiphilia through the good offices of Don Pedro, who enacts rather than preaches the principles of the rational horses: "I at last descended to treat him like an Animal which had some little Portion of Reason," snaps Gulliver (p. 271). The Houyhnhnms, of course, had evidenced this same kind of condescension to Gulliver when he began to act like a horse. Swift's readers ought to avoid the mistake Swift satirizes; they must not try to represent the Houyhnhnms as either an allegory for some one point of view or as some kind of ideal. Instead, the Houyhnhnms should be understood as literary enactments of the knowing and judging process. They implement, in the most local, most unusual of contexts, the organizing process that makes common sense out of unevaluated experience. Like the intermediate human world, the Houyhnhnms are—and are only—a mode of idealizing, judging, and explaining. They enact the transformation, in all its excellences and absurdities, of writers like John Locke from philosophers to a philosophizers. Their story is a story about the perpetual implementation of continually revised philosophical ideas.

Like Dryden and Locke, Swift is concerned to treat real things, forces, and mysteries as contributing partners in the human world. Faith in a real God or belief in theological mysteries, for example, may be irrational; it may not be supported, let alone encouraged, by the limited fund of human knowledge. Yet such a faith may nevertheless be useful when it stimulates or at least allows for that regular, moral behavior that divinely-given reason would encourage (see *On the Trinity*, pp. 161-62). More than Dryden and Locke, Swift wants to treat objective reality as a systematizing process. Locke would claim, for example, that a primary quality is both a thing and an idea, but Swift would prefer to define things and ideas as a process of reconciliation between the two. Were an angel to command Swift to believe that noon is midnight, he would rather defy the command than upset the dependable coherence of human experience (*On the Trinity*, p. 161). The most dramatic evidence, a miracle, is only useful when it shows objects in the act of conforming to systems.[30] Like Swift, Locke worries about the relations among large but not comprehensive systems like physics, ethics, and semiotics. Swift, however, would solve the problem of a comprehensive "knowledge" by refusing to hypostatize it, by treating "knowledge" as a code word for the organizing of things, for the seeing of the act of judgment in all particular experiences. Swiftian knowledge, as Shaftesbury might say, is a forming rather than a form. Like Alexander Pope, Swift prefers the production and comprehension of truth to its counterproductive apprehension. How far this flying island of formative knowledge might drift Swift was terrified to ask.

CHAPTER SIX

POPE

Confronted Systems

Swift finds himself in the sometimes unenviable position of writing about a grudgingly intelligible world. Like it or not, Swift, his characters, and his readers must translate their thoughts and experiences into a stubbornly common, aggressively straightforward language. Their every move is subject to evaluation by an omnipresent but ever-elusive common sense. However outrageous his opinions, Swift's persona is an identifiable character whom his readers can understand, categorize, and appreciate. Yet Swift's purportedly "common sense" is a highly wrought commodity. For all his talk about horse sense, Swift finds more truth in distortion and abbreviation than in raw experience. Improving on Locke, he abbreviates heroically complex ideas and attitudes into practicable and pleasing guidelines. Artificiality becomes for him a matter-of-fact affair. So readily does sense become common sense that the conversion happens almost casually, before anyone knows it, often with dire results.

Alexander Pope regards this easy transition from sense to system as a mixed blessing. Like his friend George Berkeley, Pope aims for a "compendious" way of knowing, for an abbreviated science that both knows and distorts—or knows by distorting—a "wild," expanding world. He exposes the voluntary character of human knowledge—the fact that someone, somewhere, often when least expected, must voluntarily produce the knowable, artificial, and "human" world. While Jonathan Swift shows how this casual miracle of knowledge can lead to frightening consequences, his more cheerful colleague argues that an engaged, explanatory discourse may work in both terrifying and salutary ways, that it may draw a certifying power from its alarming capacity for distortion.

In this chapter I shall present a Pope who is an empiricizing citizen of the human world but who is also a Robespierre of artificiality. Both the genius and the terror of Pope's writings lie in his acute awareness that an empirical inspection of his own character will reveal his own artificiality, that it will disclose his status as an ill-managed, even anarchic commonwealth of identity-building forces and artificially refined passions. Pope confronts his reader with a dire, exasperated project to explain Pope away, to elucidate "Pope" into the context of an intellectually comprehensive but immediately felt system for the revelation, transformation, and finally absorption of his identity. Combining a zeal for precise description with a Pandoran enchantment with the manipulative powers of explanatory discourse, Popean poetry relates the value of empirical knowledge to the degree of effort—and anxiety—expended in its formation. Mixed modes, those most labor-intensive of ideas, dominate Locke's thinking; Pope, I shall argue, examines the psychological as well as the epistemological consequences of Locke's human worldview, for he absorbs himself in the intentional production of dominating, appropriative, and, finally, psychologically crushing systems of ideas. Halifax may have asked for a "living law," a moral power behind a rule, but Pope aspires to be a lawgiving life, a systematizing force synthesized with (and finally overwhelmed by) his own universalizing systems.

I shall guard against allegorizing Pope into a ideological fiction like that devised by Laura Brown. Suspicious of commerce, protective of the individual, and never a mere personification of abstract social processes, Pope and his writings are more than the wheels of the capitalist juggernaut.[1] If we must see Pope in economic terms, I shall suggest, we should see him as someone who capitalizes himself, who, like Swift's Gulliver, converts himself into a miniature system of values, into someone who can "see" the public good in those ideas that make up his own identity. I shall take a less embittered approach to Pope, one like that adopted by Fredric Bogel, who interprets Pope's poetry as a gradual synthesis of perspectives.[2] Like many of those attracted to the ground-breaking work of Maynard Mack, Bogel is too quick to present Pope as an author "striving" to know a divinely prefabricated universe. By highlighting Pope's preference for the production over the knowing of knowledge, I hope, however, to avoid Bogel's awkward juxtaposition of a destabilized author and a prestabilized order of things.

Pope's writing, therefore, confronts the weighty problem of the status of the author, authorship, and authored systems in a human, empiricizing universe. Zealous for coherence in knowledge, Pope versifies on the intentional synthesis of relations among ideas. One well-known critical axiom holds that Pope often makes his most telling points by making comical lists of things, that, for example, he exposes the triviality of modern life by juxtaposing Bibles and billets-doux. While it may be effective as an instrument of persuasion, the light-hearted and occasionally sarcastic listing and jumbling of common-places in Pope's two poetic "essays" has discouraged critics from taking Pope's philosophy seriously. It is, however, precisely this voluntary, aggressive, and entrepreneurial relating of disparate things, ideas, and systems that constitutes Pope's explanatory mode. And it is Pope's passionate feeling for the destabilizing, irregular, and eminently personal character of explanation, his sense that an empowered, self-assured philosophizing can be fun, that nominates him as an item of interest for modern scholars of the theory of science and explanation.[3]

Dustin Griffin has directed attention to Pope's engagement *in* the making of poetry. Like Mack, however, Griffin has created a Pope who leaves the final synthesis of knowledge to God.[4] I want to suggest that Pope includes the idea of Griffin's editorially providential God *within* his ever-expanding, ever-synthesizing discourse of explanations. Hence Pope finds himself confronted with an agitating dilemma: by explaining nonhuman things like "God" in an aggressively human, overtly literary discourse, Pope increases the epistemological distance between things, their explanations, and their explainers. He makes human knowledge partly a matter of the denial of knowledge. To versify explanatory discourse is to *progress* from the private language of the mind to the conventional languages of poetry and philosophy. It is to juxtapose the incoherent poet and his ultracoherent, ultrasynthesized productions, even to pit them against each other. Pope's poetry, I shall argue, is a poetry of epistemological and psychological combat: combat between explanation and experience and between the poet and his appropriative, even cannibalistic discourse. It combines the vocative, exhortative functions of the beleaguered satirist and the exasperated didactic poet with the esoteric concerns of the philosopher and theoretician. I therefore subtitle this chapter "confronted systems" in reference to my chapter on Rochester, whom I characterized as the poet of confrontational systems. In Pope, the Rochestrian concern with the confrontation of the mind with the world gives way to a more subtle anxiety about the relation of self to systematic knowledge and about authorial control over authorial productions.

I shall divide this chapter into four sections. In the first, I shall talk about Pope's Swiftian attempt to fuse explanation with immediate experience, to treat experience not only as an object of or a precursor to explanatory discourse, but as an integral component of it. Pope doesn't explain things; for him, things are explanations. In my second section, I shall proceed to Pope's fusion of explanation with exhortation—his energizing of the passive world into an aggressive appeal for its systematization. In my third section, I shall talk about Pope's assimilation of the universe into a kind of (literary) character. I shall deal with the problems that result from this "characterization" of the cosmos. A "character" is a study in deviation and, perhaps even more perplexingly, a portrayal in stock, durable terms and conventions of eccentric persons who are never quite integrated into convention-producing societies. A "universal" knowledge that takes a form appropriate to eternal deviancy is, to say the least, a troubling prospect. In my last section, I shall discuss Pope's exploitation of despair—his use of the failure of the explaining poet to sustain the process of explanation.

ACTIVE PERCEPTION AND RESPONSIVE EXPLANATION

Pope's earliest poetry takes a pastoral turn—that is, it studies the turn away from pastoral. For the young Pope, the pastoral mode offered a convenient means of merging the highly conventionalized but seemingly empirical description of nature with the spontaneous but seemingly systematic process of explanation. Pope warns that his *Pastorals* attend to the "action" and the "character" of shepherds rather than to rural scenes. His shepherds, moreover, evidence "some skill in astronomy" (as well as other human arts).[5] Both the ideology and the manner of Pope's pastorals could be described as naturalistic rather than natural, for Popean nature never appears without the presence of complicating factors, whether technologies or witticisms.[6] In *A Discourse on Pastoral Poetry* (prefaced to Pope's *Pastorals*), for example, Theocritus is criticized for his excessive rusticity (p. 121); in *Windsor-Forest*, likewise, history is quickly completed with the early arrival of the Stuarts (1.42), and the forest itself is moving rapidly ahead in time by growing into "future Navies" (1.222). The *Essay on Criticism*, similarly, delivers a panegyric on nature in which last-minute functions, like being the "End" and "Test" of art, outnumber early duties, like being a "Source," by two to one (1.73). As late as the *Epistle to Burlington*, Popean nature is still craning into the future, once again by growing "future Navies" (1.188). Pastoral poets from Virgil to Dylan Thomas have specialized in juxtaposing the mannered and conventional with the spontaneous and bucolic, but even skeptics like Christopher Marlowe or Sir Walter Raleigh have set nature's happy world in the foreground of their poems. Like Locke, Pope postulates that a "state of nature" stands in the background of his poeticized universe, but he doubts whether that primitive condition can be described without the introduction, valuing, and even emphasis of postlapsarian notions. He preempts and revises the simple opposition of bad city and good country life on which pastoral poetry is traditionally built.

To borrow a phrase from Hollywood, the settings of Pope's early poems are "based on" rather than located in nature. Their technique is aggressively urbane; their goal a point near the climax of social history. As his Toryizing dilation on Norman monarchy (*Windsor-Forest*, 11.43-92) repeatedly proves, Pope downplays nostalgia and emphasizes progress, presenting a "nature" that exists only to be bypassed. Pope's poetry may initially be an empirical, descriptive poetry, but it is essentially a poetry of explanation. Always more than what Reuben Brower calls a "poetry of allusion," his poems do more than set up image/allusion, sign/signified, poem/tradition relations. Pope likes to package description, meaning, explanation, and response to explanation in one tight, mixed-modal bundle; from the beginning, his poems don't *make*, but *are* allusions, or are the alluding process. Gestures and relations more than presentations, they *are* approaches to nature, to poetic tradition, and to an audience.

The relational character of Pope's early poetry opens an oeuvre ever-engaged in the act of relating. Pope was a long-time friend and admirer of that most literary of philosophers, George Berkeley, and Berkeley, throughout his eccentric career, insistently defined "ideas"—sensuous presentations of experience—as part and parcel of a "Language of Nature." Berkeley didn't coin this term until late in his career, but even in an early work, his *New Theory of Vision*, he regards sensory experience as coextensive with explanatory data. As Berkeley says in one mind-boggling sentence, "It being already shewn that distance is suggested to the mind by the mediation of some other idea which is it self perceived in the act of seeing, it remains that we inquire into what ideas or sensations there be that attend vision, unto which we may suppose the ideas of distance are connected, and by which they are introduced into the mind."[7] In Berkeley's world, perception is profoundly moral and historical. It tells a story about actions that must occur over time. When percipients look at Berkeley's moon, they see a white sphere, but they also see an explanation, a statement about the distance of that orb from themselves and about the difficulty of traveling to that distant place.

Pope's poetry, like Berkeleian perception, abounds with "concrete" images, but these images, however firm and sharp, are always perceived in moral and epistemological relief, as one focus of several spatial and ethical umbras. His poems have a way of relating themselves *to* some set of actions in which readers and writers are presently involved. In *Windsor Forest*, rural scenes appear in the context of an extended, explanatory tale of British political history, a history presented directly to individual persons as their own story. Like L. Frank Baum's apple trees, Pope's timber likes to speak its mind; his forest exists in order to reveal its story and show itself the tool of various ethical and practical applications. Consider one inhabitant of this didactical woodland, Pope's happy retiree:

> He gathers Health from Herbs the Forest Yields,
> And of their fragrant Physick spoils the Fields:
> With Chymic Art exalts the Min'ral Pow'rs,
> And draws the Aromatick Souls of Flow'rs.
> Now marks the Course of rolling Orbs on high;
> O'er figur'd Worlds now travels with his Eye.
> Of ancient Writ unlocks the learned Store,
> Consults the Dead, and lives past Ages o'er.
> Or wandring thoughtful in the silent Wood,
> Attends the Duties of the Wise and Good,
> T'Observe a Mean, be to himself a Friend,
> To follow Nature, and regard his End. [ll. 241-52]

Whether encounters with local aromas or sightings of distant planets, particular sensory experiences are always conjoined with a some explanatory, historicizing modifier. "Worlds" assume "figures." They engage the eye in a prolonged "travel" narrative. "Orbs" roll through a schematized, astronomical course; chemistry applies "Min'ral Pow'rs" to specific tasks; even canonical "Writ," when "lived," moves through history, from antiquity into modernity and from uselessness into utility. Pope's complex "images" imply their interrelatedness. The listing together of fragrances, chemistry, books, and exegeses suggests that all these things and pursuits contribute to the emergence of a human system of disciplines, even though the relation between modern chemical art and ancient writ may be hard to see. Yet see it we must, for Pope, in writing a pastoral poem, makes a generic (and empirical) claim to show his ideas in the form of scenes, to communicate his thoughts first through rural vignettes, and only secondarily through more abstract techniques like argument or insinuation.

In Pope's forest, every object, every tree, stone, and flower, strives for complexity and systematicity. Relational concepts like "Forest," a set of relations among trees, displace the trees themselves. Time-tested periphrases like "figur'd Worlds" link immediate experience to a literary tradition—and, thence, to a vast complex of stock reader responses. Pope finally supplants his forest with a site, Sir John Denham's "*Cooper's* Hill" (l. 264), whose interest derives more from its poetical associations than from its geography. When Pope looks at nature, he sees, like the rest of us, fields and forests, but he also sees, like Berkeley, the way that millions of viewers have responded to, understood, and conventionalized the world.[8] Dustin Griffin suggests that Pope extended this poem in 1713 (ll. 291-434) in order to clarify his relation to Granville and to the pastoral tradition; I would add that the addition completes the progress of the poem into modern and future history. The closing paean to Granville, after all, portrays the pastoralist amidst the "Scenes of *opening* Fate" (l. 426; my italics), while the preceding vision of British empire showcases a relentless use of the future tense. The extension makes use of an allegedly natural form like pastoral to bring about the convergence of natural history and all the objects in it with a more schematic political history, and of both of these with an unending process of interpretation, explanation, and conventionalization.

Windsor Forest studies the epistemological and psychological acceleration of the civilizing process. Refining a natural, "harmoniously confus'd" wildwood into an explanatory, human world, it moves through the Lockean progress from nature to state at breakneck speed, with the result that the initial, natural condition, now existing only "in Description" (l. 8), is all but forgotten: "Thy Forests, *Windsor*! and thy green Retreats, / At once the Monarch's and the Muse's Seats, / Invite my Lays" (ll. 1-3). From a particular forest (already an arrangement of trees), Pope proceeds to "green Retreats," to a summary of the forest's moral and recreational value. He then directs attention to the forest's political and poetical implications. The whole transition from nature to state happens in twenty-four syllables. While there is nothing startling about Pope's use of figurative, invocative language, his repeated use of that language to define, compress, and accelerate a historical and social progress augments his program to assimilate sense into system. Things become contexts, contexts lead to systems. As F.E.L. Priestley explains, Pope treats even the most complex systems as "premises" from which to proceed with (still more) system building.[9]

An equally speedy progress toward relatedness is underway in Pope's early treatise on nature and poetry, *An Essay on Criticism*. "Nature" in this first of Pope's essays is already literary, for it is already oxymoronic. In reflecting the image of our mind, it immediately presents our reflective responses. *"True Wit"* is *"Nature* to Advantage drest," a *"Something"* that "gives us back the Image of our Mind" (297-300). "True" poetry serves as a kind of intellectual cellophane tape: it binds disparate objects into attractive relations; its adhesive power is felt, but it doesn't interfere with the immediate perception of the object. This quick, reflexive fusion of near objects with remote contexts also characterizes Pope's later verse. Pope can progress from one object to an entire macrocosm in ten lines (*Essay on Man* 1.259-68) or from an instinctual sex drive to a system of benevolence in one short verse-paragraph (3.109-46). Leo Damrosch is wrong to see an early poem like *Windsor Forest* as a passive contemplation of the world.[10] From first to last, Pope's poetry aggressively hastens the fusion of nature with the explanatory response to nature. It sees experience as a continuous explanatory act.[11]

This speedy progress toward an immediate sense of relatedness is important for another reason. Experience, in Pope's poems, *must* be perceived as proceeding into a moral relation with percipients. In the first verse-paragraph of *Windsor-Forest*, Windsor's woods invite a "lay" specifically from Pope. The Muses then redirect this lay specifically toward Granville. Later in this same poem, "Britannia's Standard" "flies" of a "sudden" into the air, hitting the reader in the same sudden way that shotgun fire specifically and suddenly hits a poor pheasant (ll. 109-14). Experience not only can but must compel its viewers to assume an attitude, a relation, toward experience. The possibility of disinterested observation is summarily eliminated when Pope's rendering of experience flies into the face of his startled, suddenly self-consciously particular, and reflexively responsive reader. Two of the percipients to whom Pope specifically addresses his poems are, of course, his reader and himself, both of whom are forced to take on an attitude toward and thus assume a persona within the poem, and both of whom, therefore, engage with and vitalize the work.

This personalizing power pervades social as well as natural experience. In poems like *The Dunciad* or *An Epistle to Dr. Arbuthnot*, dunces always seem to be presenting themselves to Pope. Pope himself can speak comfortably through the persona of the Goddess Dulness, to whom all writers in Pope's beleaguered world present their wares, just as they do to Pope. Readers of Pope's poems have an even more difficult task, for they are lured into creating relations among a great many parties—the author, experience, and themselves. Pope often speaks of "our mind"; he habitually flees from idiosyncracy toward common sense; but he also demands, even if that demand is redundant, that human knowledge relate to some thinking person. Someone, some particular as well as collective person, must believe in Pope's vast system of relations; his poetry of belief needs validation and support from psychological forces like certainty and from a belief-inducing world.

In order to insure that his poems solicit this type of moral support, Pope tries to concentrate more evocative meaning in his images than they might seem able to sustain. Indeed, one part of Pope's project to vitalize knowledge is to call attention to the fact that someone is packing an unusual amount of meaning into conventional scenes or low objects. In *Windsor-Forest*, the numberless relations among commerce, empire, and geography hang from a single support, the trees used in shipbuilding: "By our Oaks the precious Loads are born, / And Realms commanded which those Trees adorn" (ll. 31-32).[12] It takes some person, whether Pope or his reader, to assert that a few chunks of woods can support so big an imaginative load. All poets make startling comparisons, but Pope is doing more than spinning conceits. His metaphor and his fact are the same; he demands that some reader notice—and believe—that the real oaks just down the street at plain old Windsor are, in fact, carrying the oversize metaphor of empire into the undersize reality of history.

As the case of these nautical oaks suggests, Lockean abstraction sustains but is also transformed by Pope's panegyrical verse. In the aforementioned passage, Pope shows his reader only some features of his logs. He doesn't talk much about their bark or their susceptibility to termite infestations. Yet he more than replaces what he takes away. For Locke, everyone in the world is likely to abstract more or less the same general ideas out of the same range of experience. For Pope, the abstracting process happens immediately and in idiosyncratic ways. "Oak" is perhaps the last—and the least obvious—common denominator that the average percipient would abstract from the events that Pope is describing. Pope, in other words, enriches his stripped-down abstractions with an awareness of the abstracting person, quirks and all. In presenting his specialized, historicizing oaks as though they represented the common verdict on the character of this species of tree, Pope suggests that every idiosyncratic act of abstraction contributes to a larger, collected, and human act of schematization. For Locke, the assimilation of so many ideas into a generalized idea of trees would strip the trees of all their particularity, but Pope calls attention to the fact that he voluntarily sustains their sharp, definite identities. He asserts that *someone* can explain the relation between this tree or that forest and a comprehending imperial ideal.

Like Lockean "identities," Pope's "Oaks" retain their particularity. But that particularity resides less in their "thingness" than in the relations among such qualities as buoyancy, strength, and abundance. The breathless comprehensiveness of Pope's later poems is an extension of Pope's early desire to escape the "thingness" of things, to present knowledge as a flexible matrix of voluntary, organizational actions. The principal dilemma in Pope's thinking is the relating of general systems to those individual writers who must articulate them. Transferring identity from things to relations (and finally to relating minds) helps Pope to close this gap between self and system. Pope's lifelong dialogue on self and system reverberates through his frequent (and frequently casual) talk about "the universe" and in many similar examples of easy verbal immensity. Talking about vast spaces and vast arrays of phenomena as though they were one easily unified universe is an act of rhetorical role-modeling, a way of showing readers how to associate their idiosyncratic way of "identifying" things with that largest and most objective interplay of irregularities, "Nature":

> See plastic Nature working to this end,
> The single atoms each to other tend,
> Attract, attracted to, the next in place
> Form'd and impell'd its neighbour to embrace.
> See Matter next, with various life endu'd,
> Press to one centre still, the gen'ral Good.
> ....
> Nothing is foreign: Parts relate to whole;
> One all-extending all-preserving Soul
> Connects each being, greatest with the least;
> Made Beast in aid of Man, and Man of Beast;
> All serv'd, all serving! nothing stands alone;
> The chain holds on, and where it ends, unknown.
> [*Essay on Man* 3.9-26]

Percipients are commanded to "see" nature working toward some "unknown," orderly end, to "see" their partial perceptions as part of an unfinished depiction of an unending, ever-unfinished finishing process. Pope, indeed, could exchange the subject and object terms in most any of these statements, as he does explicitly in his comment on the reciprocal helpfulness of "Man" and "Beast." "Wholes" could relate to "parts"; attraction works in two ways. The verb, not the noun, "identifies" the meaning of the statement. Verbs signify activities; by establishing relations, they fabricate human knowledge.

Relations and the decision to write about relations define both the human world and the *"end* and *purpose"* of the individual: "I thought it more satisfactory to begin with considering *Man* in the abstract, his *Nature* and his *State*: since, to prove any moral duty, to enforce any moral precept, or to examine the perfection or imperfection of any creature whatsoever, it is necessary to first know what *condition* and *relation* it is placed in, and what is the proper *end* and *purpose* of its *being"* (Design, *Essay on Man*). Divided into four sections, each of which details some "relation" into which "man" enters, Pope's *Essay on Man* is less a description of the universe than an action by the poet to relate a whole "Man" to his several relation-defined ends.[13] Having "thought" of a plan, Pope draws attention to his decision to act—to "enforce" and "examine." Metaphysical assertions like "whatever is, is right" or "Order is Heav'n's first law" (4.49) literally *make sense*, for they epitomize a fundamental component of human perception: the voluntary decision to relate an ordering mind to an order-eliciting system.

The relational, communal, and yet voluntary character of Popean experience can support quite extravagant beliefs. Pope's first essay, on criticism, reconciles private genius with public, poetic discourse. Genius, Pope admits, is an unknowable, eccentric sort of thing. With its hundreds of often contradictory bits of advice, *An Essay on Criticism* tests to see how far one can go in asserting that deviation relates to a systematic norm. Pope's gambit is the reifying of the psychological relation between believers and the most unbelievable "objects" of belief: " 'Tis with our *Judgments* as our *Watches*, none / Go just *alike*, yet each believes his own" (ll. 9-10).[14] As a measure *of* time, the watch implies its difference from, its relationship to, and, thence, its wearer's belief in this most elusive of metaphysical commodities. This relational knowledge of time leads chronometricians to organize their collected, human experience according to a time that is, as Berkeley might say, less seen than suggested. The watch may deviate from the time that it signifies, but its deviancy is salutary. It justifies the psychic distortion of experience until experience seems to validate what must be believed before it is seen. Pope says the same thing about the soul: *"It self unseen*, but in th' *Effects*, remains" (l. 79). As a factor in the production of knowledge, the soul produces "Effects" and ideas that make their marks on experience.

Poets bring out and amplify the distorting power of images and signs; they turn an "Effect" into a cause of knowing, and, as Coleridge says, they "know" in a fully "active," transitive way (*Biographia Literaria*, ch. 12). Witty writing draws an "Image of our Mind" within "Nature" (*Essay on Criticism*, ll. 297-300); artifacts like neo-classical "Rules" are "*Nature* still, but *Nature Methodiz'd*; / *Nature*, like *Liberty*, is but restrain'd / By the same Laws which first *herself* ordain'd" (ll. 89-91). Art improves on "Nature" when it improves on natural philosophy—when it fuses "Nature" with occasionally extravagant conceptions of what nature seems or ought to be. Individual acts of critical judgment ought to be made to coalesce with *both* the reader's immediate feelings and the public's verdict on a poem—hence Pope's idea for a personal but published essay "on criticism." When an important citizen of the judging public is also a poet, the situation is still more complex; the poet's individual judgment of his poem must coincide with a better, presumably more rigorous and less complimentary judgment from the public. Self-judgment becomes a humbling, public act of self-redefinition. Pope's later essay, on man, follows a similar strategy, linking comprehensive knowledge of comprehensive systems with the conventional presentation of idiosyncratic knowledge:

> That REASON, PASSION, answer one great aim;
> That true SELF-LOVE and SOCIAL are the same;
> That VIRTUE only makes our Bliss below;
> And all our Knowledge is, OURSELVES TO KNOW.
> [*Essay on Man* 4.395-98]

Immediate self-seeing is also immediate system seeing; self-knowing, as Pope's use of the classical *gnothi seauton* trope shows, can pass as an immediate knowing of literary tradition.

SYNTHESIS AS EXHORTATION

Assuming that random experiences must, some way or other, fall into a system, Pope, like Swift, associates the casual with the teleological. Still, Pope would speed up this casual motion toward order by aggressively perceiving as many relations among things as possible. The Design for *An Essay on Man* begins by proposing a system that coordinates passivity with aggression:

> The science of Human Nature is, like all other sciences, reduced to a *few clear points*: There are not *many certain truths* in this world. It is therefore in the Anatomy of the Mind as in that of the Body; more good will accrue to

mankind by attending to the large, open, and perceptible parts, than by studying too much such finer nerves and vessels. . . . If I could flatter myself that this Essay has any merit, it is in steering betwixt the extremes of doctrines seemingly opposite, in passing over terms utterly unintelligible, and in forming a *temperate* yet not *inconsistent*, and a *short* yet not *imperfect* system of Ethics.

When the paragraph opens, Pope's "science of Human Nature" is passively "reduced" to a few clear points; when it ends, this same abridgment is being carried out in the active voice by a self-conscious "I." This wavering in the assignment of responsibility is characteristic of Pope, especially when associated with the acceleration or abbreviation of system building. Whether in happy poems like *The Rape of the Lock* or in growling indictments like *The Dunciad*, things always happen as they must happen. They may happen slowly, seeming only to happen to happen, or they may happen more quickly and intensely, when the author or some other party intervenes. But they always *do* happen, and in an orderly, predictable way. The world of *The Dunciad* would collapse with or without Pope, but Pope's participation makes the collapse happen more quickly and stylishly, or at least it seems to. Pope, as it were, is part of a system in which he apparently has no place. The one unimpaired genius remaining in the collapsing empire of Dulness, his presence in the final calamity of British culture seems to make some difference in the panache with which the final moment arrives, if only because it allows us to know, to notice, that Pope is making no difference, that the apocalypse is more heartless than expected. "Some have at first for *Wits*, then *Poets* past, / Turn'd *Criticks* next, and prov'd plain *Fools* at last" (*Essay on Criticism*, ll. 36-37); the only question is whether this natural history of folly would proceed as quickly and cleanly as it does were not Pope packing it all into twenty syllables.

Pope makes his own contribution to the "system of things" seem both aggressively voluntary and passively inevitable. "ALL subsists by elemental strife; / And Passions are the elements of Life" (*Essay on Man* 1.169-70); authorial duty consists in asserting that individual things, passions, and authors contribute to the great concord of things—especially when, promoting "strife," they seem *not* to contribute to it. Pope's pose as a satirist allows him to pretend that his rage, despite its apparent roughness, is promoting the common good and speeding the discovery of systematicity. "Great Wits sometimes may *gloriously offend*" (*Essay on Criticism*, l. 152); indeed, Pope's injunction to "Know well each ANCIENT's *Character*" (l. 119) implies that the crankiness, eccentricity, and angry deviation normally associated with "Character" must be contributing to that seamless rhetorical and critical tradition that the collective term "ANCIENT" implies. Poets are in the business of declaring that involuntary passions are, somehow, being voluntarily directed into useful works—of insisting, like Bernard Mandeville, that a complex, counterintuitive system is obvious to "common sense":[15]

> Expatiate free o'er all this scene of Man;
> A mighty maze! but not without a plan;
> A Wild, where weeds and flow'rs promiscuous shoot,
> Or Garden, tempting with forbidden fruit.
> Together let us beat this ample field,
> Try what the open, what the covert yield;
> . . . .
> Laugh where we must, be candid where we can;
> But vindicate the ways of God to Man.
> [*Essay on Man* 1.5-16]

Sooner or later this "plan" would come to light, but its advent is hastened by Pope's flushing it out. Pope recalls Colonel Sanders, who, in the heyday of health food, suddenly discovered that his chicken had always had high nutritive value. Pope's point is not simply that poetry is more adept than mere chance at discovering truth. For Pope, there is no chance. The world will "yield" something, one way or the other. To "try" experience is a matter of exhortation; explanation is a hybrid act, a mixture of passive description and aggressive incitement.

Pope's "scene of Man" represents Pope's belief that everyone shall, either voluntarily and quickly or accidentally and slowly, come to see order in experience. The imperative "see" is therefore one of his most common usages (see, for example, *Dunciad* 3.322-32 and *Essay on Man* 3.9-26, quoted above); "see" directs the attention of the more sluggish observers of nature to those order-disclosing scenes that more aggressive viewers, like Pope, have already seen. Popean "experience" is supercharged by a sense that someone—or everyone—is about to consent to its intelligibility. So strong is this sense of imminent commitment that it can almost be seen. Eminently Berkeleian, Pope would "see" nature as a favorable attitude toward the seeing of order:

> Self-love thus push'd to social, to divine,
> Gives thee to make thy neighbour's blessing thine.

Is this too little for the boundless heart?
Extend it, let thy enemies have part:
Grasp the whole worlds of Reason, Life, and Sense,
In one close system of Benevolence.
                                   [*Essay on Man* 4.353-58]

Where "Faith, Law, Morals all began / All end, in LOVE OF GOD,
and LOVE OF MAN" (4.339-40). Out there, somewhere, there is
someone or something in which all these good attitudes "began."
Someone loves God and man, but that someone is only the occasion
for the disclosure of all these productive attitudes, from faith to love.
However comprehensive, Pope's vision remains local, particular, and
immediate. Faith, law, and love are as "seeable" as the parties who
practice them. The "close system of Benevolence" tangibly "grasps"
(and perhaps strangles) "Sense." Things in experience are enveloped
by order, but it takes the right attitude to see (and see quickly) the
envelope as well as its contents.[16]

For Pope, then, explanation is exhortation, an egging on of sys-
tematizers: "Reason the card, but Passion is the gale" (*Essay on Man*
2.108). Explanation is a way of speeding up the discovery of still more
explanations, explanations that, as part and parcel of the way we see
experience, must eventually present themselves anyway. In his *Epistle
to Burlington*, Pope can only satirize (and thereby obstruct) Timon's
disconnected works, but he panegyrizes Burlington's, and, thence,
encourages Burlington in his project. By explaining, in advance, the
effects that the building will have on its future viewers, Pope can
accelerate Burlington's projects, for he can anticipate, even see, the
real, immediate, and psychological effects of Burlington's enterprises.
This kind of exhortation is in the process of becoming empirical description, for it must praise some eventually knowable, observable
thing. Burlington's building program differs from Timon's because
Burlington fuses his passive perception of the landscape with his
aggressive approach to renovation. He blends his demanding taste
with the compliant character of a place, its genius loci.[17] Exhortative
discourse like that directed at Burlington marks the outermost limits
of the empirically-grounded model of language, for it describes experience by implementing and accelerating changes in it. It also marks
the outermost limit of explanatory discourse, for it explains how to
do or see things that may be experienced only later.

The more Pope commits himself to the discovery of an extensive
order in experience, the more he commits himself to exhorting it into
being. What good is an "extensive" but visionary system of which

there are no examples? Pope may explain that self-love and social instinct drive his comprehensive system (*Essay on Man* 2.59-80; 3.95-98), but he cannot say that they appear within it. It is not so much that experience fails to reveal a design; it is, rather, that the intense, immediate, and psychological experience of the designing act, of asserting that there is a system, seems more compelling, more tangible, than the designed things:

> This light and darkness in our chaos join'd,
> What shall divide? The God within the mind.
> Extremes in Nature equal ends produce,
> In Man they join to some mysterious use. [2.203-6]

Pope's hedged, dialectical affirmation of a psychological *and* systematic use for natural conflict overshadows any discussion of nature's particular uses. The details of experience prove less interesting than the dark, aggressive, and imaginative acts that fit it to some productive, human design.[18]

Pope's job as a philosophizing poet is less the accommodating of difficult ideas to particular images than the speedy splicing of particular images into those complex systems that they suggest: "See anger, zeal and fortitude supply; / Ev'n av'rice, prudence; sloth, philosophy" (*Essay on Man* 2.187-88). Pope respects Mandeville's attempt to relate evil deeds to good results, but, as Pope's almost verbless diction suggests, he doubts whether a system so comprehensive as Mandeville's could ever *do* things like *arise* or *apply*. Pope won't even pose Berkeley's question to Mandeville—Which particular drunkard helps which particular brewer?—but only wonders here, "Which generalized vice promotes which generalized virtue?"

> All Nature is but Art, unknown to thee;
> All Chance, Direction, which thou canst not see;
> All Discord, Harmony, not understood;
> All partial Evil, universal Good. [1.289-92]

Pope is not so foolish as to present such exaggerated views in the indicative voice. His is an exhortative argument, a warning that explanation ought to push and transform as well as to describe experience.[19] Pope's admonition is directed to a "thee"; it has a moral *and* a philosophical purpose. Experience recedes from view, leaving behind a balanced battle between abstractions of disorder ("Nature," "Chance," "Discord") and abstractions of order ("Art," "Direction," "Harmony"). Experience, to use Pope's own terminology, becomes an "open field" against which he may accelerate an unending dialogue of opposites, parts, and wholes. When Pope declares that "the *Sound* must seem an *Eccho* to the *Sense*" (*Essay on Criticism*, l. 365), he means it literally, for he affirms that aural experience, physical sound, ought to *follow* rather than precede, accompany, underwrite, embody, or otherwise dominate its explanatory product, auditory and intellectual meaning. Pope affirms that *"Nature's chief Master-piece is writing well"* (l. 724), that nature, seeking posteriority, seeks to "Eccho" explanatory discourse. "Harmoniously confus'd" (*Windsor Forest*, l. 14), chaos itself can invoke a system of chaos—a system so suggestive, so exhortative, and so productive of harmony that it displaces vulgar disorder. Pope often rhetorically opens vast spaces with his poems— "from Infinite to thee, From thee to Nothing!" (*Essay on Man* 1.241)— in the expectation that the invocation of a wider field for explanation will produce a wider explanation—and, subsequently, a wider nature.

Moving his emphasis from Lockean coher*ence* to Swiftian coher*ing*, Pope assigns a higher value to knowledge that has been voluntarily synthesized than to knowledge that has been inadvertently found. An explicitly moralizing art is also a "realistic" art, for such an art displays the rendering of a subjectively experienced world into an intelligible, human form. Even Locke, after all, admits that highly processed "knowledge" like that found in Tully's essays is more real than the real people that it explained. Similarly, Pope defines man with respect to a system of knowledge far more coherent than the average person's "measur'd" wit.

> Then say not Man's imperfect, Heav'n in fault;
> Say rather, Man's as perfect as he ought;
> His knowledge measur'd to his state and place,
> His time a moment, and a point his space.
> [*Essay on Man* 1.69-72]

The knowledge possessed by particular human beings proves less interesting than its contextualization in some "state and place." No enemy of paradox, Pope suggests that human knowledge produces an idea of human knowledge that is far more impressive than human knowledge would seem to allow. Indeed, Pope forbids either thinking of or acting on the very thoughts that produce this majestic, regulative idea of an apparently super-human human knowledge. "The bliss of Man (could Pride that blessing find) / Is not to act or think beyond mankind (1.189-90). Knowledge "measur'd to his state and place" is knowledge suited to the contours and character of human experience—an experience that, in its moral immediacy and its capacity to produce bliss, proves more convincing than knowledge does. "Thro' worlds unnumber'd tho' the God be known, / 'Tis ours to trace him only in our own" (1.21-22): what Pope means by "tracing" is unclear, but it is clear that this "God" is less interesting and less useful than the production of human theories about him. It is tempting to suppose that Pope is only having fun by sporting with religious talk. No one, for example, has ever seen much "deeper meaning" in Pope's use of Rosicrucian machinery in *The Rape of the Lock*. Yet passages like the preceding, when taken in the context of his lifelong discourse about divine beings, from St. Cecilia to the Goddess Dulness, show that Pope toys with the gods for more than fun.[20] In Pope's post-Halifaxian, epistemologically supercharged world, even outrageous opinions may help to sketch the tracery of human knowledge. Always concerned to see order in experience, Pope wonders whether the experience of the collected articulation, by himself and his readership, of even absurd tenets, like those of Rosicrucianism, might yield what Shaftesbury calls a "pleasant sort of truth"—a truth productive of stimulating explanations.

THE CHARACTER OF EXPERIENCE

Pope's personalized manipulation of philosophical commonplaces is part of his overall program to link explanatory systems with those explaining characters who alone may articulate them. Pope always has the option of offering a straightforward treatise on criticism, cosmology, or any other topic. But, rather than follow the course of Blackmore and other rhyming philosophers, the philosophizing Pope casts his disquisitions in the form of addresses and conversations and puts his cosmological systems in the mouths of emphatically particular, often socially alienated speakers. Pope is no solipsist, but his lifelong commitment to large-scale explanatory works, coupled with his equally durable commitment to terse, aphoristic discourse, suggests that he regards the philosophical characterizing of the universe—the framing of a cosmological system by the relating of several salient, jarring theories about it—as the same psychological process as that underwriting the assembly of disparate anecdotes into the "character" of some person. The emergence of Pope's own persona culminates a long explanatory process in which all the irregular actions in Pope's mind are fully coordinated, in one grand system, with all the irregular actions in the objective universe. A character, after all, is an identity, and an identity, as Locke explained, is an intelligible, public product, the result of private acts of mental appropriation. Many of Pope's major late poems, accordingly, take the form of epistles. Working in the same way as the epistolary novels of the midcentury, they rely on the stylized discourse of spontaneous, individualized characters to outline the whole character of a fictional world.

For Pope, the cultivation of a "character" means the cultivation of an explanatory system. Pope's own, partial point of view, his own "psychology," can be seen as one system, one identity, within the vast system of systems. His character serves as a nucleus around which to build a more comprehensive explanatory system. A faith in the systematizing tendencies of individuals underwrites Pope's aphoristic style; individual advices and commonplaces, for example, tend to queue up into whole "essays." For these reasons, Pope spreads his *Imitations of Horace* across a frame defined by character. The *Imitations* begin and end with intimate colloquies, with character-revealing, psychotherapeutic conversations between Pope and his "friend." These framing dialogues establish a larger context in which to interpret the intervening satires. In his introductory satire, for example, Pope interprets his "lawless" "*Libels* and *Satires*" as "grave *Epistles*" (Satire 2.1.150-51); indeed, the Advertisement to the *Imitations* suggests that the entire work constitutes a framing commentary on Pope's career as an epistle writer (p. 613). While a poet like Dryden enlarges his characters until they devour his well-known enemies, Pope keeps his characters brief, permitting obscure parties to demonstrate quickly the operation of a much larger system:

> "I give and I devise, (old Euclio said,
> And sigh'd) My lands and tenements to Ned."
> Your money, Sir? "My money, Sir, what all?
> Why,—if I must—(then wept) I give it Paul."
> The Manor, Sir?—"The Manor! hold," he cry'd,
> "Not that,—I cannot part with that"—and dy'd.
> [*Epistle to Cobham*, ll. 256-61]

Euclio's truncated life explains, in brief, the operation of the whole corrupt economic system. His cameo appearance quickly discloses the miserly impulses driving it. Appearing at the climax of *To Cobham*, this uncomplimentary portrait summarizes Pope's moralizing commentary by culminating a letter on a big topic, the "Knowledge *and* Characters *of* Men." Pope's portrait thus performs two reciprocal tasks: it discloses the corrupting local influence of an inhumane economic system, but it also implies the emergence, in the background, of a more coherent system in which goods are eventually justly distributed and in which Euclio has a place.

The portrait of Euclio throws into relief Pope's and his reader's actions and judgments. Judgments like those made against Euclio emanate from individuals, yet the inevitable similarity of these judgments suggests that a common standard of judgment is in the process of formation. People like Euclio undermine any notion of a preestablished moral order, yet Pope constructs the simulacrum of such an order from this shaky ground up, by leading himself and every other individual to pass similar moral judgments. Playing particular, ugly portraits against the general, improving movement of the poem, Pope points up the freedom of the reader, for he allows readers to *decide* to experience and to *consent* to the emergence of order within the poem. In the *Epistle to Bathurst*, for example, the contrasting portraits of the miserly Sir John Cutler and his spendthrift son encourage Pope's reader to ratify Pope's favorable judgment on the moderate Bathurst, whose portrait emerges as the climax of this dialectic. Pope's portraits open the possibility that moderation is just one other possibility in a spectrum ranging from penury to prodigality; they allow readers to evaluate all approaches to wealth equally and relativistically. Yet they also suggest that the poem moves—or rather circulates—toward a proper approach to wealth and its uses, an approach discovered not so much through authorial reasoning as by leading the reader to choose it.

Partial and made up of parts—of anecdotes, characters, and aphorisms—Pope's moral and philosophical poems pass a great deal of responsibility along to the synthesizing reader. The portrait of the Man of Ross (*Epistle to Bathurst*, ll. 249-74) amounts to a detailed list of particular acts by a particular man "whose true name was almost lost," who epitomizes Pope's ethics because, in his obscurity and through his doing of occasional charities, he puts his author and audience into the act of finding him out, of assembling his anecdote-based identity and of relating that identity to the poem as a whole. Bathurst, the addressee of this epistle, specializes in making himself an obscure part of the larger synthesis. Knowing how "to value Riches, with the Art / T' enjoy them, and the Virtue to impart" (ll. 219-20), he incorporates his character as a benevolent private man into the economic system at large. As Fredric Bogel explains, a character study like that of Bathurst is a study of the conversion of an individual character into a mode of knowing.[21]

However extravagant Pope's cosmological systems, they always fit into the context of an individual character. As early as the *Essay on Criticism*, Pope situates his wandering critical system by pointing to particular persons, from Quintilian to Roscommon, who have exemplified it (see *Essay on Criticism*, ll. 665-744). Nature and Homer are "the *same*" (l. 135). Nature and nature's law appear in the context of a character, Homer; that character, as the personification of epic poetry, becomes a critical system. Truly an "identity," Homer's exemplary excellence makes him truly singular and hence necessarily individual, yet it also makes him systematic and transpersonal. When Pope goes still further and proclaims himself "TO VIRTUE ONLY and HER FRIENDS, A FRIEND" (*Imitations of Horace* Satire 2.1.121), he avoids disgusting his reader with his pomposity because he ascribes responsibility for this self-congratulatory description to "the World"—to a superpersonal character, to that collection of folks who, by their "murmuring" and "consenting," gradually appropriate the character of Pope into their common discourse and understanding.[22]

I call Pope's character "superpersonal" for two reasons: first, because it is *both* personal and public; second, because it arises from voluntary acts of self-transformation, acts by which Pope turns himself into the human image of something more than human. Explaining the whole universe through one's own benevolent behavior is a tall order, one calling for more than a phone booth in which to don the cape, leotard, and boots. A sort of philosophical vampire, Pope asks his reader to keep sustaining his ever-expanding, ever-varying cosmological system with ever-intensifying acts of commitment to it. He wants to bring out the superiority of faith to knowledge by forcing his readers to make a continuous psychological commitment to an inaccessibly grandiose, manifestly unprovable cosmology. Pope challenges his audience to convert the universe into an orderly system, but he also asks the audience to imagine that this system transcends the powers of its authors.[23] As Dr. Johnson feared, commitment to an overwhelming system like Bolingbroke's or Leibniz's could paralyze believers by numbing them into a stypefying admission of their insignificance in comparison to a system that, paradoxically, depends on the systematizing action of these same persons. "Go, teach Eternal Wisdom how to rule— / Then drop into thyself, and be a fool!" Pope scoffs (*Essay on Man* 2:29-30). Yet he performs a similar stunt in his next epistle, describing the chain of being from end to end and then claiming, in an exquisitely self-humbling rhetorical trick, that "the chain holds on, and where it ends, unknown" (3:26). Pope's optimistic description of the chain of being leads directly into a scourging attack on human presumption (1.1-42). His visions of cosmological systematicity come into sharpest focus when he compares them to bursting bubbles or fancies god hurling them into ruin (1.89-90). Pope exhorts his readers to reflect on their own smallness beside a magnificent moral and cosmological system, a system that, paradoxically, is most fully represented in their own minds or in human artifacts like Pope's poem.

Increasingly comprehensive explanatory systems make increasing demands on individual persons. Unfortunately, the character of Pope's human world is such that it demands an endless, superhuman commitment to the production of knowledge. Human capacities may fit human beings to a particular conditions, much as a "microscopic eye" fits a housefly to its lowly station (*Essay on Man* 1.189ff.), but the condition of mankind, the state of subdivinity, demands the use of systematizing powers that tend to render humanity disproportionate to itself, to make "man" imagine that "man" knows more than "man" can know. The *Essay on Man*, Pope's essayistic exercise in anthropology, after all, is concerned with much more than anthropology. It explains man through cosmological studies and situates humanity in the context of superhumanity. Still, that all-important je ne sais quoi, that genius that produces and accredits explanatory artifacts, must arise from the individual human beings. Like it or not, Pope must treat even the most depraved characters—people like Euclio— as highly abbreviated characters of the universe. So in literary criticism: "Some Lucky LICENCE answers to the full / Th' Intent propos'd, *that Licence is a Rule*" (*Essay on Criticism* ll. 148-49). It is to the individual, the freak event, or the particular innovation, that Pope looks for his most esteemed commodity: not just any old rule, but a paradoxical hybrid of genius, deviation, and rule, regularity and conformity.

Pope talks a great deal about theoretical generalities, but his own poetry erupts from the sudden metamorphoses of instincts, beliefs, and *bon chance* into believable, valuable rules. Indeed, Pope makes a remarkably post-Shaftesburian claim: that no person could possibly err in a world governed by a *universal* system:

> "The ruling Passion, be it what it will,
> The ruling Passion conquers Reason still."
> Less mad the wildest whimsey we can frame,
> Than ev'n that Passion, if it has no Aim;
> ....
> Hear then the truth: " 'Tis Heav'n each Passion sends,
> And diff'rent men directs to diff'rent ends.

Extremes in Nature equal good produce,
Extremes in Man concur to gen'ral use."
[*Epistle to Bathurst*, ll. 155-64]

Pope's diffusely universal system is exemplified by no one particular person or place. It is exemplified morally, in the working assumption, in every mind, that every particular thing, including the individual person, must be participating in some system. Self-identification as a "diff'rent" person with a "diff'rent end" amounts to the tacit recognition of a system by which differences can be defined. Pope is no totalitarian or deconstructionist, yet he presents this paradoxical consent to—or consent to the production of—this unnamed, totalizing system as an inevitable action by every individual, differentiated soul.

In Pope's later poems, explanatory verse becomes an elaborate device for the production of confident moral action. Every action, every event, and every thought is joined, for Pope, to an accompanying idea, and to the expectation that that idea can be explained by and enrolled in some system. Explanation becomes a means of generating moral certainty. It produces a belief in the eventual intelligibility and value of things, and thereby justifies the doing of good actions. Unlike persuasive philosophizing, truth-seeking philosophy can be dangerous, for it can make the individual person seem small and stupid before an immense cosmos. Pope reconceives explanation in moral and aesthetic terms; he asks himself and his reader to try *not* to realize his hypothesizing art, to avoid reducing the explaining of experience to some finished explanation and to keep on "seeing" order rather than draw specific conclusions. Hence Pope's preoccupation, throughout his poetry, with the interaction and interimplication of parts and wholes—with "the joint Force and full *Result* of all" (*Essay on Criticism*, l. 246), with the power of the whole but also with the autonomy and interplay of "all" its discrete parts. Pope asks readers to imagine that they act under the direction of a comprehending system, of a realizing, but not realized, design:

Still follow Sense, of ev'ry Art the Soul,
Parts answ'ring parts shall slide into a whole,
Spontaneous beauties all around advance,
Start ev'n from Difficulty, strike from Chance.
[*Epistle to Burlington*, ll. 65-68]

By treating experience as a prompt to poetic explanation and moral action, Pope produces a poetry of distortion, a poetry in which the true image of an object is the image of its motion away from itself

and toward its role in a system. Pope enjoys using rhetorical invo-
lutions like "See *Dionysius Homer's* thoughts refine" (*Essay on Criticism*,
l. 665) because they place the transforming—or distorting—critic before the unprocessed poet. John Locke wryly comments that everyone
evidences a tincture of insanity; but Alexander Pope spends his last
years in the study of the universal deviancy of man, trying to show
that the motion toward distortion is the motion toward systematicity
and hoping to harmonize his personal outrage with that public voice
of stable morality that drones through the clamorous experience of
The Dunciad.

THE VIGOROUS ASSERTION OF INCOMPETENCE

Pope's philosophizing rhetoric revolves around his central assertion
that man is, as Swift might say, incapable of knowledge. What could
be more perplexing than the writing of essays about what "man"
knows by someone who doubts whether "man" means anything at
all?

> His Principle of action once explore,
> That instant 'tis his Principle no more.
> Like following life thro' creatures you dissect,
> You lose it in the moment you detect.
> [*Epistle to Cobham*, ll. 37-40]

This vigorous assertion of human incompetence is a strategy for differentiating the individual mind from human knowledge and for engaging this same mind with it—for asserting that human knowledge
is less a completed thing than a completing relating to things. When
Pope talks about the immensity of knowledge, he does so not to teach
any one doctrine but to set big-scale human knowledge in a relation
of superiority to individual knowers. This strategy works bivalently;
Pope's exclamations concerning the weakness of human beings and
the strength of human knowledge are a covert way of asserting that
there is at least one weak, unconstructed person who is not quite at
the center of the omnicompetent human world. By allowing human
knowledge to appropriate all of the individual's identity, Pope ends
up allowing human knowledge to appropriate the idea of the individual's difference from and inadequacy to that "knowledge."

Pope enrolls individuals in an endless quest to relate their own,
ultracoherent human productions to their less-regular private lives—
to unite themselves with the "character" of the universe, yet to include

in this most comprehensive of characters the idea of their own incompetence and difference. "There must be," Pope muses, "somewhere, such a rank as man," some point "respecting" which "human works" and even "right" and "wrong" have a different value than they do "respecting" the remainder of the universe (*Essay on Man* 1.48-53). The mature Pope finds himself in a paradoxical role, that of private, individual assertor of public, even universal, order:

> Ask you what Provocation I have had?
> The strong Antipathy of Good to Bad.
> When Truth or Virtue an Affront endures,
> Th' Affront is mine, my Friend, and should be yours.
> Mine, as a Foe profess'd to false Pretence,
> Who thinks a Coxcomb's Honour like his Sense;
> Mine, as a Friend to ev'ry worthy mind;
> And mine as Man, who feel for all mankind.
> [*Epilogue to the Satires* 2.197-204]

The moral order that Pope claims to defend—this stark, schematized system of truths, virtues, affronts, goods, and bads—is most clearly articulated in Pope's own far less schematic experience. This poem is not ours, but, for Pope, "mine." Pope sends two conflicting messages: he desperately asserts that his own outrage is implementing a collected, public judgment about the proper order of things, but he also desperately asserts that his character differs from that of the corrupt, public state, that he lives outside of this degenerating public world. Pope makes himself the public image of self-satisfied marginalization, the personal, proprietary realization of a system that describes the whole by transforming, systematizing, expanding, and finally depreciating it.

As one target of his own depreciative rhetoric, Pope is not quite so disdainful of or different from the inhabitants of his oft-abused Grub Street world as he likes to pretend. He uses examples of deviant, inadequate behavior to make himself and his audience *assert* that deviation, destabilization, and differentiation are essential parts of the human "scene," a scene that deviant persons manufacture, enact, and energize—and from which they deviate. *The Dunciad* and the *Imitations of Horace* abound with unstable characters, none of whom can "act consistent with himself an hour" (*Imitations of Horace*, Epistle 1.1.137). Curiously, these characters draw less attention to their corruption of virtue than to their role as occasions for Pope's asserting of his opinions. In the *Epilogue to the Satires*, Pope can only ask whether vices will continue—"Shall *Ward* draw Contracts with a Statesman's skill? / Or *Japhet* pocket, like his Grace, a Will?" (1.119-20)—in the expectation that a committed audience will devise a program for revising what Swift calls "appearances." Bad examples are occasions for voluntarily seeing, in advance, the happy conclusion to the present, tragicomic story of British civilization. When Pope shows Cibber building a pyre out of ancient tomes (*Dunciad* 1.155-62), there can be no misreading Pope's delight in his own superiority to the impotent knowledge that these tomes contain. Nor can one mistake the glee beneath the irony in Pope's and Dulness's charge to "MAKE ONE MIGHTY DUNCIAD OF THE LAND" (4.604). Burning through his library, Cibber eradicates any visible evidence that enthusiastic moralizing programs—like Pope's own—have seldom succeeded in improving behavior. Cibber's arson makes for a happy ending, no matter how bad the story. His fire blazes through the dark ending of this poem. Igniting the heap of scholarship, *The Dunciad* turns modern "learning" into a quasi-classical pyre, a pyre in which an energetic, transforming fire becomes more visible, more available to sense (and common sense), than the hidden learning it consumes. Pope's indictment of modern writing amounts to a self-indictment, but Pope's burning self-contempt also saves Pope qua author, for it lets him take an omniscient, public point of view on the public consumption of his own work.

Pope's poetry involves far more than the discovery that ideals seldom fit with experience, for Pope attacks ideals and idealizing with the same fervor with which he attacks blunders and blundering. Truncated by a satirical adversary who orders "more *Essays on Man*" as though they were junk food, the long, idealizing paean to virtue that culminates the *Epilogue to the Satires*, for example, is reduced to a joke. Pope's idealizing rhetoric capitalizes on its alleged applicability to experience; his discourse both denies access to and depends on the postulation of some standard of judgment. The net product of these two countervailing motions is a poetry of hope, a poetry that suggests (and keeps on suggesting) its "truth" but denies that it can realize some final—and, hence, falsifiable and disappointing—system of the world: "Hope leads from goal to goal" (*Essay on Man* 4.341); Dulness shows

> How random thoughts now meaning chance to find,
> Now leave all memory of sense behind:
> How Prologues into Prefaces decay,

> And these to Notes are fritter'd quite away:
> How Index-learning turns no student pale,
> Yet holds the eel of science by the tail.
>   [*Dunciad* 1.275-80]

Pope speaks of learning as though it were an animate thing, a compromised, limited organism with only so much energy, so much resistance to ailments, and so great a life span. To compensate for learning's deficiencies, Pope works up an expansive, systematizing discourse that fights against its own entropic tendencies.

Yet Pope fears that an excessively enlarging rhetoric is likely to overwhelm the individual rhetorician. He finds himself in a trap, willing the production but debarring the realization of madly proliferating systems, systems that could organize—and hence fortify—an evil world. Were Pope's cohering systems really to cohere, they would only index Pope's inadequacy to his job as coherer:

> How little, mark! that portion of the ball,
> Where, faint at best, the beams of Science fall:
> Soon as they dawn, from Hyperborean skies
> Embody'd dark, what clouds of Vandals rise!
>   [*Dunciad* 3.83-86]

Pope, in the last analysis, has more in common with Dulness than anyone would like to admit. Like this dimmest of goddesses—this strange combination of satiric butt, satiric spokesperson, and Pope himself—Pope's career culminates in a comprehensive review of all the crazed systems of human thought. Seeing "round the Poles" (*Dunciad* 3.69), Pope's global vision incorporates the destabilizing possibility, outlined in the *Epistle to Cobham*, of alternative and irregular explanations for everything. Some thing, event, or behavior might be explained by a Leibnizian harmony in things; by drunkenness; by, as in Rochester, nothing at all; by the sheer desire to explain; or by all of these. Like Dulness, Pope stands at a distance from these disorganized, often competing attempts to organize human knowledge. But, again like Dulness, he is also implicated in their production. Confronted with wildly expanding, potentially crushing systems of knowledge, Pope can only engage himself in the paradoxical assertion of his disengagement from them.[24]

Pope defines, refines, and redefines the human world until, like his chaotic "clouds of Vandals," it comes to be an embodied mock heroic. His art of explanation becomes an art of depreciation and self-depreciation. His concern for the synthesis of ideas draws more attention than ideas themselves, including the idea of Pope himself. John Locke, I argued, presents "experience" as complex, modal, and system-building. He depicts "ideas" both as "things to be known" and as the first steps in a tacit progress toward their systematization and explanation. For Alexander Pope, this inevitable progress from epistemology to semiotics—toward a kind of unstoppable self-explanation in which experience screams out judgments about itself—takes on a Frankensteinian character.[25] Pope so greatly expands Locke's system of moral relations that that system nearly collapses under its own weight. He faces, nay, welcomes a new, psychologized dualism: the confrontation of the creating self with the created system. He recognizes that, in his own work, the affective, belief-inducing power of explanatory structures more often counteracts than tells the truth about the degraded world and the unimpressive people who inhabit it—that explanation wrestles with, more than discloses, the "scene of Man." As a result, Pope becomes the consummate poet of certainty: a poet who asks his overworked faith in a relentlessly expanding system to close the gap between author and authorial production that that very system opens up.

CHAPTER SEVEN

SMITH

Systematic Reclamation of the Self

The story of Alexander Pope's career is the story of Pope's confrontation with his own explanatory powers. From his early pastorals to his late satires, Pope portrays a world in which experience seems to invite explanation, a world where immediate perceptions and reflective theories appear *ensemble*. Whether describing Windsor's visionary forests or the *Dunciad*'s urban wasteland, Pope regards "neutral" experience as an impossibility. By refusing to distinguish judgment from description, Pope creates a relentlessly explanatory universe—a relational world in which everything *is* a theory, whether about itself or about its place in the cosmos. Pope's poetry engages the reader, the writer, and the world in the thrilling, wildly expanding process of poetical explanation. So lucid a poetry, unfortunately, comes at a high price. Pope's totalizing, manifestly human discourse of explanations has the apparently unanticipated consequence of diminishing, indicting, and intimidating the individual person—especially the individual writer.

Fears over the alienation of the explaining writer from the explanatory text suffuse many midcentury works, not just Pope's. One need only look to the emotionally turbocharged epics of Robert Blair and Edward Young or to the sentimentalizing tracts of Samuel Johnson and Oliver Goldsmith. This issue, however, stands at the center of Adam Smith's attention. As an economic theorist, a scholar of "sentiments," and a historian of science, Adam Smith is a professional explainer. Appropriately, the extenuating relation between philosophizing writers and philosophical systems becomes his featured topic. As its title suggests, Smith's first systematic work, *The Theory of Moral*

Sentiments, calls for a philosophical explanation of the relation between private sentiments and public morality. By promising a synthesis of epistemology, ethics, and aesthetics, Smith positions himself as the heir to a Lockean tradition in which relations are the building blocks of knowledge. By selecting the relating of disciplines as the topic of his work, he implies that epistemology itself is a relating process. More provocatively, he suggests that epistemology might become a tool for relating individual explainers to explanatory discourse.

In this chapter, I shall suggest that Smith's philosophizing begins in an urge, like Pope's, to enlarge, play with, and claim control over explanatory devices. Pope carries out his reformative program through the manipulative reiteration of a vast number of theories and pieces of advice, but Smith goes further still. By reformulating the science of explanation, he examines not only many but all theories. Smith, as Locke or Kant might say, wants to evaluate and appropriate the grounds of any possible explanation, if not by a formal critique, then by a process of accumulation. He wants to take possession of the foundations of philosophy and to turn uncertain explanations into the reassuring act of explaining. He would consolidate his authority over the human world and would make sense out of all the paradoxes implicit in it. Doing all that he can to enlarge the jurisdiction of the human world, Smith suggests—long before Pierre Duhem, Thomas Kuhn, and Hans Georg Gadamer—that everything that can be known, including passions, forces, and instincts, must be known in the context of some controllable, revisable theory. In the writings of an early philosophizer like Rochester, I have argued, rigid theories and conventions counterpoint dark, instinctive impulses. Rochester is left to speculate avidly about his own somewhat paradoxical desire to explain things. In Smith's writings, desire and power enjoy a much more comfortable relationship with systematicity. At ease with the idea of a theory of passion, Smith raises to a high but also resolving pitch that zeal for stabilizing explanation that characterizes the discourse of writers from Rochester to Pope.

Smith, I shall therefore argue, values explanatory discourse for its ability to reclaim, make knowable, and empower that most irregular of things, the self. By relating orderly knowledge to the evocatively irregular "person," Smith tries to sketch out a redemptive, public character of otherwise idiosyncratic mental states. He gives good reason why "we," collectedly, ought to believe in and act on what individual persons think. Writing a literature of certainty, he relates a certain, believing mental state to artificial, conventional explanations of the world. These explanations, moreover, take a personal form in Smith's strange, superpersonal person, the "impartial spectator." In the course of my argument I shall debunk the stock notion that Smith is a Romantic or pre-Romantic. Smith's writings, rather, invite a reassessment of Romanticism, for they warn critics to pay as much attention to Blake's public man, to Keats's classicism, and to Coleridge's statesman as they pay, say, to Wordsworth's private recollections.

My argument will have four parts. In the first, I shall discuss Smith's program to relate science and knowledge to those destabilizing but also constructive forces that make up human history. I shall talk about Smith's revolutionary attempt to empower theory, to treat explanatory discourse as a force influencing the development of "the world." My second section will counterpoint my first. This section will discuss Smith's empowering of theory with respect to the mind of the individual person. Here I shall discuss Smith's use of theory to excite psychological states like wonder. My third section will treat Smith's attempt to reconcile this psychologically empowered theory with its historicized, contextualized counterpart. Smith's "impartial spectator," I shall suggest, serves two purposes: first, he brings about the identification—in the full, Lockean sense of that word—of individual persons with large-scale, collected systems of judgment; second, he publicizes, in his character as a spectator, the subjective component in collected experience. I shall sum up with a discussion of Smith's use of "self-command" to explain, expose, and empower the explaining author. "Self-command," certain moral action, affords an opportunity to construct and to reconcile both social and individual selves, to let the explaining author take charge of the explanatory spectator.

A word needs to be said about the relation of Smith to British writers and about my selection of works from Smith's canon. Granted, Smith belongs to the so-called Scottish school. Critics like John Dwyer and Richard Sher, however, have recently argued that writers in this movement were deeply involved in the British intellectual scene.[1] Smith's place in the "empiricist" tradition of Locke, Berkeley, and Hume has also been well documented, as has his relevance to British writers with philosophical interests.[2] Smith himself admitted his debt to Berkeley's highly literary philosophy. D.D. Raphael has recently described the extraordinary success of *The Theory of Moral Sentiments* in England and has pointed to the role of Hume as an intercessor between Glasgow and London.[3] More recently still, John Mullan has detailed the influence of Smith's *Theory of Moral Sentiments* on British sentimental writing.[4] I shall limit myself to those two works of Smith's in which the issue of explanation per se is most prominent: his early essay on the history of astronomy and his *Theory of Moral Sentiments*. Smith is a man of diverse tastes and skills, and it could plausibly be argued that his *Wealth of Nations* constitutes the ultimate analysis of what I have called the "human world." Smith's economic theory, however, is too large a topic for so small a space. In bypassing Smith's other works, I once again call on the authority of his foremost interpreter, D.D. Raphael, who cites Smith's *History of Astronomy* as the only work comparable, in scope and quality, to Smith's two great treatises on sentiment and political economy.[5]

KNOWLEDGE AS HISTORY: ENGAGING ASTRONOMY

Smith's history of astronomy is precisely that: a *history*. It is not an eschatology. Documenting the rise and fall of several explanatory systems, it details a succession of contexts in which those systems have flourished. It avoids the notion that science makes a direct "progress" from inferior to superior theories. Smith, for example, accepts Aristotle's old-fashioned notion that all phenomena may be assimilated into increasingly general taxons—into those "ideas which in the schools are called Genera and Species, and those abstract and general names, which in all languages are made use of to express them."[6] "Mobile" creatures move into the family "animal"; animals and inanimate objects enter the class "substances." These bursts of conservatism, surprisingly, reinforce Smith's relativistic outlook. His respect for Aristotelian taxonomy leads him to deprive science of its privileged position. Science must submit to Smith's classifying process; its history is just another set of phenomena waiting to be organized. The discipline of astronomy, for example, is always observed in some historical context. A timeless, placeless astronomy has yet to be invented. When applied to science, Aristotelian taxonomy becomes far more than a dry, technical matter. Different species of scientific activity can actually be *seen* in history. Like science in general, taxonomic systems can influence the shaping of the world (and of human knowledge). So wholly fused are science and society that to observe one is to observe the other. Smith, therefore, classifies scientific revolutions by their historical contexts rather than their theoretical innovations. He argues that all explanatory devices, whether taxonomic terms like "species" or theoretical entities like "natural coherences," register the influence of cultural forces. To use Cowley's terminology,

Smithian science produces human "Creatures" that relate to (as well as signify) the real essences of things.

For Smith, the historical relativity of science is not bad news. The contextualizing of astronomy exemplifies his project to redefine "science" as a constructive process rather than as a mere accumulation of objective knowledge. Smithian science aims to construct coherent relations between people, society, and nature. Knowledge may be its goal, but the production of a "knowing" society is its essence.[7] Smith, accordingly, reinterprets the role of empirical experience in science. From his hero, George Berkeley, Smith borrows the idea that experience "suggests" interpretations. Like Berkeleian nature, Smithian nature is plentiful; it suggests many theories, but different "suggestions" are taken at different moments in history. Science, in other words, is more than the determinate product of social forces or natural evidence. In taking a suggestion from nature, scientists voluntarily accelerate the production of this or that explanation out of the many alternatives. Once selected by a scientist, a suggested theory acquires a life of its own. It may correct, interfere with, or even determine either natural experience or those scientists who selected it. Consider Ptolemy's "Equalizing Circle": "Here, at last, they enjoyed that tranquility and repose which they had pursued through all the mazes of this intricate hypothesis; and here they beheld this, the most beautiful and magnificent part of the great theatre of nature, so disposed and constructed, that they could attend, with ease and delight, to all the revolutions and changes that occurred in it" (*History of Astronomy*, p. 62). The "Equalizing Circle" differs from all the other epicycles, cycles, and concentrics in the Ptolemaic system. These latter explanatory devices have been suggested by one phenomenon or another. The equalizing circle, however, derives from no particular phenomenon. A suggestion made by a series of suggestions, it culminates an epistemological history in which particular suggestions have made, with help from Ptolemy and his colleagues, still other, more extravagant suggestions.

Smith, moreover, says that the Ptolemaics "beheld" their circle. His choice of words—his speaking as he would speak of empirical experience—is no mistake. History involves a kind of artificial perception—what one might call "spectation." Ptolemy and his associates always assert that their theories, no matter how extravagant, emerge from some experience and announce themselves in a way that appeals to the senses. The history of the equalizing circle, the sequence of perceived suggestions, can, in some specialized, Popean sense, be seen. Smith, one must remember, holds equally startling views about moral "things," which can be seen through a special "moral sense." He improves on Locke's mixed modes, for his complex moral and philosophical concepts succeed in making themselves visible. Smith, in effect, shows us modal ideas, ideas like, say, the idea of coherence. The equalizing circle draws together in one coherent image all the possible perceptions, from all possible points of view, of the solar system. It presents what *could* be sensually (and coherently) represented. So great an explanatory force does this magic circle carry that Smith values it more than data gathered through direct observation.[8]

Smith's discussion of the equalizing circle epitomizes his early assertion of the voluntary, empowering character of explanation. Smith gives to the circle the power to reshape our perceptions of those phenomena that fail to suggest an adequately coherent explanation. The equalizing circle is a figure of desire, a visible demand that experience live up to its explicated, theoretical image. One might even go so far as to compare Smith's Ptolemy to Alexander Pope. Both Ptolemy and Pope depreciate experience at the same time that they ask experience to suggest a relentlessly coherent (and purportedly commonsensical) standard of judgment. Both Pope and Ptolemy see a "common" sense that no other mortal has the capacity to see.

Smithian science is a rhetorical strategy, a way of asserting that irregular experience presents itself as a demand for a regular, hence distorting, "knowledge." Later in his career, Smith cautions that "though our brother is upon the rack," "it is the impressions of our senses only, not those of his, which our imaginations copy."[9] Sense impressions do not so much represent or verify as invoke an explanation. The sight of a man on a rack does not disclose his pain; it points up our interpretation of and response to it. To put it in Lockean jargon, the sight of torture is always accompanied by two other ideas, that of one's own moral pain and that of one's plan for correcting an ugly situation. Perception elicits what might be called "formalized feeling"; it brings out feelings that are not the original feelings, but that move the viewer into organized, remedial action: "We sometimes feel for another, a passion of which he himself seems to be altogether incapable; because, when we put ourselves in his case, that passion arises in our breast from the imagination, though it does not in his from the reality" (*Theory of Moral Sentiments*, p. 12). Such ultraempathic perception leads the percipient to interfere with and thus to change the "objects" perceived. Happy sights demand as much interference as unhappy ones. A sense of approval leads the percipient to promote the doing of more good deeds. There is more to Smith's view than the simple discovery that people encourage goodness and hate badness. Smith never allows the possibility of a neutral perception. *Every* experience leads to a distorting, if systematic, course of action; vision *is* revision.

Smith thus reconciles the most intense skepticism with the most engaging optimism. He allows that we are insurmountably ignorant concerning, for example, the feelings of another person. By the same token, this chronic ignorance confers a provisional certainty on the individual moral judgment.[10] Percipients cannot avoid seeing the world in some distorted, morally provocative way. They always, reflexively, act in a way consistent with their "imaginary" reconstructions of external experience. One can see a similarly buoyant faith in Smith's treatment of his predecessors. Locke's "natural coherence of ideas," for example, turns into the "natural career of the imagination": "the ideas excited by so coherent a chain of things seems, as it were, to float through the mind of their own accord" (*History of Astronomy*, p. 40). Lockean perception becomes a highly charged moral process, a process that naturally posits a pliable, provocative relation between percipients and the world. For similar reasons, Smith refuses to dismiss our old friend the equalizing circle simply because it misrepresents experience. "Experience" *is* a demand for the framing of novel theories. The "verification" of human knowledge is a moot issue, for all experience appears as a demand for a distorting, albeit moralizing, reconstruction. "Constructive misrepresentation" describes the true character of human knowledge.

The story is the same in Smith's ethics as in his astronomy. The passions register natural needs, but they also drive an intensifying, distorting search for finer gratifications, for finer arts *of* gratification, and, finally, for wholly new, superior desires:

To a man who from his birth was a stranger to society, the objects of his passions, the external bodies which either pleased or hurt him, would occupy his whole attention. The passions themselves, the desires or aversions, the joys or sorrows, which those objects excited, though of all things the most immediately present to him, could scarce ever be the objects of his thoughts. . . . Bring him into society, and all his own passions will immediately become the causes of new passions. He will observe that mankind approve of some of them, and are disgusted by others. He will be elevated in the one case, and cast down in the other; his desires and aversions, his joys and sorrows, will now often become the causes of new desires and new aversions, new joys and new sorrows; they will now, therefore, interest him deeply, and often call upon his most attentive consideration. [*Theory of Moral Sentiments*, p. 110-111]

Smith never leaves nature in the driver's seat. His civilizing passions seem to distort themselves, to produce a system of social checks on instinctive, selfish, and passionate behavior. The passions are most fully gratified—are most fully themselves—when they distort themselves into a system for their own management and fulfillment. In his *Lectures on Rhetoric*, Smith sums up his case by observing that audiences desire to experience conventions rather than passions— that, for example, they react more strongly to the minor pains of a theatrical king than to the real woes of a real peasant.[11] Smith's person does not really live out his passions, no more than he really feels the pain of the "brother" on the rack. Feeling his way into an artificial model of *how* the passions *ought* to operate *on* experience, he feels the conversion of wayward passions into sociable impulses.

PSYCHOLOGICAL ASTRONOMY: WONDER

It may be a long trip from Smith's sentimentalizing to twentieth-century popular psychology, yet it is fair to say that Smith concerns himself with the individual's "feelings" about explanatory systems. Smith's *History of Astronomy*, I have just argued, connects the history of science with a series of historical contexts. Smith's historicism, however, is not a dead-end street in the ghost town of ideology. By contextualizing science, Smith aims not to subsume science into some monolithic theory of history, but to affiliate it with those particular persons who implement those social mores and ethical precepts that coincide with scientific reasonings. Smith's "history" of science brings about the psychological enabling rather than relativizing of knowledge.[12] Fusing knowledge with value means fusing knowledge with the function of value; for Smith, the function of value is to pique personal moral desires and to elicit personal feelings about systems of knowledge. Were Smith a cocktail lounge singer, then "Feelings," that anthem of conventionalized spontaneous sentiment, would be his opening number. Like the science of musicology, philosophy aims to produce an appreciative sensibility—a feeling for a system of harmonies: "By long attention to the connections which have ever been presented to his [the philosopher's] observation, by having often compared them with one another, he has, like the musician, acquired, if one may say so, a nicer ear, and a more delicate feeling with regard to things of this nature. And as to the one, that music seems dissonance which falls short of the most perfect harmony; so to the other, those events seem altogether separated and disjointed, which fall short of the strictest and most perfect connection" (*History of Astronomy*, 44-45). The hard sciences also produce intense personal desires for gratifying explanations. Science aims to produce not knowledge but wonder and anxiety. As A.S. Skinner has suggested, Smithian science is a "trade," a brokering of the psychological commodities of curiosity and uncertainty.[13]

The conjunctions among natural phenomena prove less important for Smithian science than do the disjunctions, the gaps in explanatory systems. Disjunctions motivate research and keep science exciting. Science is a pleasant process of curing intellectual pain. Disjunctions may have caused this pain, but they also initiate an exciting motion toward imaginative pleasure, a motion that completely counteracts the misery in which it began. This emotional response to disjunctions Smith calls "wonder." Wonder, a state of awed confusion, a nervous but stimulating uncertainty about an unexplained phenomenon, may even be pursued "for its own sake" (p. 50). Wonder drives a cycle of worry and joy—of disjunctions, wonder, insight, relief, and renewed confusion—an orderly cycle that, because it converts "pains" into precursors of future intellectual pleasures, can be described as not only therapeutic but also systematic.

Smith's "wonderful" science specializes in the discovery of conjunctions between the system of nature and the system of psychology: "A system is an imaginary machine invented to connect together in the fancy those different movements which are already in reality performed" (p. 66). In Smith's psychology of science, the exciting potential for order may prove more attractive than order itself. The natural disorderliness of the natural world is especially good at evoking wonder. Alexander Pope liked to see order in experience, but Smith likes to see both order and disorder; he likes to see the flawed world as a call for the exciting production of an improving science. The most competent scientists are those who make the most of their incompetence, those who keep relating their known but incomplete science to bigger, currently unknown wonders.

Smith asks his beleaguered scientists to spend a lot of time in the cultivation of deficiencies, to search far and wide for wonder-inducing gaps in explanatory systems. Smith asks philosophers to review carefully such familiar processes as the transformation of bread into human bodies, for a careful examination of such complex but familiar processes could open up tremendous, explanation-inducing gaps in the understanding (*History of Astronomy*, p. 44). A "stop" in the "career of the imagination," a major gap in a system, turns out to be the "whole essence" of wonder (p. 41). Science runs on the breakdown of science; the interruption of science encourages the doing of more science. Will turns out to be the most important mental faculty in Smithian science, for investigators must voluntarily seek out conjunctions and disjunctions: "The supposition of a chain of intermediate, though invisible, events, which succeed each other in a train similar to that in which the imagination has been accustomed to move, and which link together those two disjointed appearances, is the only means by which the imagination can fill up this interval, is the only bridge which, if one may say so, can smooth its passage from the one object to the other" (pp. 40-41). This voluntary "supposition" of "links" between phenomena serves both scientific and psychological purposes. It explains nature by smoothing the "passages" of the mind. When experience fails to suggest a link between two phenomena, scientists should intervene and devise one, preferably by comparing unfamiliar phenomena to familiar theories. Smithian science extends analogies while it domesticates unfamiliar or anomalous data. The more mysterious and unfamiliar a phenomenon, the more science tries to square it with a familiar paradigm. The more dramatic this analogy between the strange event and its familiar explication, the greater the need for a willful scientist.

Some disjunctions are more suggestive than others. The gap between self and society appeals to Smith because one of its boundaries is the self. The self/society dichotomy is doubly engaging: wonder makes the imagination anxious to intervene between its two terms, while one of these terms, the self, is engaged in its political context. Smith's citizens begin their "careers" as self-interested, deviant parties, but theirs is a deviation with a difference. Smithian deviation opens a wonder-producing gap between self and society, a gap that Smith's citizens want to cross. The self, Smith tells us, likes to cross gaps; in this case, it seeks the approbation of other selves. A comparison between Smith and the Marquis of Halifax can make the case clear. For Halifax, the inertia of society buffers the influence of deviant parties. Radical ideas must be expressed in a common, normalizing language. Smith treats this same process in internal, psychological terms. Whenever individuals "wonder" at their deviation from the norm, they want to devise a "science" for "connecting" the self with the state.

Smith's treatise on the history of astronomy could, accordingly, be treated as a study of the relation of individual scientists to the collected tradition of science (and to society). Consider Newton's career:

His principles, it must be acknowledged, have a degree of firmness and solidity that we should in vain look for in any other system. . . . Can we wonder then, that it [Newton's system] should have gained the general and complete approbation of mankind, and that it should now be considered, not as an attempt to connect in the imagination the phaenomena of the Heavens, but as the greatest discovery that ever was made by man, the discovery of an immense chain of the most important and sublime truths, all closely connected together, by one capital fact [gravitation], of the reality of which we have daily experience. [*History of Astronomy*, p. 108]

The darling of enlightened society and the final link in an "immense chain" of scientific reasonings, Newton was destined to pass from his role as a deviant innovator to his role as the grand master of human knowledge. By distancing Newton's "sublime truths" from raw "phaenomena," Smith portrays Newton as someone who both opens and overleaps vast gaps. Newton's own identity seems to become a subsystem of Newton's philosophy. Taking on an identity of its own, his system becomes a discovery that "was made by man"; so powerful a system needn't wait to be discovered, but may declare that it had a discoverer, then proceed to suggest, to the imagination, what that mighty discoverer might have been like. Newton's is a system that can imagine its discoverer's psychology. Smith's paean to Newton ends in an accolade to "daily experience," for daily experience (and the perception of it) has been appropriated by Newton's system. Through the experience of gravitation, a collected "we" can feel, daily and directly, the certainty of Newton's laws.

Newton is only one of a thousand scientists from the past. Sir Isaac stands out because lesser researchers have failed to complete a "progress," like his, from their roles as individuals to new roles as personifications of theories and worlds. The requirements for scientific success are formidable: theories can make no headway, Smith cautions, unless they are translated into a language fitted to their historical contexts. Such an accommodation of theories, alas, makes them less satisfying to "wonder" (pp. 46, 51). Scientists fail when their personally understood, totalizing theories come into conflict with the compromising theories held by society at large. Smith, fortunately, is a never-say-die sort of fellow. He can see a use even in a failure. A conflict between the individual researcher and his or her social context opens a gap between the private science of the individual experimenter and the "common sense" science established in a given culture. The resulting disjunction elicits a useful project like Smith's own *History of Astronomy*. It invokes a science of science—a natural and psychic history of disputes between scientist and science.

Smith's eminently human science is a process in which the assertions of a few innovators are gradually translated into the established science of a whole culture. In Smithian science, the eccentric becomes the norm, and while it is the norm, while it is established science, it may wholly transform "nature": "For, though it is the end of Philosophy, to allay that wonder, which either the unusual or seemingly disjointed appearance of nature excites, yet she never triumphs so much, as when, in order to connect a few, in themselves, perhaps, inconsiderable objects, she has, if I may say so, created another constitution of things, more natural indeed, and such as the imagination can more easily attend to, but more new, more contrary to common opinion and expectation, than any of those appearances themselves" (pp. 75-76). A "natural," "easy," and commonsensical understanding of the world represents so total a transformation of experience that it makes both isolated innovator and establishment researcher seem like grubby naturalists. Smithian science builds a "nature" that reckons with the collected psychology of science, a science that considers the way in which people "attend" to nature and in which all points of view become part of the transforming whole. Politicizing, Smith's science eventually puts things and views together; as Halifax would also say, it "constitutes" things.

This constitutive process can be time-consuming. New theories, like Copernican astronomy, "naturally" offend the popular imagination, at least initially. A startled reaction to science is part of the system of science. Established science was once new; it, too, was once evocative and offensive. "Wonder" at irregularities is, after all, at the foundation of any system. Established science remains "connected" to those original acts that led to its synthesis. It continues to act, working night and day to filter out crank innovations while admitting sound discoveries. When Newton produced "another constitution of things," for example, the popular imagination accepted it, even while it rejected other proposals. Smith's history has proved that the public often endorses a science that grossly distorts raw experience. His public likes wonder and wants compelling theories. Smith's collected human world will always support those explanatory systems that recognize the whole process of research, that account for the convergence of psychology and natural history into a comprehensive system of knowledge.

The Theory of Moral Sentiments could be described as an attempt to have one's cake and eat it too. The sentimentalizing Smith accepts Locke's notion that the self is a complete system of ideas. Yet Smith's theory, his explication of the self, must, like all theories, be motivated by wonder, and wonder results from disjunctions—from incoherences in systems. *The Theory of Moral Sentiments* attempts to reconcile the self in its character as a system with the self in its character as an impassioned producer, observer, and admirer of its own system. Microcosmically, Smith's self tries to systematize the gap between the mind's impulsivity and the mind's systematicity; macrocosmically, the self tries to account for the apparent disjunction between the small system of the mind and the enormous system of human knowledge.

Throughout Smith's *Theory*, the "system" of individual identity has a way of interacting with, substituting for, and struggling against the larger system of human knowledge. Smith postulates a wonder-inducing gap between the two selves—between the colloquial, individual self, and the enlarged self, the "impartial spectator." An empiricist prototype of Michael Riffaterre's superreader, this impartial spectator can index the whole system of human knowledge. "He" can make a judgment about anything. Epistemology is at the soul of both the impartial and the individual selves; self and spectator alike are systems of ideas.

Despite his epistocentrism, Smith thinks of the relation between the two selves in ethical and emotive terms. He fears, for example, that too close a comparison between the deeds of the weak individual and the moral ideals of a faultless judge may lead to "a certain melancholy dejection" (*Theory of Moral Sentiments*, p. 139). Smith's self, admittedly, carries a heavy load: "Though our effectual good offices can very seldom be extended to any wider society than that of our own country; our good will is circumscribed by no boundary, but may embrace the immensity of the universe. We cannot form the idea of any innocent and sensible being, whose happiness we should not desire, or to whose misery, when distinctly brought home to the imagination, we should not have some degree of aversion" (p. 235). It is no wonder that one needs a second self to bear such a burden. The feelings of individuals interact with all the universe. When someone forms an idea of a fellow creature, he or she also forms an idea of that creature's feelings and devises a plan for increasing its happiness. The simplest feelings have a way of turning into complex schemes and concepts. Smith *understands* feeling; from an idea of others' experiences, he forms an idea of what his own feelings would be, then explains how anyone beset with such a feeling ought to act. A mind full of these empathic but intellectualized feelings is a mind that has related itself, in a very direct and feeling way, to most of the system of the whole. Smith's self, in other words, is always systematizing itself out of its own individuality. It expresses its citizenship in the human world by systematically surpassing its identity as an individual citizen.

The impartial spectator helps to make sense out of this systematic sentimentalism. This "inmate of the breast" presents "himself" as an advocate for the collected judgments of all society about every thing, person, or problem. He can "voice" an objective (or at least unanimous) judgment for every possible problem, and he can do so in the context of the individual mind. An embodiment—or perhaps disembodiment—of common sense, he allows the individual self to hear, feel, and experience omniscience in a strikingly immediate way. This social spectator contains the smaller system of personal identity. The "true" man, he defines us.[14] Neither embodying nor allegorizing particular opinions, this spectator implements and empowers what might be called the whole attitude of a culture. He knows, for example, how most people in a culture will organize their ideas, and he knows how most people will evaluate an action. A living mixed mode, he is omnicompetent in the sciences of judgment and organization.

The relation between the spectator and the self is not a simple or stable one. The spectator is not so much *in* as *in the act of addressing* the individual mind. "Self-command," about which I shall speak more fully in the next section, is one of several devices for responding to this address—for addressing the spectator:

In proportion to the degree of the self-command which is necessary in order to conquer our natural sensibility, the pleasure and pride of the conquest are so much the greater . . . it must be acknowledged, at least, that this complete enjoyment of his own self-applause, though it may not altogether extinguish, must certainly very much alleviate his [the wise man's] sense of his own sufferings.

In such paroxysms of distress, if I may be allowed to call them so, the wisest and firmest man, in order to preserve his equanimity, is obliged, I imagine, to make a considerable, and even a painful exertion. . . . When he follows that view which honour and dignity point out to him, Nature does not, indeed, leave him without a recompense. He enjoys his own complete self-approbation, and the applause of every candid impartial spectator. [*Theory of Moral Sentiments*, pp. 147-48]

Self-command is a way of addressing oneself, of imagining how a judging spectator might speak about one's actions. No one person can ever *be* the collected "self," but anyone can act and speak like this "wisest and firmest man." A perfect imitation, a complete identifying of the self and the spectator, would, in any case, terminate the exciting process of imitation. By focusing on the act of self-approving, by touting "exertion" rather than virtue, Smith promotes a "complete self-approbation" over a complete moral knowledge. A self-sustaining process, self-approbation is most complete when it goes on indefinitely, when ongoing "self-applause" never terminates in genuine hand clapping.[15] Continuous sympathizing, likewise, is preferable to completed sympathy. The impartial spectator advises us to "struggle to keep down our sympathy with the sorrow of others" (p. 44). An excess of sympathy for any one sufferer might stop Smith's expansive sympathizing by making it into a painful process.

   The omnicompetent spectator is a man of the future and of possibilities. Sympathizing "in advance" with any possible situation, he feels his way into unrealized actions and contexts. The spectator lacks a constitutive power, but he can define the limits of moral judgment by declaring which events will merit his attention: "The propriety of every passion excited by objects peculiarly related to ourselves, the pitch which the spectator can go along with, must lie, it is evident, in a certain mediocrity. If the passion is too high, or if it is too low, he cannot enter into it." (*Theory of Moral Sentiments*, p. 27). As the norm of all judgments, the spectator can only "enter into" well-tempered, moderate actions. It is not that the spectator cannot understand intemperate actions, but that Smith wants to temper the spectator himself, to dedicate this giant being to mediocre human experience. The spectator, accordingly, instructs individual persons to look at the moderate character rather than at the particular details of a situation. He speaks to the self in a language at once particular and general, explaining when and how to respond, in general, to any particular situation. The spectator observes moderately processed, judgeable contexts; he teaches individuals to see "things" as evaluated situations. Judgment relies on principles both immediate and reflective, principles both intuited in experience and learned from the spectator: "It is thus that the general rules of morality are formed. They are ultimately founded upon the existence of what, in particular instances, our natural sense of merit and propriety, approve, or disapprove of" (p. 159). Smith's moral sense allows for the immediate experience—the engagement—of the science and the whole history of moral experience. This sense always acts immediately, but it has been refined and fine-tuned through centuries of "natural" use. The development of the spectator culminates this history, yet the spectator himself always acts immediately.

One critic has claimed that Smith "simply didn't know what he was doing,"[16] but many of the apparent contradictions in his thinking can be explained in light of this sense of the immediacy of history. For Smith, judgments take place either immediately, through sympathy, or quickly, through a conversation with the spectator. The art of judgment is learned "immediately" from a mediate, historical construct, the spectator. Judgment may be immediate, but a system of judgment works itself out over time, through a series of immediate acts. Smith, therefore, favors complex, comparative standards of judgment, standards like, say, the tests of time and experience (*Theory of Moral Sentiments*, pp. 26, 123). It is, after all, the spectator, not the individual, who actually makes judgments and who is, consequently, immediately engaged in history. The most personal of experiences has no meaning at all unless it is also preexperienced by the spectator. When a "violator's" "passion is gratified, and he begins coolly to reflect on his past conduct, he can enter into none of the motives which influenced it" (p. 84). Even the most impassioned action would disappear from consciousness unless a spectator were to connect the past motive, the future consequence, and the omniscient point of view with the present act. In the arts, likewise, the individual self does not so much experience a work as reenact, in an immediate way, the spectator's critical response to it. Someone or something must connect the individual person to that complex system of conventions and criteria by which a work can be judged. Smith, as a critic, is a closet conservative; he identifies himself with an established, historically based ground of judgment. Yet he also looks for a wonder-producing disjunction in this identification of self and spectator. Smithian critics always evidence some degree of originality; they are always slightly deviant. Eccentrics who support the regime, they are always identifying, but never identified with, the spectator.

With a name like "spectator," Smith's superman has got to stand at a good distance from the good, the true, the beautiful, and, indeed, from everything. The spectator may provide a foundation for judgment, but he also looks down on that foundation from a privileged loge. The spectator, in other words, embodies the monolithic autonomy of human knowledge. Individual persons may identify themselves with this portable god, but they must also magnify him to so high a degree that they could never live up to his example. Ordinary people most resemble the spectator when they conceive of themselves in the most impersonal way, when, like Pope, they imagine that their judging "inmate" is vastly superior to themselves. The most personal judgments are made through the eyes of "other people": "We can never survey our own sentiments and motives, we can never form any judgment concerning them, unless we remove ourselves, as it were, from our natural station, and endeavour to view them as at a certain distance from us. But we can do this in no other way than by endeavouring to view them with the eyes of other people, or as other people are likely to view them. Whatever judgment we can form concerning them, accordingly, must always bear some secret reference, either to what are, or to what, upon a certain condition, would be, or to what, we imagine, ought to be the judgment of others." (*Theory of Moral Sentiments*, p. 110). Proper judgment takes place in a human but also impersonal context. Smith's collected "judgment of others," for example, makes no reference to any one judgment by any one person. Authors, critics, or judges, as a result, must present themselves as spokespersons for *all* humanity: "How amiable does he appear to be, whose sympathetic heart seems to re-echo all the sentiments of those with whom he converses, who grieves for their calamities, who resents their injuries, and who rejoices at their good fortune!" (p. 24). Smith is no Marxist; the individual is indispensable to this vastly communal experience. Smith's point is that the individuals must experience judgment (here, for example, the resentment of injuries) in the context of the collected acts of many individuals. Only individuals—never "society"—may imagine themselves into the role of the spectator. The spectator, accordingly, is an individual person.

Alienation is an impossibility in Smith's protocapitalist worldview. Every judge and every observed person may perceive himself in the context of the observing, value-producing spectator. Even the downtrodden may take on the privileged viewpoint of the spectator in order to "exert that recollection and self-command which constitute the dignity of every passion, and which bring it down to what others can enter into!" (*Theory of Moral Sentiments*, p. 24). Victims are empowered to experience the production of value and, thence, to tone down their pain to a dignified, spectatable mediocrity: "In such cases, this demigod within the breast appears, like the demigods of the poets, though partly of immortal, yet partly too of mortal extraction" (p. 131). Smith's comparison of the spectator to classical demigods is more than a rhetorical flourish. Like God, the spectator or the spectatorial pose suffuses all creation. Everything spectates everything else. Observed as well as observer observe. Yet the divinized spectator works in a human way, reducing everything to a moderate scale. He serves, as it were, as the household demigod of mediation.

It is his very enormousness and collectivity that makes the spectator so avid a defender of individuality. Smith declares the spectator to be the "real" man, for the spectator *realizes* the human world. He is a fiction about putting real individuals into psychological control over a transpersonal human world. Smith recognizes that an artificial human world started with individual artists. For John Locke, human knowledge developed almost on its own. So many people participated in its formation that no one person could have done much about it. Smith expands the human world beyond Locke's wildest dreams, yet he is careful to allow to individuals an immediate "moral sense" of their participation in the production of "Mans Creatures." As an individual himself, the spectator embodies the eminence of the individual throughout human society. Smith, admittedly, allows that no one individual may hope to reenact, single-handedly, all of the history of human consciousness. Yet, happily, the "inmate in the breast" is in the business of doing things vicariously—of "connecting" particular, immediate actions with oft-repeated situations, thereby accomplishing things no one real person could do. Further, he will not deceive us: "If we place ourselves completely in his situation, if we really view ourselves with his eyes, and as he views us, and listen with diligent and reverential attention to what he suggests to us, his voice will never deceive us" (*Theory of Moral Sentiments*, p. 227). All knowledge, according to Smith, implies a point of view and a person who takes that point of view. The spectator is nothing but a connecting of persons and viewpoints, and, hence, a connecting of the components of knowledge. The spectator connects the idea—the identity— of a person to all other identities. He links knowledge and knower. Indeed, he connects the citizens of the human world in a system of knowable, even friendly, relations. Mediating between self and system, the spectator identifies the self as the foundation of systematicity and systematicity as the foundation of self.

SELF-COMMAND: EXPLANATION AS EXHORTATION?

Smith's impartial spectator is a point of convergence, a central, mixed-modal idea through which self and system try to represent each other. The totalizing spectator and the differentiated individual, alas, resist this reconciliation with one another. In practice, judgment is never a simple process performed by a simple judge; it always involves the individual, the spectatorial, and possibly other points of view: "The sense of merit seems to be a compounded sentiment, and to be made up of two distinct emotions; a direct sympathy with the sentiments of the agent, and an indirect sympathy with the gratitude of those who receive the benefits of his actions" (*Theory of Moral Sentiments*, p. 74). In theory as well as in practice, a simple judgment—an unqualified statement like "This action is good"—is impossible. A judgment must always be somewhat perplexed, for multiplexity is a central issue in the psychology of judgment. Smith's judging self, for example, is a self-appropriating self. When making a judgment, this self tries to annex all its divided impulses into a simple, straightforward opinion. This self tries to blend many different feelings into one final verdict; it tries to annex its own complexity—its own vast and various resources—into a single, assessable "person." Seeing well beyond deconstruction, Smith aspires to a superspectatorial point of view. He constructs a third, unifying viewpoint, a viewpoint that combines the omniscient viewpoint of the spectator with the differentiated viewpoint of the individual:

When I endeavour to examine my own conduct, when I endeavour to pass sentence upon it, and either to approve or condemn it, it is evident that, in all cases, I divide myself, as it were, into two persons; and that I, the examiner and the judge, represent a different character from the other I, the person whose conduct is examined and judged of. The first is the spectator, whose sentiments with regard to my own conduct I endeavour to enter into, by placing myself in his situation, and by considering how it would appear to me, when seen from that particular point of view. The second is the agent, the person whom I properly call myself, and of whose conduct, under the character of a spectator, I was endeavouring to form some opinion. The first is the judge; the second the person judged of. But that the judge should, in every respect, be the same with the person judged of, is as impossible, as that the cause should in every respect, be the same with the effect. [p. 113]

One cannot, of course, "see" or "spectate" from this point of view. One can only experience it in polyvalent discussions like this one, in which Smith tries to speak, from some epistemological vanishing point, about both himself and his spectator—and about some implied reconciliation of his two personalities.

The value of a Smithian "person" is measured by the intensity of his or her activity. As the preceding passage shows, Smith pays more respect to the active judge than to the passive judged. The more active the person, the more likely that his judgments will appropriate the greatest possible number of viewpoints. Smith's chain of being tempers Pope's chain; Pope ranks beings according to their magnitude or intelligence, but Smith ranks them by their vitality and fictionality. At the top of Smith's scale is a sort of spectator of spectators, an "invisible hand" that combines the omnicompetence and fictionality of the impartial spectator with the vitality and the differentiating power of the individual person. Wealthy citizens, for example, "are led by an invisible hand to make nearly the same distributions of the necessaries of life, which would have been made, had the earth been divided into equal portions among all its inhabitants, and thus without intending it, without knowing it, advance the interests of the society, and afford means to the multiplication of the species" (*Theory of Moral Sentiments*, pp. 184-85). On the one hand, the invisible hand makes particular distributions to particular parties; on the other, its natural habitat is a theoretical work on aesthetics.[17] Taking into account such extrahuman influences as the availability of mineral resources or unusual weather, the hand fits nature and the human world to one another. This hand pens an enlarged and enlarging definition of human nature. It draws the individual person as a mediate relation, as an engaged, explicable, and explaining link between an overwhelming, hypersynthetic spectator and a chaotic, unknowable nature. Invisible and flexible, complex yet direct, the hand implements and explains the relation of the self, society, the spectator, and even experience itself.

The most extensive, artificial explanatory systems, then, have a way of interacting with as well as describing real experience. These forays of fiction into fact usually depend on the idiosyncratic actions of individual persons. Soldiers, for example, "cheerfully sacrifice their own little systems to the prosperity of a greater system" (*Theory of Moral Sentiments*, p. 236). To imagine that the average sad sack thinks of himself as a self-sacrificing system is, to say the least, to think a fiction. Yet Smith's propositions do account for what happens on the battlefield. Soldiers do engage themselves in the defense of some cultural system; their identities are "systems" in Smith's Lockean sense.[18] The more one thinks about Smith's explanation, the more difficult it is to refute; the more one feels it is right, the more it influences real action. Similarly, Smith's harsh discussion of representative meter—his claim that its effects are only the result of "custom" (p. 197)—is not as derogatory as it might seem. "Custom," for Smith, is always led, by the invisible hand, into some coherent, if arbitrary, relation with the system of the world. Representative meter, with all its self-consciousness and misrepresentation, accurately represents the systematizing nature of things. Experience cannot be understood or even experienced unless it is manipulated by some fictional creature, whether that creature be the invisible hand or the metrical technique of Alexander Pope.

Like Alexander Pope, Smith seems to delight in comparing inadequate things, especially himself, to his ultracoherent hands and spectators. The greater the contrast between the incompetent self and the competent judge, the more wonderful the resulting mediating system. Smith prefers the fictional applause of the spectator to the vulgar applause of a real audience (*Theory of Moral Sentiments*, p. 116). The greater the distance between the deed and reward, the greater the effort that the agent must expend in explaining (to himself!) the connection between his action and his applause. "Men have voluntarily thrown away life to acquire after death a renown which they could no longer enjoy"; experience shows that many people take on perilous missions out of a lust for an imaginary acclaim. Histories "concerning the perfidy and cruelty of a Borgia or a Nero" (p. 76) hold more interest than more balanced studies of less extreme characters, for the worldly successes and psychological complexities of wicked characters demand more of an explanation than do those of virtuous persons. The best history is a lying history, a history that elicits an evocative form from the lives of the most irregular, most despicable characters. Enterprising historians assume the posture of the impartial spectator. They aggressively spectate evil characters from countless viewpoints, thereby asserting that these malefactors may be connected to a superior, synthetic rendering of themselves.[19] The greatest historians are the ones who explain those persons and events that seem to defy explanation.

The "great source of pleasure" in art is therefore the "disparity between the imitating and the imitated object" ("On Imitative Arts," in *Essays*, p. 141). Unlike Alexander Pope, Smith considers the distortions of topiary shrubbery to be more beautiful than nature. Pyramidal yews put the Egyptian pyramids to shame; geometric forms, Smith smiles, are more unnatural to leaves than to stones, and "disparity between the imitating and the imitated object" is "the foundation of the beauty of imitation" (pp. 141, 144). This kind of corrective distortion is at a premium in Smith's moralized economy: "Thus man is by Nature directed to correct, in some measure, that distribution of things which she would herself otherwise have made. The rules which for this purpose she prompts him to follow, are different from those which she herself observes" (*Theory of Moral Sen-*

timents, p. 168). Like Smith's topiary gardener, the spectator prunes the natural order of things into a more obvious moral form. The raw materials remain the same; the same economic forces are at play in both nature and human nature; yet nature is forced to take on a different form, to appear in both its natural state and its improved, explained, and human state. Nature and man, Smith continues, share the same goal, equity, yet man must make nature fit that idea of natural justice that "he himself conceives for it."

There is always the danger, of course, that Smith's moral topiary might go too far. The "disparity" in the relations between, say, an epic and an outhouse might not prove as beautiful as our seriously mock-heroic Smith might expect. Smith is therefore always alert to the threat of bathos: "What a tragedy would be that of which the distress consisted of a colic!" On the other hand, some medical needs (as well as other low ideas, scenes, or images) can be morally, aesthetically, and epistemologically glamorized to an extraordinary degree. The "bodily pain" of a character like Hippolytus ought to be extrapolated into a spiritual pain, a "romantic wildness" (*Theory of Moral Sentiments*, p. 30). The distinction between the colic sufferer and Hippolytus is simple. The topiary distortion of bitter experience into beautiful psychological states must be precisely that: *distortion*. A colic has nothing to do with pity and terror; a distortion must be related to the experience that it distorts. Ethics and epistemology converge, for Smith, in literature, for literature specializes in the explanation of inadequate or unlikely phenomena but filters out irrelevant or unconnected materials. Tragedies, for example, preserve a "pleasant anxiety" by organizing a series of "displeasing events" into a clarifying form. Arranged properly, "miseries" can be more "affecting" than "pleasure," which "could be dispensed with" (*Lectures on Rhetoric*, pp. 80-82).

The best writers are those who, like Alexander Pope or George Berkeley, can literally "see" such distortions in a close relation to or even *in* experience. Smith could have enrolled in the graveyard school, for he can relate the most sublime emotions to the most skeletal imagery: "The idea of that dreary and endless melancholy, which the fancy naturally ascribes to their [the dead's] condition, arises altogether from our joining to the change which has been produced upon them, our own consciousness of that change, from our putting ourselves in their situation, and from our lodging, if I may be allowed to say so, our own living souls in their inanimated bodies, and thence conceiving what would be our emotions in this case" (*Theory of Moral Sentiments*, p. 13). Gothic meditations link the numbing fact of death with an animating, immediate sense of "their condition." So wholly engaged is Smith in the enlivening experience of this conventional imagery that he claims a practical purpose for it. Fantasies about death "guard and protect the society" of those who might take rash actions; fear of death discourages injustice, while melancholy literature provides an incentive to live!

Smith's "imitator" of the "divine artist" is always balancing on the boundary between systematicity and alternatives to systematicity—between, as above, pragmatic concerns and gothic sublimities. Judgment is a matter of intensely patrolled borders. People may judge themselves by one of two neighboring standards: either a supersystematic standard of perfection, or a proportionate, socially relative system of normative values. The first standard always pronounces a work, whether moral or artistic, to be a failure; the second standard is limited to works evidencing Smith's "pleasant mediocrity" (*Theory of Moral Sentiments*, pp. 247-48). Only the mild, normative standard, fears Smith, will allow for progress in the arts. Still, Smith declares the perfectionist standard to be the choice of the "wise man" (p. 249). Comparing himself to Boileau, he sets his own works against an unreachable ideal, opens a huge, wonder-producing gap between work and life, and, at last, cultivates a sublime vision of the imaginary failure of his own endeavors.

Smith's humbling recourse to an absolute standard of judgment might seem to contravene his search for a more human judge like the impartial spectator. Yet the impartial spectator himself is in many ways more of an absolutist than a relativist. Standing on the border between contexts and absolutes, assimilating both into a still more comprehensive idea of the humanized universe, he is both structuralist and deconstructionist, both man of possibilities and man of boundaries. It is possible in Smith's system to formulate a judgment that is fully reliable—fully certain—and yet that, relativistically, takes into account the variations in the human community, those "different degrees of attention, which our different habits of life allow us to give easily to the several parts of those complex objects" and those "different degrees of natural acuteness in the faculty of the mind to which they are addressed" (*Theory of Moral Sentiments*, p. 19). Even private, relativistic judgment is at its best when it is "suited to its object," when it is decorously conventional but also relativistically particular.

So great are the demands of this polycapacious spectator that the private person might well need to look elsewhere for a practical moral guide. The character of the spectator, after all, implies not only a motion from particular cases to general laws but also from the ultimate spectatorial person to the limited individual whom he spectates. No matter what he says in his more theoretical passages, Smith, talking about day-to-day practice, tends to treat the spectator as a sort of intermediate step between the individual person and an absolute foundation of judgment, whether that absolute be God, truth, or beauty. Particular problems are only partially solved by this wisest of judges. Half-real and half-artificial, the protean spectator bears some of the hallmarks of an objective standard of judgment—including that of being too hard to understand.

Smith, consequently, often finds himself in the awkward position of looking for a substitute for something that is already a substitute—of finding a miniature version of the spectator when the spectator himself proves too unwieldy or elusive. Smith settles on what he calls "self-command." Self-command amounts to the freely undertaken decision to see one's own actions as part of a comprehending system of things and to see oneself as a substitute for the spectator. Finding, like Pope, that human knowledge has enlarged beyond human comprehension, Smith qua self-commander assumes that any and all of his actions are spectated, that his every deed implies, in advance, a favorable judgment by the unwieldy, elusive spectator. All individual acts "re-echo" some judgment by *some* spectator, whether the "inmate" in his breast, in some other breast, or, perhaps, in the breast of society at large. Smith's strategy is an emancipating one. It empowers judgment, for any judgment, any act of knowing, carries the credentials conferred by the omniscient spectator. Yet it keeps the judging person free of the spectator's heavy duties—and, more importantly, free of his disturbing need to stand at a distance from particular, engaging contexts.

Through self-command, the imposing person of the spectator becomes more personalized. "Self-command" is a shorthand term for the conscious representation *of* oneself *to* oneself *as* a spectator:

The man who acts according to the rules of perfect prudence, of strict justice, and of proper benevolence, may be said to be perfectly virtuous. But the most perfect knowledge of those rules will not alone enable him to act in this manner: his own passions are very apt to mislead him; sometimes to drive him and sometimes to seduce him to violate all the rules which he himself, in all his sober and cool hours, approves of. The most perfect knowledge, if it is not supported by the most perfect self-command, will not always enable him to do his duty. [*Theory of Moral Sentiments*, p. 237]

Self-command is not an ordinary passion, for it masters passion; it is not knowledge, for knowledge, lacking enforcement powers, cannot command. Rather, self-command is a moderating passion for order. A desire to implement the judgments of the spectator, self-command *is* the engagement of epistemology. It *is* the injecting of a totalizing, systematic, and panoptical knowledge into morally significant, historical contexts.

The development of an impartial spectator is only the first step toward Smith's abbreviation, consolidation, and subjugation of his enormous system of human knowledge. Locke's vague, unspecified "powers," for example, take on a clean-shaven look among the self-commanders. Looking beneath the idea of "red" or the idea of "monarchy," Locke's reader finds "the power to produce the idea of red" or "the power to constitute a government." Looking beneath the same ideas, Smith's readers also find these diverse (and vague) Lockean powers, but they also find a unified self-command. These latter readers find, beneath ideas, a decision to believe in the relation between thing, power, and perception—and to treat this relation as the "thing" to be known. Self-command certifies that an omnicompetent judge would regard this relation as valuable, if not true. It redeems percipients from solipsism and relativism, for self-commanders assert that their judgments, no matter how personal or particular, enact the remote judgments of an impartial arbitrator. Smith, for example, often speaks as though the faculties of the individual were those of the impartial spectator:

Every sense is supreme over its own objects. . . . Whatever gratifies the taste is sweet, whatever pleases the eye is beautiful, whatever soothes the ear is harmonious. The very essence of each of those qualities consists in its being fitted to please the sense to which it is addressed. It belongs to our moral faculties, in the same manner to determine when the ear ought to be soothed, when the eye ought to be indulged, and when the taste ought to be gratified, when and how far every other principle of our nature ought to be indulged or restrained. What is agreeable to our moral faculties, is fit, and right, and proper to be done; the contrary wrong, unfit, and improper. The sentiments which they approve of, are graceful and becoming: the contrary, ungraceful and unbecoming. The very words, right, wrong, fit, improper, graceful, unbecoming, mean only what pleases or displeases those faculties. [p. 165]

Self-commanders must make two assumptions: that their personal judgments anticipate those of the spectator and that the spectator will guarantee some relation between those judgments and the judgments of others. The preceding passage, for example, explains that words can derive consistent meanings from quite different sources. Spontaneous feelings of approval and overworked common usage can assign the same meanings to words like "right," "fit," and "graceful." Personal experience constantly confirms the spectator's collected, schematic rendering of the world; a living, acting person is a spectator in miniature.

Smith, then, both invents and bypasses the spectator. By assuming that every action contributes to the formation of a moral system, Smith can bypass time-consuming efforts to abstract a whole system of knowledge. Systematicity is everywhere; why waste time talking about its inevitable emergence when one can be implementing its precepts? "Self-command," the self-initiated but also spontaneous and reflexive implementation of systematic, spectatorial systems by the individual person, "is not only itself a great virtue, but from it all the other virtues seem to derive their principal lustre" (*Theory of Moral Sentiments*, p. 241). Like Halifax's "living law," the spectator, whatever he might be, speaks best through action. Smith awards high marks to "Buccaneers," mariners who bypass normative ethical standards in order to practice a steely self-command (p. 240). Smith awards especially high marks to himself, whom he presents as a buccaneer of explanatory discourse, as a philosophizing writer who never fears to turn lucky license into literary rules:

The rules of justice may be compared to rules of grammar; the rules of the other virtues, to the rules which critics lay down for the attainment of what is sublime and elegant in composition. The one, are precise, accurate, and indispensable. The other, are loose, vague, and indeterminate, and present us rather with a general idea of the perfection we ought to aim at, than afford us with any certainty and infallible directions for acquiring it. A man may learn to write grammatically by rule, with the most absolute infallibility; and so, perhaps, he may be taught to act justly. But there are no rules whose observance will lead us to the attainment of elegance or sublimity in writing; though there are some which may help us, in some measure, to correct and ascertain the vague ideas which we might otherwise have entertained of those perfections. And there are no rules by the knowledge of which we can infallibly be taught to act upon all occasions with prudence, with just magnanimity, or proper beneficence: though there are some which may enable us to correct and ascertain, in several respects, the imperfect ideas we might have entertained of those virtues. [pp. 175-76]

This kind of morally coherent system of human knowledge has been the collected goal of all the writers that I have assessed. By making a sublime, personalized spectator into the foundation of judgment and by playing up the commandeering, potentially destabilizing character of judges, Smith suggests that comprehensive coherence must, paradoxically, exceed the limits of any one limited, differentiated, and potentially deviant system. A completing, cohering system must apply itself to some other thing, even if it must turn that thing into a "human creature" or, like Smith's spectating system, must generate that thing—that ultimate sense of otherness and engagement—out of its own resources.

To counterbalance the limitations inherent in any system, a Smithian philosophizer must rely on some "person" to enliven and enact the process of knowing. As a living, differentiated counterpart to an equally differentiated, if more generalized, spectator, such a person can interpret his or her engagement with the system of knowledge as a sign of this system's moral value—as a sign that so truly human a world may inspire, despite its limitations, a committed, certain program of action. As apprentices to the distant spectator, practitioners of self-command may stand apart from and stabilize the human world; as actors, they may voluntarily participate in the never-ending progress toward a comprehensive human knowledge. As the consummate practitioner of a simultaneously empiricist and explanatory discourse, Smith tries to produce an engaged, moralizing system of knowledge that also allows for disinterested observation. Appropriately, Smith acts out his dizzying project by observing, judging, and explaining the construction, failure, and finally reconstruction of his impartial spectator in a newly humanized self—in the character of the acting individual.

EPILOGUE

Adam Smith's writings show that a history of explanation should terminate not by terminating but by asserting the value of a continuing process of explanation. I would therefore like to close my study by making a few assertions concerning worthwhile directions for the future study of past literary periods. I suspect that my comments bear some relation to what I have said in this book, but I offer them in an occasional manner, as an antidote for an excessive dose of systematicity. I leave them for more able (and, I hope, not wholly invisible) hands to manipulate.

The story that I have told, of the enlargement and psychological reclamation of explanatory discourse, is similar to the story of our own era. Ours is an era in which explanatory discourse is discovering—and sometimes running afoul of—an immense, virtually omniscient collection of information, judgments, and opinions. What Adam Smith would call "imaginary" explanatory devices—whether terms like "light years," "hyperspace," and "eons" or tools like libraries holding 10^7 books—have both enlarged and impoverished knowledge. They have systematized what could never, as Locke might say, be understood; they have, in effect, given a verbal, theoretical, and institutional form to uncertainty. Criticism, fortunately, can treat these humbling circumstances as an opportunity to reform itself. Matthew Arnold's reputation has fallen on hard times, yet criticism today enjoys an unprecedented opportunity to act, as Arnold had hoped, as a master discipline, as a system for understanding, coordinating, and judging the interplay of theories and as a means of escaping the limits of any one system or ideology. Put simply, criticism needs a new credo. It needs an explanation and a justification—an assertion of reasons why it ought to be believed, especially when it faces so much competition and draws so little attention. Writers like Halifax and Pope have already set a fine example. These writers took advantage of what they feared was the unintelligibility of the world; they used the breakdown of knowledge as an occasion to multiply theories or to provide a theory for any occasion that might arise. Their sense of the productive limitation of explanation, of the need to restrict some theories to specific contexts, is sadly lacking in contemporary criticism. Its absence accounts for the failures of Marxism and deconstruction, two monolithic theories from two relatively small segments of intellectual history, to provide not only a coherent but a believable and satisfying interpretation of the world; its continued absence will continue to account for the failure of any future theory that commits itself to any impersonally dogmatic, relentlessly all-encompassing framework.

What is boded in Smith's critical theorizing is a criticism of constructive refusal: a commitment to limit belief in any one critical system while also engaging belief in explanatory activity. Dryden's unresolved debates define the negative pole of "constructive refusal"; Rochester's gingerly endorsement of any and all theories defines the positive pole. During the eighteenth century, in other words, truth was often treated in a systematic rather than a realistic way. Pope could truthfully describe a real "time" that, by his own admission, none of his devices could explain or measure (thus deconstructionists commonly believe that what they say is true, although truth has little meaning in their approach). A belief in the possibility of truth was, for a writer like Alexander Pope, a necessary condition of the systematizing act, even despite the fact that Pope's own multiplying of explanations was making the attainment of truth an impossibility.

I suggest, therefore, a frank confession that the conditions of critical knowledge—the fact that critics live and work in a context that compels them to know something about an earlier one—might compel the limiting of belief not only in some one theory or ideology, but in all theories and ideologies, especially in theories that refuse to let us at least consider commonsense notions about humanity's place in the objective world, to take into account—to use old-fashioned words—nature and majority opinion. John Locke, for example, leaves his reader with three partial sciences, three accounts of human nature, each of which compels belief *part of the time*. Locke expects his reader to devise a "living" law that denies the omnicompetence of any one of these disciplines, that refutes an approach to human nature when that approach stands in the way of the construction of a "common" sense of things. Locke's constructively refutative criticism would be appropriate, for example, for a writer like Swift. It could offer a post-phenomenalist, postpsychoanalytic reading of Swift, a reading in which the hard edge of his plain prose foils a will to believe in those systems and ideologies that he satirically refutes. Such a Lockean criticism would serve a moral purpose, for it would cultivate what Smith calls the "real" or "true" self. By granting an increased prestige to common sense, it would empower those moral impulses that work just beyond the edge of critical discourse.

Authors from Rochester to Smith also teach the lesson of sympathy for systems of explanation. By "sympathy" I mean an appreciation of the believability of any theory—for that fascinating feature of reader and writer psychology that makes any assertion, at least initially, more credible than incredible. The tendency to believe, as Smith points out, is "natural." Pope, for example, could not simultaneously believe every maxim that he declaimed, for his pieces of advice often contradict one another. Yet a constructive criticism of Pope's writings takes into account Pope's feeling for the believability of the many theories that he addresses. Pope never doubts that he might commit himself at some time to some one of his theories; he shows us that the sheer presentation of an idea is a way of making it intellectually seductive.

Literary criticism like that in the "new critical" or deconstructionist tradition is dishonest when it exiles authors and their beliefs from texts. Critical texts themselves both declare and pique belief and disbelief. By confronting explanatory discourse, writers from Rochester to Smith were confronting the inevitability of belief. They were facing up to the fact that one could not argue for anything, not even for skepticism, without eliciting at least an initial desire to believe in it (and affirm its value). Among critics of our day, this sympathetic criticism might take the form of a renewed interested in the generating as well as the description of beliefs, values, and opinions. It would offer a truly public psychology of history. Going beyond the person-oriented analyses of Freudian criticism and resisting the collectivist approach of socially oriented disciplines like anthropology, it would discuss the production of culture from the interaction of idiosyncratic attitudes.

Such an enterprise need not focus on high culture; work has already begun on sectarian movements and their literatures, and more work could be done on the rhetoric of political dissent. The key to success in a constructive critique of early literature is not the elimination of ideology. Rather, critics need to subordinate ideological interpretation to the sympathetic analysis of those motivations that lead to the production of theories and ideologies and that support belief in them. The term "interpretive community," for example, is presently enjoying a certain currency in literary circles: To make sense of this term, it will be necessary to examine what people commonly believed about themselves—and what we, overburdened with ideologies, must refuse to believe about them. Critical pluralism, I therefore suggest, may be a pluralism with standards. It may be a way of recognizing all the facts about early literature, including the irreducible fact that earlier writers *did* hold beliefs, often in theories that we, presently and irreducibly, *do not* believe. Pope, for example, believed, at least for the duration of one line, that sublimity was a real psychological force. No amount of critical ingenuity can completely resolve that irreducible, if limited, act of moral certainty into a mere exemplification of those many literary theories in which, as Dryden might say, the literary scholars of our era also "must believe," if only for a line.

Attention to *all* the means of production, including the psychological ones, could shed light on a number of troubling questions in eighteenth-century studies. One need not select a cheerful topic like "certainty"; no one, for example, has investigated Smith's suggestion that the eighteenth century had a developed notion of the psychological origins of war. A book might be written on spontaneous literary productions of the eighteenth century—on, say, street demonstrations. I myself hope to produce a book on the generating of genres during the eighteenth century. A "generative" approach might also direct attention to the old question of the relation between genre and mode. Explanation, I have argued, is a kind of master mode, but other literary procedures merit attention. Shaftesburian ridicule would be one candidate mode; dialogue another; laughter, that strange combination of power and comedy, would be a third; and the mode of making modes, the literary technique of devising literary techniques, a fourth. A more "modal" criticism would, for example, attempt to work out a sentimental or a satiric mode in drama; it would avoid procrustean pronouncements about "eighteenth-century comedy," but it wouldn't shy away from the use of several texts or authors to assemble a collected idea of the way in which most persons *believed* comedy was formed. A modal criticism would encourage more collected critical efforts; it would promote collections of essays on issues as well as on authors, collections by individual authors, like Michael Seidel's *Exile and the Narrative Imagination*, or collections of essays, by various hands, on topics like liberty, allegory, or rhetorical theory. A modal criticism would thus open up new ground for comparative studies. It would authorize cross-generic studies like, say, a comparative analysis of philosophical texts from assorted national literatures.

In a moment of religious enthusiasm, Benjamin Whichcote warns that "if reason may not *command*, it will *condemn*"; in a moment of secular enthusiasm, Shaftesbury announces that "there is no such thing as a partial skepticism," that one must either believe or disbelieve a proposition.[1] In a recent, exasperated paper, Peter Firchow declares that "we are all new critics"—that all contemporary critics begin their inquiries with the goal of illuminating a literary work, and then—only then—think about philosophical or political issues.[2] Weary of this sort of aestheticism, the so-called "new historicism" has attempted to stir up interest in early literature by declaring all literary texts and all literary canons to be the tools of special-interest groups. In the process, unfortunately, this "school" has managed to imply—in contravention of its own goals—that interest in and engagement with literature is slightly naughty. Belief in the values inscribed in a text shows that the believing writer or reader has something to gain from them, usually at someone else's expense. This secret fear of prosperity, ironically, encourages an aestheticism more restrictive than that of the new critics. Deviations from a unifying social process end up offending a delicate moral sense. So puritanical a criticism would hold little value for writers like Dryden and Locke, writers who made at least two assumptions: first, that the production of any work or ideology, *as* a productive act, always improved society (hence Dryden's respectful reflections on deviant doctrines in works like *Religio Laici*); second, that the inevitable, if only initial, belief in the value of a work, like the passion for explanation, was nothing to be ashamed of, indeed was a precondition of the construction of a society. Rochester, Dryden, and their colleagues could be described as the greatest of new critics, for they assumed that the vast array of social and intellectual forces led to a culminating work, to the endless, unifying job of explanation.

If the study of early literature is to survive the numbing contemporaneity of our own culture, then criticism must ask itself to ask what historical movements *mean*, both to the people who participated in them and to us. It must speak to the heart by knowing the heart of the past; it must, in current literary jargon, relate "engagement" to epistemology. A simple humanism, a concern for grand old values, is not the answer. Such a nostalgic approach is impossible in our immense world. Talking about the busy beehive of society, both

Alexander Pope and Bernard Mandeville wryly comment that one can equally well explain the universe as a system for serving the needs of mankind or as a system for serving the needs of a goose. A more-than-humanist criticism would keep this caveat in mind. Like Alexander Pope's verse essays, it would experiment with possible explanations, and it would assume that possible theories might possibly be true as well as false. It would not be afraid to propose an abundance of new explanations for past, historical experience, but, like Smith's invisible hand, it would present both past and present explanations as part of a series of theories that certainly leads up to a certain understanding of the whole. I say "certain" because the multiplicity characteristic of explanatory activity precludes a complete or superhuman knowledge yet encourages an indivisible faith in the value and validity of explanation. Like Ptolemy's equalizing circle, criticism demands the positing of the possibility of truth, not just as a distant, Hegelian synthesis, but also as an immediately felt, motivating device, as a spur to explanation. Within eighteenth-century studies, for example, it is time for a book that reevaluates, with the help of our own de-Romanticized, demythologized notions, the eighteenth-century conception of that "real" object of explanation, nature. Rose Zimbardo's recent book on dramatic imitation, *A Mirror to Nature*, has opened this inquiry; other writers will, I hope, follow her example.

In closing, I want to suggest that writers from Rochester to Smith make possible not only an understanding but also a revision of our own self-styled "information age." These writers regarded knowledge, whether of a historical or semiotic variety, as important but not morally sufficient. What they regarded as self-sustaining was the certifying of knowledge—the use of knowledge to reconstruct individual identity and to construct a society in which individual belief, certainty, was sovereign. Knowledge, for those who followed Rochester, turned into power; information became the occasion for belief. It will be of great importance for eighteenth-century studies to explore the belief-compelling quality of eighteenth-century literature, to show why we ought to believe what was said in that faraway time and how we might reclaim authority over our own enlarging, ultrahuman world of information.

Notes

PROLOGUE

1. Lincoln Faller, *Turned to Account: The Forms and Functions of Criminal Biography in Late Seventeenth- and Early Eighteenth-Century England* (Cambridge: Cambridge Univ. Press, 1987), pp. x, 41.

2. See, for example, Paul J. Korshin, "The Intellectual Context of Swift's Flying Island," *Philological Quarterly* 50 (1971): 630-46.

3. See, for example, Heinz-Joachim Müllenbrock, *Popes Gesellschaftslehre in "An Essay on Man": Eine Untersuchung der dritten Epistel* (Göttingen: Vandenhoeck and Ruprecht, 1977), esp. pp. 15-34. Particularly commendable among recent studies is Howard Erskine-Hill's attempt ("Pope and the Origins of Society," in G.S. Rousseau and Pat Rogers, eds., *The Enduring Legacy: Alexander Pope Tercentenary Essays* [Cambridge: Cambridge Univ. Press, 1988], pp. 79-93) to show both the range and the particularly of Pope's acquaintance with political philosophy.

4. Barbara Shapiro, *Probability and Certainty in Seventeenth-Century England* (Princeton, N.J.: Princeton Univ. Press, 1983), p. 9.

5. See Abraham Cowley, *Complete Works*, ed. Alexander B. Grosart (Lancashire, England: Chertsey Worthies Library, 1881), p. 285; and Thomas Sprat, *History of the Royal Society*, ed. Jackson I. Cope and Harold W. Jones (St. Louis, Mo.: Washington Univ. Publications, 1958), pt. 2, sec. 11, pp. 81-83.

6. On "moral certainty" and "constructive skepticism" in these authors, see Henrik van Leeuwen, *The Problem of Certainty in English Thought, 1639-1960* (The Hague: Nijhoff, 1963), pp. 13-89; and M. Jamie Ferreira, *Scepticism and Reasonable Doubt: The British Naturalist Tradition in Wilkins, Hume, Reid, and Newman* (Oxford: Clarendon, 1986), pp. 12-31.

7. See Douglas Lane Patey, *Probability and Literary Form* (Cambridge: Cambridge Univ. Press, 1984), pp. 3-74.

8. See A.D. McKillop, *English Literature from Dryden to Burns* (New York: Appleton-Century-Crofts, 1948), pp. 15-17 and passim; and George Sherburn, in A.C. Baugh, ed., *A Literary History of England* (New York: Appleton-Century-Crofts, 1948), p. 733 and passim.

9. See Basil Willey, *The Eighteenth Century Background* (London: Chatto and Windus, 1939), index and p. 99ff.; Leroy Loemker, *Struggle for Synthesis: The Seventeenth Century Background of Leibniz's Synthesis of Order and Freedom* (Cambridge, Mass.: Harvard Univ. Press), pp. 4-27; Paul Fussell, *The Rhetorical World of Augustan Humanism* (Oxford: Clarendon, 1965), pp. 4-9 and passim; and Donald Greene, *The Age of Exuberance* (New York: Random House, 1970). See also Van Leeuwen, *Problem of Certainty*.

10. Greene, *Age of Exuberance*, pp. 90-96.

11. Shapiro, *Probability and Certainty*, p. 9; Patey, *Probability*, p. xii.

12. Eric Rothstein, *Systems of Order and Inquiry in Later Eighteenth-Century Fiction* (Berkeley: Univ. of California Press, 1975).

13. For an exposition of this approach, see Arthur O. Lovejoy, *The Great Chain of Being* (1936; reprint, Cambridge, Mass.: Harvard Univ. Press, 1966), pp. 3-23.

14. So Marjorie Nicolson offers a fascinating, if flawed, record of the influence of Newton, in *Newton Demands the Muse* (1946; reprint, Princeton, N.J.: Princeton Univ. Press, 1966); and so Richard Foster Jones, in *Ancients and Moderns* (Washington: Washington Univ. Studies in English, 1961) credits Francis Bacon with responsibility for most of early modern intellectual history. To Jones's credit, however, he deletes "background" from the subtitle of the second edition of his book.

15. Walter Jackson Bate, *From Classic to Romantic* (Cambridge: Harvard Univ. Press, 1946).

16. Louis Althusser, *Essays in Self-Criticism*, trans. Grahame Lock (London: NLB, 1976), pp. 133-34.

17. Max Horkheimer and Theodor Adorno, *Dialectic of Enlightenment*, trans. John Cumming (London: Allen Lane, 1973), pp. 127-29.

18. Antonio Gramsci, *Selections from Prison Notebooks*, ed. and trans. Quintin Hoare and Geoffrey Nowell Smith (New York: International Publishers, 1971), p. 9.

19. Arnold Kettle, *Literature and Liberation*, ed. Graham Martin and W.R. Owens (Manchester: Manchester Univ. Press, 1988), pp. 122, 126.

20. Sir Lewis Namier, *Crossroads of Power* (London: Hamish Hamilton, 1962), pp. 1-6.

21. J.C.D. Clark, *Revolution and Rebellion: State and Society in the Seventeenth and Eighteenth Centuries* (Cambridge: Cambridge Univ. Press, 1986), p. 23.

22. See for example Pierre Macherey, *A Theory of Literary Production*, trans. Geoffrey Wall (London: Routledge and Kegan Paul, 1978), pp. 28, 85.

23. "For this reason the *senses* of the social man are *other* senses than those of the non-social man. Only through the objectively unfolded richness of subjective *human* sensibility . . . [are these senses] either cultivated or brought into being. For not only the five senses but also the so called mental senses . . . come to be by virtue of the object, by virtue of *humanized nature*" (Karl Marx, *Economic and Philosophical Manuscripts of 1844*, in *Karl Marx and Frederick Engels on Literature and Art*, ed. Lee Baxandall and Stefan Marawski [New York: International General, 1974], pp. 51-52).

24. See M.M. Goldsmith, *Private Vices, Public Benefits: The Social Context of Mandeville's Political Thought* (Cambridge: Cambridge Univ. Press, 1985), p. 125.

25. Derek Attridge, *Peculiar Language: Literature as Difference from the Renaissance to James Joyce* (Ithaca, N.Y.: Cornell Univ. Press, 1988), p. 7.

26. Hazard Adams, *Philosophy of the Literary Symbolic* (Tallahassee: Univ. Presses of Florida, 1983), pp. 355-56.

27. Jonathan Culler, *On Deconstruction* (Ithaca, N.Y.: Cornell Univ. Press, 1982), pp. 22.

28. Jacques Derrida, *Of Grammatology*, trans. Gayatri Chakravorty Spivak (Baltimore, Md.: Johns Hopkins Univ. Press, 1976), p. 50.

29. Paul de Man, "The Epistemology of Metaphor," *Critical Inquiry* 5 (1978): 28-29.

30. Michel Foucault, *The Archaeology of Knowledge*, trans. A.M. Sheridan-Smith (New York: Random House, 1972), p. 127.

31. Reevaluations of the Scots influence are now beginning to appear. See Richard

B. Sher, *Church and University in the Scottish Enlightenment: The Moderate Literati of Edinburgh* (Princeton, N.J.: Princeton Univ. Press, 1985); and John Dwyer, *Virtuous Discourse: Sensibility and Community in Late Eighteenth-Century Scotland* (Edinburgh: John Donald, 1987).

32. See John Steadman, *The Hill and the Labyrinth* (Berkeley and Los Angeles: Univ. of California Press, 1984), pp. 113-23.

33. See John J. Richetti, *Philosophical Writing: Locke, Berkeley, Hume* (Cambridge, Mass.: Harvard Univ. Press, 1983), pp. 4-47.

34. See Edward O. Wilson, *Sociobiology: The New Synthesis* (Cambridge, Mass.: Harvard Univ. Press, 1975), pp. 3, 7, 548, 564.

35. Michael Ryan, *Marxism and Deconstruction* (Baltimore, Md.: Johns Hopkins Univ. Press, 1982), p. 43.

36. The most searching discussion of "internal processing algorithms" is Pawel Lewicki's *Nonconscious Social Information Processing* (Orlando, Fla.: Academic Press, 1986), pp. 28-37 Lewicki also provides a comprehensive review of other attempts to reconstruct consciousness, the unconscious, and the nonconscious processing of information (pp. 13-26). Howard Gardner, *The Mind's New Science: A History of the Cognitive Revolution* (New York: Basic Books, 1985), pp. 386-88, is at pains to remind "cognitivists" that a systematic representation of the mind must avoid vulgar analogies—for example, that the mind recalls a computer. Gardner recommends instead a model of the mind as a complex of systems, some of them registering social context, others monitoring biological activity, and still others performing computations. See also the excellent collection of essays assembled by Kenneth S. Bowers and Donald Meichenbaum, eds., *The Unconscious Reconsidered* (New York: Wiley, 1984).

CHAPTER ONE. ROCHESTER

1. M.H. Abrams et al., eds., *The Norton Anthology of English Literature*, 5th ed. (New York: Norton, 1986), p. 1957.

2. See Dustin Griffin, *Satires Against Man* (Berkeley: Univ. of California Press, 1973), p. 16; Kristoffer Paulson, "The Rev. Edward Stillingfleet and the 'Epilogue' to Rochester's *A Satyr Against Reason and Mankind*," *Philological Quarterly* 50 (1971): 657-63; C.F. Main, "The Right Vein of Rochester's *Satyr*," in Rudolf Kirk, ed., *Essays in Literary History* (New Brunswick, N.J.: Rutgers Univ. Press, 1960), p. 99; J.W. Johnson, "Lord Rochester and the Tradition of Cyrenaic Hedonism," in Theodore Besterman, ed., *Transactions of the International Congress on the Enlightenment* (Oxford: Voltaire Foundation, 1976), p. 1154; David Farley-Hills, *Rochester's Poetry* (Totowa, N.J.: Rowan and Littlefield, 1978), p. 161; Raymond K. Whitley, "Rochester: A Cosmological Pessimist," *English Studies in Canada* 4 (1978): 188; and Thomas H. Fujimara, "Rochester's 'Satyr Against Mankind,' " *Studies in Philology* 55 (1958): 578-81.

3. See Howard Erskine-Hill, "Rochester: Augustan or Explorer?" *Renaissance and Modern Essays* 48 (1966): 54. See also Charles Knight, "The Paradox of Reason: Argument in Rochester's *A Satyr Against Reason and Mankind*," *Modern Language Review* 65 (1970): 254-60, who argues against the tendency to see Rochester's later satires as grim examples of skepticism rather than as brilliant exercises in argumentation.

4. G. Douglas Atkins, *Reading Deconstruction, Deconstructive Reading* (Lexington: Univ. Press of Kentucky, 1983), p. 11.

5. Bishop Gilbert Burnet, *Some Passages of the Life and Death of John, Earl of Rochester* (Menston, England: Scolar Press, 1972), p. 7. Subsequent citations of this edition are

incorporated into the text. On the varieties of contemporary dualism and their relevance to Rochester's interest in the problem of belief, see David Vieth, "Divided Consciousness: The Trauma and Triumph of Restoration Culture," *Tennessee Studies in Literature* 22 (1977): 46. On the seriousness of Rochester's pose, see Carol Righter, "John Wilmot, Earl of Rochester," *Proceedings of the British Academy* 53 (1969): 68; K.E. Robinson, "Rochester's Dilemma," *Durham University Journal* 71 (1979): 228; Reba Wilcoxon, "Pornography, Obscenity, and Rochester's Imperfect Enjoyment," *Studies in English Literature* 15 (1975): 389; and Griffin, *Satires*, p. 18.

6. "Rochester's poetry is written out of the tension between a disbelief in any metaphysical sanction for orderliness and the social need for an aristocrat to insist on the inherited conventions that guaranteed his position and defined him as a social being" (Farley-Hills, *Rochester's Poetry*, p. 4).

7. See ibid., p. 141; Griffin, *Satires*, pp. 27-28; and Alvin Kernan, *The Cankered Muse* (New Haven, Conn.: Yale Univ. Press, 1959), passim.

8. See Righter, "Wilmot," p. 49. Johnson, in "Lord Rochester," argues that Rochester's love of complex and sometimes contradictory guises evidences his split allegiance to Roman Catholicism and Protestantism, but I would argue that the concern for guises comes first, the religious concerns second.

9. A satire of the Gondibert stanza constitutes a subtle attack on Dryden, Davenant, and the heroic mode. See Griffin, *Satires*, pp. 50-52. On Rochester's favorite dichotomies, see Carole Fabricant, "Rochester's World of Imperfect Enjoyment," *Journal of English and Germanic Philology* 73 (1974): 345-46; Whitley, "Rochester," p. 183; and Griffin, *Satires*, p. 16.

10. John Adlard, *The Debt to Pleasure* (Cheadle, England: Carcarnet Press, 1973), p. 127, for example, quotes a conversation in which Rochester couples a confession of extravagance with an assurance of his rejection of atheism.

11. *The Complete Poems of John Wilmot, Earl of Rochester*, ed. David Vieth (New Haven, Conn.: Yale Univ. Press, 1968). Subsequent citations of the Vieth edition are incorporated into the text.

12. On Rochester's disdain for *actual* solutions, see Fredelle Bruser, "Disproportion: A Study in the Work of John Wilmot, Earl of Rochester," *University of Toronto Quarterly* 15 (1946): 389; and Farley-Hills, *Rochester's Poetry*, p. 48.

13. Fabricant, "Rochester's World," p. 338, selects this passage as an example of Rochester's practice of "counter-transubstantiation," a descent from coherent ideas to disunited objects.

14. Rochester's poetic and sexual performances are often interrupted by an icy, antiexperiential logic. See Ronald Berman, "Rochester and the Defeat of the Senses," *Kenyon Review* 26 (1964): 359.

15. Griffin, *Satires*, p. 102, notes that, in the Ovidian love songs, pain becomes desirable, for it harkens the arrival of pleasure.

16. Robinson, "Rochester's Dilemma," p. 225, analyzes Rochester's psychological dilemma: gratification is a form of slavery to external determinations; therefore, freedom results from willing the opposite of what one desires.

17. See Griffin, *Satires*, pp. 227-28.

18. See Fujimara, "Rochester's 'Satyr,' " p. 588. Barbara Everett, "The Sense of Nothing," in Jeremy Treglown, ed., *The Spirit of Wit* (Oxford: Blackwell, 1982), pp. 7, 9, describes Rochester's poems as instances of "startled paradoxical self-undermining wit" in which "elegant verse often resounds with the crash of breaking glass."

19. David Vieth, "Towards an Anti-Aristotelian Poetic," *Language and Style* 5

(1972): 142, notices that Rochester never lets us touch base at any one local point in experience; indeed, he centers his poems a few lines off center in order to upset the sense of locality.

20. Farley-Hills, *Rochester's Poetry*, p. 207, identifies the trouble in *Artemesia to Chloe* as stemming from our total reliance on the perceptions of Artemesia, which are merely idiosyncratic. Griffin wonders whether an ideal term like "satire" applies to such a de-intellectualized university (*Satires*, pp. 153-54). Vieth notes that we can never answer the question the poem poses—which character represents the paradigm of happiness?—because each character is too defective to offer a model of any kind ("Anti-Aristotelian Poetic," p. 136). Berman, "Rochester and the Defeat," p. 367, deems the poem a mad effort to propose an individual ideal for every action, the ideal being thus reduced to particulars.

21. On Hobbes's account of freedom, see Robinson, "Rochester's Dilemma," p. 224. On the impossible conclusion, see Whitley, "Rochester," p. 191.

22. See Burnet, *Passages*, p. 35.

23. In one subtle parody of Renaissance theosophy, Rochester argues that infinite sexual engagement allows us to imitate the full infinity of God. See Berman, "Rochester and the Defeat," p. 368.

24. On sudden devaluations in Rochester's poetry, see Paul C. Davies, "Rochester and Boileau: A Reconsideration," *Comparative Literature* 2 (1969): 348-55; Vieth, "Anti-Aristotelian Poetic," pp. 126-29.

25. Main, "Right Vein," p. 110, quips that the remarkable thing about the *Satyr* is that the standard of behavior is so low, yet man still falls away from it.

26. See Griffin, *Satires*, p. 233.

27. Fujimara, "Rochester's 'Satyr,' " pp. 579-81, reads the *Satyr* as an abortive attempt to graft together all rationalistic philosophies into an objective worldview. The particular philosophies tapped are reviewed by Johnson, "Lord Rochester," p. 1154; Griffin, *Satires*, pp. 210-28; Main, "Right Vein," p. 99; and J.F. Croker, "Rochester's *Satire Against Mankind*," *West Virginia University Studies* 3 (1937): ii and passim.

28. Farley-Hills, *Rochester's Poetry*, p. 177, calls *Upon Nothing* an effort to build "the world upon a point."

CHAPTER TWO. HALIFAX

1. See Walter Raleigh's Introduction to *The Complete Works of George Savile, First Marquess of Halifax*, ed. Walter Raleigh (Oxford: Clarendon, 1912), p. ix. Very little has been written about Halifax. Raleigh's Introduction and Helen Foxcroft's *The Life and Letters of Sir George Savile, Bart., First Marquis of Halifax* (London: Longmans, 1898) remain the best studies. The latter appears in an abridged version, *A Character of the Trimmer* (Cambridge: Cambridge Univ. Press, 1936), but this book is more concerned with Halifax's life and times than with his works. See also Kevin L. Cope, "Halifax and the Art of Power," *Rocky Mountain Review* 39 (1985): 241-50.

2. On the evidences for and against the existence of a "trimming" or moderate party, see D.R. Benson, "Halifax and the Trimmers," *Huntington Library Quarterly* 27 (1964): 133-34. For Halifax's contemporaries, trimming was suspect; while trimming, the art of balancing and compromising, had a great deal of practical value, it could only define itself as the balancing of other influences, and thus seemed to betoken

either noncommitment or equivocation. Suspected trimmers were often accused of plotting, just as were the victims of the Popish Plot hysteria.

3. L'Estrange even identified the perennially moderate Ralph Cudworth as an extremist. On the background of Halifax's works, see Mark N. Brown, "The Works of George Savile, Marquis of Halifax: Dates and Circumstances of Composition," *Huntington Library Quarterly* 35 (1972): 143-57. On L'Estrange's political strategies, see Thomas Faulkner, "Halifax's *The Character of a Trimmer* and L'Estrange's Attack on · Trimmers in *The Observator*," *Huntington Library Quarterly* 37 (1973): 71. Variations in the application of "Trimmer" are recorded by Mark N. Brown, "Trimmers and Moderates in the Reign of Charles II," *Huntington Library Quarterly* 37 (1973): 312, 316, 319. Brown observes that most of what are now called the Cambridge Platonists were named in the anonymous satirical broadside (written between 13 November 1682 and 7 July 1684), "The Trimming Clergy" (Nottingham Univ. Library, #PwV1078) ("Trimmers and Moderates," 326). See also Faulkner, "Halifax's *Trimmer*," passim.

4. Halifax, *Moral Thoughts and Reflections*, p. 230. All of the quotations from Halifax are taken from Raleigh's edition of the *Complete Works*. Subsequent citations of this edition are incorporated into the text.

5. Halifax was criticized for treating the law of nature disrespectfully. See David Wykes and B.D. Greenslade, " 'The Trimmers Character': A Further Reply to Halifax," *Huntington Library Quarterly* 35 (1972): 214.

6. M. Brown, "Dates and Circumstances," p. 145, distinguishes "The Trimmer" as a literary character from Halifax himself. Benson, in "Halifax and the Trimmers," pp. 125, 132, corroborates this view with evidence that few people at court suspected Halifax of trimming.

CHAPTER THREE. DRYDEN

1. Louis Bredvold, *The Intellectual Milieu of John Dryden* (Ann Arbor: Univ. of Michigan Press, 1934).

2. Gerard Reedy, S.J., *The Bible and Reason* (Philadelphia: Univ. of Pennsylvania Press, 1985), p. 88.

3. See Ruth Salvaggio, *Dryden's Dualities* (Victoria: English Literary Studies, 1983), p. 77

4. James Winn, *John Dryden and His World* (New Haven, Conn.: Yale Univ. Press, 1987), pp. 377-78; David Hopkins, *John Dryden* (Cambridge: Cambridge Univ. Press, 1986), p. 8.

5. Sir Herbert Grierson, *Cross Currents in English Literature of the Seventeenth Century* (London: Chatto and Windus, 1929), p. 317.

6. See Beno Straumann, *John Dryden: Order and Chaos* (Zurich: Juris-Verlag, 1973), pp. 25, 37, and passim; Jackson I. Cope, "Dryden vs. Hobbes: An Adaptation from the Platonists," *Journal of English and Germanic Philology* 57 (1958): 444; Hoyt Trowbridge, "The Place of Rules," in H.T. Swedenberg, ed., *Essential Articles for the Study of Dryden* (Hamden, Conn.: Archon, 1966), p. 128; and David W. Tarbet, "Reason Dazzled: Perspective and Language in Dryden's *Aureng-Zebe*," in Paula R. Backscheider, ed., *Probability, Space, and Time in Eighteenth-Century Literature* (New York: AMS, 1979), p. 189.

7. See Bernard N. Schilling, *Dryden and the Conservative Myth* (New Haven, Conn.: Yale Univ. Press, 1961), p. 33.

8. See Sanford Budick, *Dryden and the Abyss of Light* (New Haven, Conn.: Yale Univ. Press, 1970), p. 33.

9. See Anne T. Barbeau, *The Intellectual Design of John Dryden's Plays* (New Haven, Conn.: Yale Univ. Press, 1970), pp. 3-24 and passim. Philip Harth, in "Religion and Politics in Dryden's Poetry and Plays," *Modern Philology* 70 (1973): 240-42, claims that Barbeau's embodied ideas are better understood as the old commonplaces of love and honor. Still, this motion toward the presentation of conflict as part of a system of conventions points up the reconciling power of Dryden's style. See also Robert McHenry, "Dryden's *Religio Laici*: An Augustan Drama of Ideas," *Enlightenment Essays* 4 (1973): 60-64.

10. Donald Benson, "The Artistic Image and Dryden's Conception of Reason," *Studies in English Literature* 11 (1971): 432-33.

11. John Dryden, *Religio Laici*, ll. 400-405. All quotations from Dryden's poetry, prefaces, and treatises are from *The Works of John Dryden*, general editor, H.T. Swedenberg, Jr. (Lost Angeles: Univ. of California Press, 1956-). Quotations of works in prose are from *John Dryden: Of Dramatic Poesy, and Other Critical Essays*, ed. George Watson (1971; reprint, London: Everyman, 1962). Subsequent citations of these editions are incorporated into the text.

12. See Donald Benson, "Theology and Politics in Dryden's Conversion," *Studies in English Literature* 4 (1964): 411; and Michael Conlon, "The Passage on Government in *Absalom and Achitophel*," *Journal of English and Germanic Philology*, 78 (1979): 27, 30.

13. Stephen Zwicker, *Politics and Language in Dryden's Poetry* (Princeton, N.J.: Princeton Univ. Press, 1984), p. 75, points out that the Gondibert stanza in Dryden's hands undercuts "initial and primary meanings with ambiguities" as part of a "dialectic of assertions and qualification." Hence Dryden never permits his Cromwell to ascend completely into myth. See also Michael West, "Shifting Concepts of Heroism in Dryden's Panegyrics," *Papers on Literature and Language* 10 (1974): 384. Dryden views Christ himself as less a redeemer than an embodiment of an orderly "scientific Christianity." See Jackson I. Cope, "Science, Christ, and Cromwell in Dryden's *Heroic Stanzas*," *Modern Language Notes* 71 (1956): 483-85. In *Dryden and the Tradition of the Panegyric* (Berkeley: Univ. of California Press, 1975), p. 150, James Garrison warns that the Gondibert tradition is not the only one at work here. Dryden's poem may also be read as an example of other forms, for example a classical oration.

14. Hence Dryden's concern for moral progress, which language itself makes inevitable. See Earl Miner, "Dryden and the Issue of Human Progress," *Philological Quarterly* 40 (1961): 125.

15. David Vieth, "Concept as Metaphor: Dryden's Attempted Stylistic Revolution," *Language and Style* 3 (1970): 200.

16. Michael McKeon has also pointed to the complexity of roles in *Annus Mirabilis*: God is seen in relation to his people; English leaders are likened to God; and providence works through the fate of individuals. See McKeon's *Politics and Poetry in Restoration England: The Case of Dryden's Annus Mirabilis* (Cambridge, Mass.: Harvard Univ. Press, 1975), p. 63

17. Richard Wendorf, "Dryden, Charles II, and the Interpretation of Historical Character," *Philological Quarterly* 56 (1977): 97, draws attention to Dryden's interest in dissolving the tenant of an office into the office. See also K.E. Robinson, "A Reading of *Absalom and Achitophel*," *Yearbook of English Studies* 6 (1976): 59.

18. See Benson, "Theology and Politics," p. 405.

19. On Dryden's alleged skepticism, see Thomas H. Fujimara, "Dryden's *Religio*

Laici: An Anglican Poem," *PMLA* 76 (1961): 207; Elias Chiasson, "Dryden's Apparent Scepticism in *Religio Laici*," *Harvard Theological Review* 54 (1961): 107-21; Bredvold, *Intellectual Milieu*, passim; and Philip Harth, *Contexts of Dryden's Thought* (Chicago: Univ. of Chicago Press, 1968).

20. See Gerald B. Kinneavey, "Judgement in Extremes: A Study of Dryden's *Absalom and Achitophel*," *University of Dayton Review* 3 (1966): 25.

21. John Dryden, *The Life of Plutarch*, ed. George Saintsbury, in vol. 17 of *The Works of John Dryden* (New York: Scribners, 1904), p. 32.

22. On mute Scripture and living laws, see Harth, *Contexts*, chap. 5 and p. 38, and Benson, "Theology and Politics," p. 400.

23. Benson, "Artistic Image," 435.

24. On Dryden's use of academic skepticism, see Richard LeClerq, "The Academic Nature of the While Discourse of *An Essay of Dramatic Poesy*," *Papers on Literature and Language* 8 (1972): 28.

25. See Edward N. Hooker, "Dryden and the Atoms of Epicurus," *ELH* 24 (1957): K.W. Gransden, "What Kind of Poem Is *Religio Laici*?" *SEL* 17 (1977): 397; and A.E. Wallace, "Dryden and Pyrrhonism," *Notes and Queries* 4 (1957): 251-52. On Dryden's sources for these philosophical figures in *Religio Laici*, see Victor M. Hamm, "Dryden's *Religio Laici* and Roman Catholic Apologetics," *Periodical of the Modern Language Association* (1965): 192-98.

26. On Dryden's ambiguous attitude concerning the hereditary transmission of authority, see Alan Roper, "Dryden's *Medall* and the Divine Analogy," *ELH* 29 (1962): 403-4.

27. Vieth, "Concept as Metaphor," p. 200n, notes that line 136 "is rendered tongue-in-cheek by the word 'must.' It does not mean 'kings can do no wrong' or 'we believe kings can do no wrong,' but rather something like 'for practical purposes, we must act as if kings could do no wrong.' "

28. Paul J. Korshin, *Typologies in England, 1650-1820* (Princeton, N.J.: Princeton Univ. Press, 1982), p. 80, points out the degree of distortion in Dryden's typology. Dryden is fond, for example, of postfiguration, in which a more recent type refers back to a more acceptable typology. Howard D. Weinbrot, " 'Nature's Holy Bands' in *Absalom and Achitophel*: Fathers and Sons, Satire and Change," *Modern Philology* 85 (1988): 373-75, also rails at the tendency to take Dryden's typology too straightforwardly.

29. David Bady, in "The Exact Balance of True Virtue," *Dissertation Abstracts International* 33 (1973): 5712-13A, shows that Dryden uses ironizing tropes like syncrisis, the comparison of a greater to a great man, to convert the mere great man into the greatest. See also Peter McNamara, "Clothing Thought: Dryden on Language," *Tulane Studies in English* 20 (1972): 59. Concerning the ambiguous opening of *Absalom and Achitophel*, David Hopkins, *Dryden*, p. 87, states simply that Dryden is "inviting us to entertain speculations rather than take up a point of view." See also Thomas H. Fujimara, "Dryden's Poetics: The Expressive Values in Poetry," *Journal of English and Germanic Philology* 74 (1975): 207.

30. See Miner, "Human Progress," p. 128.

31. See Chiasson, "Dryden's Scepticism," p. 215, and Sanford Budick, "New Light on Dryden's *Religio Laici*," *Notes and Queries* 16 (1969): 377.

32. Chiasson, "Dryden's Scepticism," p. 209, identifies as a common strategy among latitudinarians the framing of a reasonable system of belief followed by a surprise announcement that this system is identical to that prescribed by tradition.

33. See Victor M. Hamm, "Dryden's *The Hind and the Panther* and Roman Catholic

Apologetics," *PMLA* 83 (1968): 400-415, for a discussion of the role of persuasion and argument in *The Hind and the Panther*.

CHAPTER FOUR. LOCKE

1. John Yolton has offered a complete account of the many ways in which the term "idea" was used during the later seventeenth century. Few of these stressed subjectivity. See his *John Locke and the Way of Ideas* (Oxford: Oxford Univ. Press, 1956).

2. See Ernest Tuveson, "Locke and the Dissipation of the Ego," *Modern Philology*, 52 (1955): 161.

3. John Locke, *An Essay Concerning Human Understanding*, ed. Peter Nidditch (Oxford: Clarendon, 1975), 1.1.8. All quotations from the *Essay* are from this edition. Quotations from the *Second Treatise* are from John Locke, *Two Treatises of Government*, ed. Peter Laslett, 2nd ed. (1967; reprint, Cambridge: Cambridge Univ. Press, 1970). Subsequent citations of these editions are incorporated into the text.

4. On Locke's distinction of the ideas in thought from the act of perception, see Jonathan Bennett, "Substance, Reality, and Primary Qualities," in Charles Martin and D.M. Armstrong, eds., *Locke and Berkeley: A Collection of Critical Essays* (London: MacMillan, 1968), pp. 89, 100-101. Joel Weinsheimer calls attention to Locke's "complicated" epistemology, in which "experience" is the ultimate judge but in which experience can only be known through signs (*Imitation* [London: Routledge and Kegan Paul, 1984], pp. 22, 26-28).

5. In Locke, "ideas of sense are tied up with ideas of external causes of sense, this relation producing certain knowledge of objects," says A.P. Woozley, "Some Remarks on Locke's Account of Knowledge," in I.C. Tipton, ed., *Locke on Human Understanding* (Oxford: Oxford Univ. Press, 1977), pp. 144-46.

6. For a discussion of the same criteria in Locke's moral theory, see John Yolton, "Locke on the Law of Nature," *Philosophical Review* 67 (1958): 482-83. Locke's thinking overall, John Dunn suggests, is suffused with the idea of force. The word, Dunn comments, trembles through Locke's vocabulary. See John Dunn, *The Political Thought of John Locke* (London: Cambridge Univ. Press, 1969), pp. 167-68. Neal Wood, in *John Locke and Agrarian Capitalism* (Berkeley: Univ. of California Press, 1984), pp. 52-53, points outs not only the dynamic character of Locke's philosophy but also Locke's energetic style.

7. See Locke's tract on Malebranche in *The Works of John Locke* (London: 1801), vol. 9, sec. 46, p. 246. On Locke's comparison of the formats of divine and human knowledge, see John W. Lenz, "Locke's *Essay on the Law of Nature*," *Philosophy and Phenomenological Research* 17 (1956): 106-7. Francis Duchesneau, "Locke et la savoir de probabilité," *Dialogue* 11 (1972): 192-93, 200, notes that Locke is fond of drawing such analogies, indeed that for Locke analogy, the voluntary association of unlike things, counts as one of the most reliable sources of knowledge. On Locke's refusal to segregate simple, complex, and relational ideas, see Willis Doney, "Locke's Abstract Ideas," *Philosophy and Phenomenological Research* 16 (1956): 406. Locke even tried to equate words with the ideas of sounds. See Norman Kretzmann, "The Main Thesis of Locke's Semantic Theory," in Tipton, *Locke on Human Understanding*, p. 135.

8. Douglas Greenlee, "Locke and the Controversy over Innate Ideas," *Journal of the History of Ideas* 33 (1972): 252, claims that Locke cared little about the problem of innate ideas. Locke did, however, want to argue that even latency implies productive

processes. See also Greenville Wall, "Locke's Attack on Innate Knowledge," in Tipton, *Locke on Human Understanding*, p. 23.

9. See Leo Strauss, "On Locke's Doctrine of Natural Right," *Philosophical Review* 61 (1952): 490.

10. Max Milam, "The Epistemological Basis of Locke's Idea of Property," *Western Political Quarterly* 20 (1967): 26, comments that Lockean property per se has no material component. Property is only "the care and power" exerted in cultivating it. Milam warns (p. 28) that this systematizing activity occurs as automatically for property as it does for perception. See also William G. Batz, "The Historical Anthropology of John Locke," *Journal of the History of Ideas* 35 (1974): 663-70, for an account of Locke's sources for his ideas concerning the pre-contractual state of society. Locke, explains Batz, doubted whether the motion toward civilization could be reversed and hence whether a natural person could ever be found; no one could *stay* in a state of nature.

11. Jerry Weedon, "Locke on Rhetoric and Rational Man," *Quarterly Journal of Speech* 56 (1970): 382-83, is correct in arguing that Locke wants to treat relational ideas as principles of motivation.

12. *An Examination of P. Malebranche's Opinion of Seeing All Things in God*, sec. 45, in *The Works of John Locke*, vol. 9, sec. 45, p. 244.

13. See David P. Behan, "Locke on Persons and Personal Identity," *Canadian Journal of Philosophy* 9 (1979): 65-66.

14. On the public character of certainty, see Duchesneau, "Savoir de probabilité," p. 186-90; Douglas Odegard, "Locke's Epistemology and the Value of Experience," *Journal of the History of Ideas* 26 (1965): 421; and Rosalie Colie, "The Social Language of John Locke," *Journal of British Studies* 4, no. 2 (1965): 29-51.

15. On Locke as an instrument in the seventeenth-century reevaluation of testimony and evidence, see Shapiro, *Probability and Certainty*, pp. 179, 193.

16. On the similarity of moral and natural ideas, see Robert L. Armstrong, "John Locke's Doctrine of Signs: A New Metaphysics," *Journal of the History of Ideas* 26 (1965): 378-79.

17. See Milam, "Locke's Idea of Property," pp. 19-20.

18. Locke's vision of a perfect state, declares Yolton, in "Locke on the Law of Nature," 492-96, is normative and nominal, not prescriptive: "Man in primitive social organizations has insufficient direction and safeguards; those in more complex political units have the wrong sort of direction and safeguards. In short, the concept of the state of nature is a normative device used by Locke to indicate the deficiencies of all forms of social organization save that a civil society."

19. See Herman Parret, "Ideologie et semiologie chez Locke et Condillac," in Werner Abraham, ed., *Ut videam: Contributions to an Understanding of Linguistics* (Lisse: Peter de Ridder Press, 1975), p. 242.

20. David Givner, "Scientific Preconceptions in Locke's Philosophy of Language," *Journal of the History of Ideas* 23 (1962): 341, observes that Locke considered language and science as objects of the same study. Both science and language publicize arrangements of experience that are devised by smaller segments of (or individuals in) society.

21. This accounts for Locke's surprising claim that government has priority over popular will. Popular will can only make itself known through the channels (and the language) generated by the governmental system. John Dunn, "Consent in the Political Theory of John Locke," *Historical Journal* 10 (1967): 156, 173, observes that Locke never means to govern by consent, only to integrate consent into a legal system. See also Martin Seliger, *The Liberal Politics of John Locke* (London: Allen and Unwin, 1968), p. 267.

22. In *John Locke* (London: Allen and Unwin, 1978), pp. 104-5, Geraint Parry explains that an heir, for example, could not secede with his property, for the social system that supports property takes precedence over the right of possession that property institutionalizes. Strauss, "Locke's Doctrine of Natural Right," pp. 498-99, suggests that, for Locke, the material components of property are far less important in the formation of this construct than is the acquisitive process.

23. Strauss, "Locke's Doctrine of Natural Right," p. 501, contends that Locke is so interested in his *program* for man that he despises results: "The starting point of human effort is misery: the state of nature is a state of wretchedness. The way toward happiness is a movement away from the state of nature . . . freedom is negativity. . . . Life is the joyless quest for joy." James Tully, however, takes a more positive view. He argues that Locke moves away from nature, but toward the realization of imperatives like benevolence and enjoyment. See Tully's *A Discourse on Property* (New York: Cambridge Univ. Press, 1979), p. 176.

CHAPTER FIVE. SWIFT

1. F.P. Lock, "Swift and English Politics, 1701-14," in Claude Rawson, ed., *The Character of Swift's Satire* (Newark, N.J.: Univ. of Delaware Press, 1983), p. 127.

2. A number of critics have described Swift's concern to "involve" or "entrap" the reader in a developing artifact. Through entrapment, Swift uses a psychological state, reader interest, to draw readers into contexts with which they would otherwise have never become involved. See Carl R. Kropf, "Editor's Comments," *Studies in the Literary Imagination* 17 (1984): 1, and, in the same volume, Frederik N. Smith, "The Dangers of Reading Swift: The Double Binds of Gulliver's Travels," pp. 35-38, 46-47.

3. See John Traugott, "*A Tale of a Tub*," in Rawson, *Swift's Satire* pp. 85-86, 124. In his third endnote, Traugott explicates in detail three methods used to tame Swift: making him the product of a background (Phillip Harth, *Swift and Anglican Rationalism* [Chicago: Univ. of Chicago Press, 1961]); resolving his rhetoric into generic techniques (Edward W. Rosenheim, *Swift and the Satirist's Art* [Chicago: Univ. of Chicago Press, 1963]); and intellectualizing him to the point that he is safely inaccessible to anyone but an initiated scholar (Ronald Paulson, *Theme and Structure in Swift's Tale of a Tub* [New Haven: Yale Univ. Press, 1960]). J. Alan Downie has lately tried a fourth method, arguing that Swift "impersonates various characters, moulding aspects of each into the corporate narrator," and thereby establishing a closer connection between the author and his "nightmares" than the use of a simple persona might allow (*Jonathan Swift, Political Writer* [London: Routledge and Kegan Paul, 1984], p. 96).

4. See David Nokes, *Jonathan Swift, A Hypocrite Reversed* (Oxford: Oxford Univ. Press, 1985), pp. 318-22.

5. Irvin Ehrenpreis, for example, seems to be of two minds with regard to the explanation of Swift. In his discussion of *A Tale of a Tub*, he is ready to accept a pious Swift who presents a model of Christian gentility (*Mr Swift and His Contemporaries* [1962; reprint, London: Methuen, 1964], pp. 190, 216); but in his analysis of *Gulliver's Travels* (*Dean Swift* [Cambridge, Mass.: Harvard Univ. Press, 1983], p. 455), he is comfortable with a Swift who offers so radical a critique of humanity that he ends up affirming nothing at all. Ehrenpreis's apostasy should put one on guard against a wild assertion like Nokes's (*Swift*, pp. 44-52) that once one penetrates the smoke screen of "paradoxes and parodies," one will find a true-blue, fully Anglican Swift.

6. See Ehrenpreis, *Dean Swift*, p. 456.

7. See W.B. Carnochan, "*Gulliver's Travels*: An Essay on the Human Understanding," *Modern Language Quarterly* 25 (1964): 18-19; and Alexander Allison, "Concerning Houyhnhnm Reason," *Sewanee Review* 76 (1968): 484.

8. Jonathan Swift, *A Tale of a Tub*, p. 46. Quotations from Swift's prose are taken from Jonathan Swift, *Prose Works*, ed. Herbert Davis (Oxford: Blackwell, 1939-1968). Subsequent citations of this edition are incorporated into the text.

9. See Jonathan Swift, *The Church of England Man*, p. 18. Here Swift argues, against Hobbes, that there is no difference between a king de jure and a king de facto, for "king" is, by definition, a de jure entity.

10. Frederik N. Smith, *Language and Reality in Swift's A Tale of a Tub* (Columbus: Ohio State Univ. Press, 1979), pp. 95-96, points to Swift's lifelong fascination with madness and death through insanity as examples of his doubts concerning his (or anyone's) ability to separate ideas from one another.

11. On Swift's attitude toward personal identity and authorship, see David Vieth, "The Mystery of Personal Identity," in Aubrey Williams and Louis Martz, eds., *The Author in His Work: Essays on a Problem in Criticism* (New Haven, Conn.: Yale Univ. Press, 1978), pp. 245-62.

12. On the conflict between the nominal and the commonsense notions of man, see Irvin Ehrenpreis, "The Meaning of Gulliver's Last Voyage," *Review of English Literature* 3 (1962): 30.

13. For a critique of Mack's positivistic model of satire, in which a self-assured spokesman asserts confidently believed community values, see my essay "The Conquest of Truth: Wycherley, Rochester, Butler, and Dryden and the Restoration Critique of Satire," *Restoration* 10 (1986): 19-40.

14. See Maurice J. Quinlan, "Swift's 'Project for the Advancement of Religion and Reformation of Manners'," *PMLA* 71 (1956): 206; and Robert W. Otten, "The 'Ill-Grounded Quarrel with Nature': The Projector as Metaphor in the Writings of Jonathan Swift," *Dissertation Abstracts International* 35 (1974): 2950A.

15. For keys to the satire of the flying island, see Nora Mohler and Marjorie Nicholson, "The Background of Gulliver's *Voyage to Laputa*," *Annals of Science* 2 (1937): 299-334; Korshin, "Swift's Flying Island," pp. 630-46; David Renaker, "Swift's Laputans as a Caricature of the Cartesians," *PMLA* 94 (1979): 936-44; Anne E. Patterson, "Swift's Irony and Cartesian Man," *Midwest Quarterly* 15 (1974): 342; and Kathleen Williams, *Jonathan Swift and the Art of Compromise* (Lawrence: Univ. of Kansas Press, 1958), p. 168.

16. Swift always suffered from deep doubts whether science could describe reality. His "Astronomer's Cave" on Laputa, a parody of Bacon's "Idols of the Cave," spoofs Verulam's attempt to set science on a solid foundation. See Denis Todd, "Laputa, The Whore of Babylon, and the Idols of Science," *Studies in Philology*: 75 (1978): 95. John A. Yunck, "The Sceptical Faith of Jonathan Swift," *Personality* 42 (1963): 543-44, goes a bit overboard in arguing that Swift admired skeptics like Montaigne or Rouchefoucauld.

17. James E. Gill, "Discovery and Alienation, Nature and Reason in *Gulliver's Travels*," *Tennessee Studies in Literature* 22 (1977): 96, remarks that the third book of the *Travels* is unique, for in it Gulliver is never fully assimilated into any of the cultures that he visits. So, too, the Laputans are unable to participate fully in their own contradiction-ridden civilization.

18. More than any other English author, says Robert W. Uphaus, Swift exploits the capacity of language to distort meaning and deploys an army of rhetorical devices in order to produce epistemological disorientation. See Uphaus's "*Gulliver's Travels, A Modest Proposal*, and the Problematic Nature of Meaning," *Papers on Language and Literature* 10 (1974): 273.

19. See F. Smith, *Language and Reality*, pp. 9-11.

20. See Jonathan Swift, *On the Trinity*, pp. 164-66. See also George R. Potter, "Swift and Natural Science," *Philological Quarterly*, 20 (1941): 110, 117-18.

21. On the possibility that the universality of folly yields a certain inverted harmony, see Clive T. Probyn, *Jonathan Swift: The Contemporary Background* (New York: Barnes and Noble, 1979), p. 73.

22. On the nonnatural character of the Houyhnhnms, see John H. White, "Swift's Trojan Horses: 'Reasoning but to Err,' " *English Language Notes* 3 (1966): 189.

23. So in state religion all *particular* practices become things indifferent. See Ricardo Quintana, *The Mind and Art of Jonathan Swift* (London: Methuen, 1953), p. 73, and Elias Chiasson, "Swift's Clothes Philosophy in the *Tale* and Hooker's Concept of Law," *Studies in Philology* 59 (1962): 78. Louis Landa calls Swift's equine economy a "mosaic" of agrarian ideas and primitivistic attitudes. See Landa's "The Dismal Science in Houyhnhnmland," *Novel* 13 (1979): 49.

24. See K. Williams, *Art of Compromise*, p. 191, and Allison, "Houyhnhnm Reason," p. 484, who take the Houyhnhnms as a serious but limited ideal, an ideal for one part of experience. See also Quintana, *Mind and Art of Swift*, p. 321; K. Williams, *Art of Compromise*, p. 192; John F. Reickert, "Plato, Swift, and the Houyhnhnms," *Philological Quarterly* 47 (1968): 191; and William Halewood and Marvin Levitch, "Houyhnhnm Est Animal Rationale," *Journal of the History of Ideas* 26 (1965): 278-80.

25. Swift exploits the familiar technique of grouping together nonequivalents, explains Clive T. Probyn, "Gulliver and the Relativity of Things," *Renaissance and Modern Studies* 18 (1974): 66-67. In *Contemporary Background*, pp. 74-78, Probyn adds that Swift extended this process to the phonemic level, using homophonic puns to assert the identity of utterly unrelated things.

26. On the contrast of Gulliver and Don Pedro, see Ralph E. Hitt, "Antiperfectionism as a Unifying Theme in *Gulliver's Travels*," *Mississippi Quarterly* 15 (1962): 168.

27. Likewise, laments Douglas H. White, in "Swift and the Definition of Man," *Modern Philology* 73 (1976): iv, 52-53, the highest religious truth that can mesh with the depraved nature of man is the fear of punishment in the next life.

28. See James Brown, "Swift as Moralist," *Philological Quarterly* 33 (1954): 380-84.

29. On "angelic" or intuitive reasoning, see Carnochan, "*Gulliver's Travels*," p. 15; Reickert, "Plato, Swift," pp. 180-81; Allison, "Houyhnhnm Reason," p. 485; and Quintana, *Mind and Art of Swift*, p. 323. "Demonstrative" reasoning is, for Locke, simply a slower version of its intuitive counterpart. Both forms of reasoning amount to the intuitive apprehension of relations among ideas. Demonstrative reasoning, however, requires more intermediate steps between the ideas in the premises and those in the conclusion. On the debate over the meaning of the Houyhnhnms, see n. 24 above.

30. J. Brown, "Swift as Moralist," pp. 385-86, thinks of Swift's theology as a process in which faith commands the admission of some truths that we cannot conceive, even while reason holds up, in the background, a standard from which theology cannot veer too far. Because all these processes take place in the mind, Brown says, Swift's religion is ultimately a psychology, a format by which the individual mind is integrated into a greater system of truth. F.M. Darnall points out, however, that Swift cites biblical support for the admission of contradictory mysteries into religion ("Swift's Religion," *Journal of English and Germanic Philology* 30 [1931]: 381).

CHAPTER SIX. POPE

1. This thesis is argued by Laura Brown in *Alexander Pope* (Oxford: Blackwell, 1985). A similar line has been taken by Wallace Jackson in his *Vision and Re-Vision in*

Alexander Pope (Detroit, Mich.: Wayne State Univ. Press, 1983). Jackson, however, re-members that Pope's "vision" is in charge of his "tradition," and not vice versa.

2. See Fredric V. Bogel, *Acts of Knowledge: Pope's Later Poems* (Lewisburg, Pa.: Bucknell Univ. Press, 1981), pp. 16-18, 222.

3. See, for example, David Porush, *The Soft Machine: Cybernetic Fiction* (New York: Methuen, 1985), p. 76 and passim, for an excellent discussion of attacks by Polanyi and others on the "positivistic-mechanistic-reductionist" approach to man and science.

4. See Dustin Griffin, *Alexander Pope: The Poet in the Poems* (Princeton, N.J.: Prin-ceton Univ. Press, 1978), p. 141.

5. Alexander Pope, *Pastorals*, pp. 119-20. All quotations from Pope are from *The Poems of Alexander Pope*, ed. John Butt (New Haven, Conn.: Yale Univ. Press, 1963). Subsequent citations of this edition an incorporated into the text.

6. In discussing the role of nature in Pope's early poetry, it is important to dis-tinguish the "nature" of pastoral poetry in general from Pope's use of a "naturalistic" mode. The *Oxford English Dictionary* points out that "naturalistic" means "based on nature" or, more recently, "in accord with naturalism (an ethics based on the cultivation of natural impulses)." Pope's early poems are also "based on" nature. They describe a landscape, but a landscape that is in the process of becoming an atlas of politics, history, and philosophy. Pope is "turning away" from the pastoral, in the sense that he presents a rural setting that is accumulating social, literary, and philosophical sig-nificance. Conventional pastoral, on the other hand, always esteems nature. W.W. Greg finds in the pastoral "the conception of a golden age of rustic simplicity" and "the recognition of a contrast . . . between pastoral life and some more complex type of civilization" (*Pastoral Poetry and Pastoral Drama* [New York: Russell and Russell, 1959], pp. 4, 6). D.M. Rosenberg talks of a naturalistic pastoral in which "the natural landscape of pastoral poetry is objectively real . . . [but] functions subjectively," where "nature in the golden world is restored nature created by art" (*Oaten Reeds and Trumpets* [Lew-isburg, Pa.: Bucknell Univ. Press, 1981], p. 19). E.W. Tayler points to "the habitual pairing of Nature and Art" (*Nature and Art in Renaissance England* [New York: Columbia Univ. Press, 1964], p. 4). Anthony Low comments on "the typical view that country life should be a life of leisure" (*The Georgic Revolution* [Princeton, N.J.: Princeton Univ. Press, 1985], p. 24). James Sambrook, speaking on one of Pope's poetic models, argues that "in Sir John Denham's *Cooper's Hill* (1642) we find the pastoral opposition of city and country, when the avarice, noise, dirt, and Puritan fanaticism of London are con-trasted with the beauty, security, and innocence of the countryside . . . pastoral poetry is the kind of poetry that takes as its subject shepherds or other rustics and generally represents them as free from the vices and sorrows of men living in more complex societies" (*English Pastoral Poetry* [Boston: Twayne, 1983], p. 94). Finally, Harold Toliver offers a schematic chart of the natural elements in pastoral poems (*Pastoral Forms and Attitudes* [Berkeley: Univ. of California Press, 1971], p. 3).

7. George Berkeley, *New Theory of Vision*, par. 16, in *The Works of George Berkeley*, ed. A.A. Luce and T.E. Jessop (London: Nelson, 1948), vol. 1.

8. This accounts for Pope's fear that words, which always work in a suggestive, allusive context, might lead readers to mistake language for things. See Carl R. Kropf, "Education and the Neo-Platonic Idea of Wisdom in Pope's *Dunciad*," *Texas Studies in Literature and Language* 14 (1973): 596-97.

9. F.E.L. Priestley, "Pope and the Great Chain of Being," in Miller Maclure and F.M. Watt, eds., *Essays in English Literature from the Renaissance to the Victorian Age*, (Toronto: Univ. of Toronto Press, 1964), p. 218, suggests that, to Pope, the "chain of

being" is only a premise, not a conclusion. On Pope's poetry as a response to "the system of credit, risk, insurance, paper money," and other aspects of the "final system," see Margaret Anne Doody, *The Daring Muse: Augustan Poetry Reconsidered* (Cambridge: Cambridge Univ. Press, 1985), pp. 15-16.

10. Leo Damrosch, *The Imaginative World of Alexander Pope* (Berkeley: Univ. of California Press, 1987), p. 217.

11. Pope doesn't mind describing natural objects, but his true interest is in talking about the place of images in theoretical schemes. See Patricia Spacks, "Pope's Satiric Use of Nature," *Studies in the Literary Imagination* 5 (1972): ii, 44. Geoffrey Tillotson, however, insists that Pope, despite his generalizing rhetoric, will not stray too far from the empirically observable. Pope suggests the universal by discussing a large but not wholly comprehensive segment of mankind, using, for example, "doctors" to mean "man." See Tillotson's *Pope and Human Nature* (Oxford: Oxford Univ. Press, 1958), pp. 121-22. Pope, likewise, avoids talking about mighty abstractions like "infinity," preferring more palpable conceptions like "immensity" or "extent." See Ernest Tuveson, *"An Essay on Man* and 'The Way of Ideas,' " *English Literary History* 26 (1959): 379.

12. On the oppressive loading of meaning into commonplace imagery, see Laura Brown, *Pope*, pp. 29-30, and Tuveson, "Way of Ideas," p. 372.

13. As John Sutherland says, in his "Wit, Vision, and *An Essay on Man*," *Modern Language Quarterly* 30 (1969): 362-63, Pope sees man never as an individual phenomenon, but always as a member of a species. See also Nancy K. Lawlor, "Pope's *Essay on Man*: Oblique Light for a False Mirror," *Modern Language Quarterly* 28 (1967): 311. G. Douglas Atkins, in *Quests of Difference* (Lexington: Univ. Press of Kentucky, 1986), pp. 51-53, warns that membership in a class or group allows for relative perfection. "To reason right" by submitting means not to relinquish all power but to accept the degree of perfection proper for one's situation. Maynard Mack, in *Alexander Pope: A Life* (New Haven, Conn.: Yale University Press, 1985), pp. 170-71, talks about Pope's "pervasive concern for corporateness," for the treatment of diverse views, for the responsibility of the individual to the whole, and for the discussion of ideas in the context of a community.

14. On the watch metaphor, see Paul Ramsey, "The Watch of Judgment: Relativism and *An Essay on Criticism*," in Howard Anderson and John Shea, eds., *Studies in Criticism and Aesthetics, 1660-1880* (Minneapolis: Univ. of Minnesota Press, 1967), p. 137.

15. On *discordia concors*, the discovery of order in disorder, as a central theme in Pope's philosophical poems, see Howard D. Weinbrot, *Alexander Pope and the Traditions of Formal Verse Satire* (Princeton, N.J.: Princeton Univ. Press, 1982), p. 181.

16. Tillotson points out (*Human Nature*, p. 7) that Pope regards perception as a willful, not an accidental, process. On the influence of the psychology of the passions on perceptual theory, see Richard Goldgar, "Pope's Theory of the Passions: The Background of Epistle II of the *Essay on Man*," *Philological Quarterly* 41 (1962): 730-43.

17. See Peter E. Martin, "The Garden and Pope's Vision of Order in the *Epistle to Burlington*," *Durham University Journal* 34 (1973): 257. See also Martin's *Pursuing Innocent Pleasures* (Hamden, Conn.: Archon, 1984), p. xx. On the genius of the place as a principle in both landscape architecture and ethics, see Mack, *Pope*, p. 532, and Rebecca Ferguson, *The Unbalanced Mind: Pope and the Rule of Passion* (Brighton, Sussex: Harvester, 1986), p. 67. On the genius of the place as a "principle of unity," see Morris Brownell, *Alexander Pope and the Arts of Georgian England* (Oxford: Clarendon, 1978), pp. 108-9.

18. See F.E.L. Priestley, "Order, Union, Full Consent of Things," *University of Toronto Quarterly* 42 (1973): 7-8.

19. See John H. Miller, "Pope and the Principle of Reconciliation," *Texas Studies in Language and Literature* 9 (1968): 185-92.

20. Arguing against the hasty dismissal of Pope's sportive passages, Ernest Tuveson, "*An Essay on Man* and the 'Way of Ideas': Some Further Remarks," *Philological Quarterly* 40 (1961): 268, and Martin C. Battestin, "The Transforming Power: Nature and Art in Pope's *Pastorals*," *Eighteenth-Century Studies* 2 (1969): 183-204, have agreed that Pope denies the sufficiency of human knowledge in order to encourage the creation of as many provisional truths as possible.

21. Bogel, *Acts of Knowledge*, pp. 61-71. On the embodiment of virtue by an excellent but worldly person as a convention of epistolary satire, see Weinbrot, *Pope and the Traditions of Formal Verse Satire*, p. 174.

22. Barbara Lauren, "Pope's *Epistle to Bolingbroke*: Satire from the Vantage Point of Retirement," *Studies in English Literature* 15 (1975): 420, 427, 430, explains that Pope's retirement allowed Pope to develop a persona that could speak from afar but also with a public authority—a character that, *because* it was private, was engaged in a public discourse.

23. Pope had a continuing interest in the relinquishing of control over one's perceptions. Surrender of the self to the self's perception was a common explanation for insanity. See David B. Morris, *Alexander Pope: The Genius of Sense* (Cambridge, Mass.: Harvard Univ. Press, 1984), pp. 272-74.

24. Morris, *Pope*, p. 275, explains that the chatter of Dulness and the dunces is a deliberate act of satirical mimicry in which Pope planned to make his own work, like that of his fellow dunces, fade through time. Pope expected that all the historical detail of his poem would sink into the obscurity of footnotes, taking the dunces along with it.

25. Deborah Jacobs has recently drawn attention to the importance of what could be called the "Frankenstein myth," the story of self-multiplication and "synthesis" into society, for writers throughout the eighteenth century ("Urbanization: A Monster of Our Own Making," paper delivered at the South-Central Society for Eighteenth-Century Studies, Shreveport, La., February 1989).

CHAPTER SEVEN. SMITH

1. Dwyer, *Virtuous Discourse*; Sher, *Church and University in the Scottish Enlightenment*.

2. For an assessment of the influence on Smith of Berkeley, Hume, Locke, and other philosophers, see Ray Edward Cain, "David Hume and Adam Smith: A Study in Intellectual Kinship," *Dissertation Abstracts* 24 (1963): 724; Andrew S. Skinner, "Adam Smith: Science and the Role of the Imagination," in William Todd, ed., *Hume and the Enlightenment* (Edinburgh: Edinburgh Univ. Press, 1974), p. 164; and A.W. Coats, "Adam Smith: The Modern Reappraisal," *Renaissance and Modern Studies* 6 (1962): 31.

3. D.D. Raphael, *Adam Smith* (Oxford: Oxford Univ. Press, 1985), pp. 16-18.

4. John Mullan, *Sentiment and Sociability: The Language of Feeling in the Eighteenth Century* (Oxford: Clarendon, 1988), pp. 44-50 and passim.

5. Raphael, *Adam Smith*, p. 107.

6. Adam Smith, *History of Astronomy*, p. 36. All quotations from the early essays are from *The Early Writings of Adam Smith*, ed. J. Ralph Lindgren (New York: Adam Smith Library, 1967). Subsequent citations of this edition are incorporated into the text.

7. See Joseph Cropsey, *Polity and Economy: An Interpretation of the Principles of Adam Smith* (The Hague: Nijhoff, 1957), p. 45, and Raphael, *Adam Smith*, p. 31.

8. T.D. Campbell, in *Adam Smith's Theory of Morals* (Glasgow: Univ. of Glasgow Press, 1971), pp. 34-38, describes Smith's science as a form of "covering law" theory. For Smith, a phenomenon is not satisfactorily explained by a simple description. It must be related to a general law, whether or not there is any empirical evidence for that law.

9. Adam Smith, *Theory of Moral Sentiments*, ed. D.D. Raphael and A.L. Macfie (Oxford: Clarendon, 1976), p. 9. All quotations from the *Theory* are from this edition. Subsequent citations an incorporated into the text.

10. Cropsey notes (*Polity and Economy*, p. 20) that Smith allows for perfect moral knowledge. All creatures synthesize some model of *their* experience, which becomes an infallible guide for *their* action. Skinner, the "Role of the Imagination," p. 173, adds that, for Smith, all theories must be evaluated with regard to their moral value. See also M.L. Myers, "Adam Smith as Critic of Ideas," *Journal of the History of Ideas* 36 (1975): 284.

11. Adam Smith, *Lectures on Rhetoric and Belles Lettres* (Carbondale: Southern Illinois Univ. Press, 1971), pp. 120-21. Subsequent citations from this edition are incorporated in the text.

12. A.L. Macfie, in *The Individual in Society: Papers on Adam Smith* (London: Allen and Unwin, 1967), p. 86, suggests, for example, that Smith regards reason as little more than a kind of calculator—as a tool that lacks value unless affiliated with other psychological forces.

13. Skinner, "Role of the Imagination," pp. 169, 226, argues that the management of "wonder" is a "trade" that Smith allocates to a special class of employees, "who are, in turn, regulated by the system of economics." See also A.D. Megill, "Theory and Experience in Adam Smith," *Journal of the History of Ideas* 36 (1975): 80-82.

14. See Robert B. Lamb, "Adam Smith's System: Sympathy Not Self Interest," *Journal of the History of Ideas* 35 (1974): 676. See also Megill, "Theory and Experience," 86.

15. As Cropsey comments, *Polity and Economy*, p. 11, Smith promotes benevolism, but not any particular action. See also Robert Lee McGowan, "Sympathy and Conscience: A Study of Adam Smith's Ethical Theory," *Dissertation Abstracts* 24 (1968): 3787.

16. Hazard Adams, personal communication, May 1982.

17. Contrary to popular belief, the invisible hand did not first appear in Smith's economic treatises. On the various ways in which Smith uses "the invisible hand," see A.L. Macfie, "The Invisible Hand of Jupiter," *Journal of the History of Ideas* 32 (1971): 595-99, and also his *Individual in Society*, p. 104.

18. Richard H. Powers, "Adam Smith: Practical Realist," *Southwestern Social Science Quarterly* 37 (1956): 23, points out that a Smithian society aims to promote the welfare of the individual, but it may do so through forceful, even ruthless means, such as "rooting out" deviant persons.

19. Vincent M. Bevilacqua, in "Adam Smith and Some Philosophical Origins of Eighteenth-Century Rhetorical Theory," *Modern Language Review* 63 (1968): 559-68, finds that Smith uses similar tactics in his *Rhetoric*. Smith argues that poets should systematically practice associating corporeal images with "spiritual" ideas, thus accustoming themselves to fitting any and all appearances to any and all explanations.

EPILOGUE

1. Benjamin Whichcote, *Moral and Religious Aphorisms*, ed. W.R. Inge (London: Elkin Mathews and Marrot, n.d.), p. 13 (Century I, Aphorism 98); Anthony, Earl of

Index

Swift, Jonathan, 115-39; on Locke, 115-16, 130, 134-35, 137-39; as "philoso-phizer," 116, 211 n 5; "clothes" phi-losophy, 116, 119-20; role of philosophy in writings of, 117; "The Progress of Beauty," 118, 128; *The Bat-tle of the Books*, 118; use of allegory, 118-19, 128-29, 138-39; delight and in-struction, precepts of classicism, 119; *A Tale of a Tub*, 119-21, 126, 128-29, 131-32, 133; grounding of belief in sys-tem, 120; "Digression on Madness," 120-21; systematization of peculiarities, 121; *A Modest Proposal*, 121; on iden-tity, 121-22, 136; *Gulliver's Travels*, 121-33, 135-38; coherence and consistency criteria in, 122, 123-24; decaying form of his satire, 122, 131, 134, 212 nn 13, 17; *Verses on the Death of Dr. Swift*, 122; normative prose style, 123; attitude to-ward projectors, 123; on prefatory writings, 126; teleological character of his language, 127; *On the Trinity*, 127, 139; "The Day of Judgement," 127; *The Church of England Man*, 128-29, 137; *On the Testimony of Conscience*, 129-30, 136; on irony, 131-32; *Critical Essay upon the Faculties of the Mind*, 133; *A Project for the Advancement of Religion*, 136; *Thoughts on Religion*, 137; on miracles, 139; on relations of faith, reason, and theology, 213 n 30. *See also* Brobding-nagg; empiricism; explanation; Houyhnhnms; Lagado; Laputa; Lilli-put; persona; reader entrapment; rela-tions; Struldbruggs; Yahoos
syncrisis, 208 n 29
synopsis: as genre of literary criticism, 6-9; as encyclopedia, 7; as background book, 7-8; as progress, 8-9

Tayler, E.W., 214 n 6
Temple, Sir William, 115, 118

theriophily, 30, 40
Thomas, Dylan, 143
Tillotson, Geoffrey, 5
Tipton, I.C., 94, 209 n 5
Toliver, Harold, 214 n 6
Traugott, John, 117, 211 n 3
trimmers and trimming. *See* Halifax, George Savile, Marquis of
"Trimming Clergy, The" 206 n 3
truth in literature, 1, 9; and truth in sys-tems, 12
Tully, John, 94, 211 n 23
Tuveson, Ernest, 94

Uphaus, Robert, 212 n 18

Van Leeuwen, Henrik, 7
Vieth, David, 41, 208 n 27
Virgil, 80, 143

Weinbrot, Howard, 1
Weinsheimer, Joel, 209 n 4
Whichcote, Benjamin, 199
Whitley, Raymond, 22
Wilkins, John, 5, 6
Willey, Basil, 7
Wilmot, John. *See* Rochester, John Wil-mot, Earl of
Wilson, Edward O., 16
Winn, James, 66-67, 83, 89
Wood, Neal, 94
Wordsworth, William, 170
Wycherley, William, 7

Yahoos, 132
Yolton, John, 94, 209 n 1, 210 n 18
Young, Edward, 168

Zimbardo, Rose, 200
Zwicker, Stephen, 207 n 13